What They Are Saying

I am fortunately not a member of The Red Dot Club myself; but, Robert Rangel struck a cathartic nerve in me in his second addition to *The Red Dot Club* series with *The Red Dot Club—Victims' Voices*! Mr. Rangel adroitly tells the stories of many peace officers, who while answering their calls to duty to protect and serve society's own victims, become physical and emotional victims themselves. After extensive and intense interviews, Mr. Rangel tells the officer's true stories, documented in their original voices so that nothing is lost in translation! *The Red Dot Club* series should be required reading for all law-enforcement academy students and encouraged reading for every non-LEO in all our communities!

—Jeff Kirkpatrick,
Chief-Retired
City of Seal Beach Police Department, CA

Robert Rangel's collection of multiple life-threatening encounters transports the reader to a "virtual experience." As an insider, Rangel was able to gain the trust of the officers he interviewed, freeing them to reveal the gripping and sometimes painful details of those incidents. This will be an eye-opener for many readers.

—Kevin Rogan
Assistant Inspector General
Los Angeles Police Commission

The Red Dot Club—Victims' Voices is a raw, thought provoking read. Honored to have worked with several whose stories you'll read, in a single day they witnessed more compassion and heroism than most experience in a lifetime.

—Mike Hall
Chief of Police (Ret.)
Medal of Valor, 1980

Robert Rangel's latest book takes us to a place very few know about, including many police officers. This isn't a script. It's not an idea for TV. It's too real for that. This is a rare opportunity for the reader to sit down, one on one and learn what it is society is really asking of our law enforcement officers and what they are willing to do to deliver on the promise to protect and serve. A sincere debt of gratitude is owed these men and women for what they have endured and for their willingness to go there again, to share their stories and their most intimate thoughts and fears. I thank them for their humility and selflessness in allowing us to see them in their most terrifying moments. Robert's closing comments come at a critical time in this country. He asks us to set aside our preconceived, often media driven notions about how cops think, act and do what they do. Read this book and decide for yourself.

—Steve Towles
Vernon Chief of Police, retired

As an officer survival instructor at a regional law enforcement training academy there are books I recommend to the recruits as outside reading. There are few that I make mandatory reading. This is one of them. The author has captured, through his own experience and the accounts of others, the essence of what it takes to survive the deadliest of encounters on the street. The reading of this book will help law enforcement officers develop the mindset needed to prevail when their lives are on the line. This is not, however, a book just for cops. Anyone reading it will be exposed to the reality of police work, not the distorted version so often portrayed in the media.

—Jerry Boyd
LASD Sergeant 1972-1975
Irvine PD Captain 1978- 1981
Coronado PD Chief of Police 1981-1991
Martinez PD Chief of Police 1991-1996
Baker City (Oregon) Police Reserve Commander 2012 to present

The Red Dot Club—Victims' Voices takes the reader on riveting journeys through the survivor's eyes and emotions, the men, and women of law enforcement, often unsung heroes, who protect the public 24/7. These experiences can only be described as intense, emotional, adrenaline driven, heart-wrenching, impactful moments that last far beyond the event itself. Guardians forced to be Warriors in a blink of an eye, fighting for their lives and the lives of their partners.

Author Robert Rangel shares these stories in only a way, a survivor himself, could. These stories offer a glimpse into a world of emotions that few will ever know and feel. A must-read not only for those considering a law enforcement career but those who have already joined.

—Paul Cooper, Police Chief (Retired)
32 years Claremont Police Department

The men and women who tell us their stories in Robert Rangel's *The Red Dot Club—Victims' Voices* come from large and small law enforcement agencies. They tell us who they were before they joined their departments. We read about their heroic actions, while they speak of their sorrow. We admire their bravery, while they live with their regrets. We learn from them that wounds don't always heal, and officer survival never ends. Bravery and sacrifice come with a price, and we are so lucky these officers were willing to pay it. We asked these officers to protect us. The least we can do is listen to them.

—Michael J. McAndrews
Attorney, Hartford, Connecticut
Lieutenant (Retired) in charge of
Los Angeles County Sheriff's Academy Class 217

This book takes you to the heart of the officer's experience and exposures to life altering events. Unlike other documented accounts, this opens you up to the raw emotions and experiences while placing you squarely in the arena the officers find themselves. This book tells it with brutal reality, having been involved in such critical incidents myself. The relevant side of the officer's mindset and thoughts are shown here. An important and worthwhile read for those both in or closely associated to the Law Enforcement profession.

—Ward Smith
Police Chief, (Ret.)
City of Placentia Police Department, Orange County, CA

ALSO BY ROBERT RANGEL

The Organ Grinder's Monkey
The Red Dot Club

The Red Dot Club

Victims' Voices

by

Robert Rangel

The homicide detective walked into the interview
room where the officer was waiting.
"How're doing? You okay?"
The young man looked up, obviously shaken,
"I don't know what to say, I just killed a man."
And the homicide detective stared him in the eyes,
"It's okay."
The young officer's blank stare spoke volumes. His unresponsiveness
was louder than any words that could be spoken.
The homicide detective continued to lock eyes with the young man.
"You're the victim. Understand that someone tried to kill
you tonight. You're just a better shot than he was."

Taken from an actual event as told by homicide detective
Joe Holmes
Retired Los Angeles County Sheriff

Dedication

Doing hard time refers to someone who is in prison for a long, long time.

Convicts will sometimes say, "Oh two years? I can do that standing on my head."

Being shot and fighting for your life is like doing hard time. I say this because the incident of being shot seems to take forever and is so horrifying and traumatizing the effects last forever.

However, you say, "But Robert, all the shootings I've seen on YouTube last maybe two or three seconds. How bad can that be?"

You are right, they usually only last seconds. But those seconds seem like hours and hours. In this book, you will read how a lifetime can pass in seconds.

Here's what happens physiologically when a threat to your life occurs, and a pouring of adrenaline enters your system: Adrenaline is dumped into your brain. Your brain starts processing information at superhuman speed. This is its attempt to find a way out, to survive. Things begin to happen that are not humanly possible under normal circumstances. Your brain ramps up your senses to their maximum. It turns on acute vision, to where you might see a bullet coming at you. You might see bullets entering clothing. It turns on acute hearing where you might hear gunfire from someone who is shooting you, but you might not hear your own gunfire. You might become superhumanly strong. You might be able to ignore the pain that otherwise would debilitate you. You might be able to run faster and jump higher than ever before. You might experience tunnel vision where all objects to the side of your vision are cut off and become nonexistent. Since your brain is thinking so unbelievably fast, it seems like the world around you slowed down. Like super-duper slow. If you are running while in this state you might feel like you are running in knee-high mud. If you are trying to flick the safety off your gun, it might seem a little flick of the thumb is taking ten minutes. Unless a person has studied it, when they go through it, they think they are going crazy. It can also scare the hell out of you because it makes you think, "I'm getting killed and I can't move fast enough to stop it."

This is not something you can train for. To get this amount of outpouring of adrenaline takes a real and credible threat to your life. It cannot be duplicated.

The closest that can be duplicated to this is some very, very stressful training. For a peace officer, a full stress academy, in my opinion, is necessary.

A peace officer must be able to think through a situation that might end his or her life in order to survive. That is the ultimate stress, and not everyone can do it. I thank the Lord every day I went through the Los Angeles County Sheriff's Academy. We lost a lot of nice people in our academy class that should not have been peace officers. They couldn't handle the stress. This was probably a blessing for them, their partners and even society. If someone can't handle the hard as steel training in the academy, then they might give up during a life and death fight in the streets. They or their partners or a citizen might pay with their lives.

Some refuse to acknowledge to win against violence, one must actually become more violent than the war being waged upon them. It is ugly in the extreme and to think this way is not politically correct. Sorry, and I know it is hard to acknowledge, but there are times when your stalwart young and sometimes not so young men and women officers become more violent than you would like to know about.

This book is as real as it gets. I refused to pull any punches. To my knowledge, everything you will read is 100% true. So...I give you all warning, when someone is trying to kill you and when you are fighting for your life people curse. When cops get shot, they do not hold up their pinky finger and say, "That's not cricket old boy!" How else can you understand the horror unless I take you there all the way?

So, this is my warning, my clarification, my caveat to you, the heroes in these pages cuss and sometimes use metaphors that might be disturbing to those with tender sensibilities. In reading these accounts, some might want to call these officers, "animals." Just remember these are the same animals who have gone into your burning house and risking their own lives dragged you out, or have given you C.P.R. or who have fought criminals to the death to make your world better. Sometimes they go home at night and have nightmares, sometimes they cry. They are your neighbors, sons, daughters and they sit next to you in church.

My sincere hope is you will not only enjoy this book, but it will give you understanding and insight into a world where heroes live.

As we ran the hills of East Los Angeles we sang;

> "Eighteen weeks of living hell, just to work the county jail.
> But I won't cry, and I won't moan,
> I'll soon be in the riot zone.
> If I die in the riot zone,
> Box me up and ship me home.
> Pin a medal upon my chest,
> Bury me in the lean and rest!
> Lef, right, lef."

This book is dedicated to my drill instructors of the Los Angeles County Sheriff's Academy Class 217:

Thank you for making us bleed, throw up, and curse you. Your methods, harsh though they were, were correct.

Due to the hard, hard training, I credit you with saving my life on the evening of June 6, 1991.

Thank you,

Robert Rangel
Los Angeles County Deputy Sheriff, Retired
Los Angeles County Sheriff's Academy, "The Hill."
Class 217
Graduated September 29, 1983

Red Dot Club Definition:

This is a very exclusive club. It has very few members in relation to the population of the world. No one wants to be a member, and the mark of the red dot is forced upon those who after receiving it become members. This is the mark made on the human body after being shot.

Taken from Robert Rangel's personal homemade dictionary.

Contents

Foreword

There are approximately 900,000 law enforcement officers in this great nation. Most of them will serve their entire careers without becoming involved in a shooting. About 150 will die in the line of duty each year while 50,000 of them will be assaulted every year. Sadly, and not nearly so well understood, is that more of these men and women will die at their own hand than will be murdered.

Every hour of every day, people will call for their assistance when the situation has deteriorated to such a point that reasonable people cannot handle events without intervention. When they call, we send them young men and women to try and rectify situations that are years in the making and may involve drugs, alcohol or mental illness. These young people are nearly always successful, and when they are not, they are on the front page of your local newspaper.

They see things that can never be unseen – and while they are well trained to handle emergency, life-threatening events, they are not trained to deal with the emotional or mental aftermath of such experiences.

Robert Rangel's new book gives us insight into the terrible realities that every one of these men and women experience, and the memories they must carry and cope with. It illustrates clearly a profound need for training and protocols to prepare for and deal with these lasting events.

Dennis Slocumb
LASD (ret.)
Vice President Emeritus, International Union of Police Associations

Victims' Voices

"So, what?" asks a number of our society. "The number of peace officers who get shot every year in relation to the number of peace officers is minimal. There are criminals, and it is a dangerous job. Officers are going to get shot."

I say, just one officer shot is too many. I know. I was shot. And if you are the one who is shot, one is too many.

Now let me put some things in perspective. Being shot and fighting for your life is, well, out of this world. If you've read this book or my first book in the series, *The Red Dot Club*, you have a glimpse of what it is like.

It's like this. Before you become a cop, you've seen the cop movies, and you are an expert. I've heard them all before. Comments such as, "Why didn't that cop just shoot the gun out of his hand?" or "Why did the cop keep shooting?" Or, "Why didn't they just shoot him in the arm or the leg?"

I ask the follow-up question. Have you ever shot a gun?

Invariably the answer is, "No, but what's that got to do with it?"

My response is, "Because if you have ever shot a gun, you would know how much it takes to hit a target. It is a combination of vision, breath control, steady legs, steady arms, steady hands, and while doing this only moving your finger. Because any other movement means you will miss. If you tried to do this on the range, it is difficult enough. Try it when someone is intent on killing you."

My next question is, "Have you ever had to stop someone who was 100% committed to killing you?"

Again, invariably the answer is, "No, but when you shoot someone it's over. Why keep shooting them?"

My answer to you is, look at any of the chapters in this book, especially, "Fighting a Zombie."

The fight isn't over until it is over. The issue is not always so clear-cut in the milliseconds of a gunfight.

Let me lay out the degrees. Before you become a cop, you see the cop movies, and you know what it is all about. Then you get into the academy, and they issue you your gun. Yes, they issue you a gun. They tell you don't load it. Don't play with it. You are not trained yet.

You actually snap to attention, 'YES, SIR!' is your silent answer because it is becoming real. You have it. The instrument to end life. To save life. Your life, your partner's life, an innocent person's life.

You have it. It is heavy. You could beat someone to death with it, or you could shoot bullets traveling faster than the speed of sound into a living person. The realization of what you have in your hands is heavy. It is literally life and death.

Now, this scares the shit out of many people. The absolute power of the gun. It scares the shit out of the cadet or recruit. But we are not even there yet. We haven't even begun to experience it. We just moved from non-cop to the in-between role of, "you have a gun." It's like moving to a different state where people have a different accent.

Within the week the cadet or the recruit is at the range. Before that, you get lessons upon lessons. You learn about the capability of the weapon you now possess. The gravity of the words hits you like the weight of the universe, "Once the bullet leaves the gun, you cannot call it back. Be sure."

After the lectures, you go to the firing range. The question from the staff comes out, 'Who here has fired a gun before?'

Your hand goes up. You want to shoot. The drill instructors call those who have shot a gun before, forward. It is not that many. The twenty or so cadets go to the firing line. Instructions are given on loading your gun. You follow precise instructions step by step.

Now you are on the firing line. Your gun is pointed away in front of you toward the target. You've been told the words to listen to signifying you can shoot. You hear them, "Ready on the right, ready on the left, all ready on the firing line."

The other cadets are behind the firing line. They too are experiencing it. They know they are next.

As you concentrate on steadying your breathing, as you concentrate on keeping your legs still, as you concentrate on keeping your arms still, as you concentrate on keeping your hands still, as you concentrate on your two-handed grip on the gun, as you concentrate on keeping the sights aligned and on your target, you think of the incredible power you now possess and as you slowly squeeze the trigger you think, "This might one day be a real person you will do this too." When the gun goes off, you are surprised at it bucking in your hand. You are surprised even though your ears are plugged, how loud it is. You are surprised you can feel the concussion of the air being displaced by the explosion. The sheer force.

And you realize the sanctity of life. And you vow to do your best to always remember when you use this tool. You have now moved to the next stage; you have now moved to another country where the people speak another language.

Oh, but I am not done. Not by a long shot.

You are fortunate enough to be one of the few who made it. Two or three out of one hundred who apply actually get through the academy.

Test after test and literally blood sweat and tears determine if you get hired and make it through the academy.

You are now a street cop. You are trying to meld all you learned into actual practice. Just getting in and out of the radio car can be a challenge with all the gear you are wearing.

Then the call comes out. In south central Los Angeles, they come out all the time. They did not teach us in the academy most cops only pull out and point their guns at someone once every 20 years because south central Los Angeles is not like that. It is not unusual to pull out and point your gun at someone every 20 minutes. In 1985 it seemed like the gangs were robbing and shooting and killing everyone, everything. In 2014 the area I worked was dubbed Death Alley. My first week in patrol there were six murders. That's not counting the people who were shot, stabbed, or beat who didn't die.

Anyway, the call comes out. It was a man with a gun. I was with my training officer, and when we got there, there was a man who matched the description of the call of the man with the gun. He was standing on the sidewalk. We pulled up and got out. My gun was in my hand, pointed down. My training officer got pissed. "POINT YOUR GUN AT HIM!!!"

Of course, he was right. Damn right, point your gun at him. You see folks, basically for a non-violent person to point a gun at someone is a hard thing to do. It can mean death. To go from pulling your gun out to pointing it at someone is a huge step. You have just entered the next stage and moved off earth. You are no longer in another country you are now on the moon.

Have you had enough? I don't think so. Let's travel down the real road. The road many people don't want to think about.

You get the call. It's the same call like the one I just described. A man with a gun. You get there, and there is the man described in the call. You get out of the car, and he has a gun in his hand. But it's not pointed at you. You are using the door of your radio car for cover. You know it's not much, but it's better than nothing, you hope. You are yelling at him to drop the gun. Of course, you are well past the stage of being worrisome about pointing your gun at someone. And you are. You have your gun pointed square at his chest. You are fifteen feet away. He doesn't drop the gun. You are focused on it, on the barrel. You feel you have time. But not too much time. You remember all you learned about reaction time. How long it takes the brain to recognize the threat and react to it. Basically, he's got you if he wants you. You know if he decides to shoot you, you don't have enough time to shoot him first. You will get some shots off, but he will fire first. And the reality of it scares you. So, you start to squeeze the trigger. Things are moving in microseconds now. You realize you are squeezing the trigger and you know you are being filmed. Someone is filming you. They film everything. You know no one will understand. Not the lawyers, not the district attorney's office, and certainly not the citizens. They know nothing of reaction time or how you can shoot someone seven times or more, and they are still a threat. You feel alone, even though your partner is with you it is your decision; yours alone. Your partner is reacting to his own interpretation of the threat he or she sees. Then the man drops the gun. The situation is over. You stop squeezing and realize it was fractions of a second away. You have now moved to another solar system, not another state, not another country, not the moon, but to another solar system.

I'm not done. Not by a long shot.

You get a call of a man with a gun. You get there, and the man described in the call has a gun. You get out and get behind your car door for cover. You point your gun at him, and he has the gun in his hand. You are giving him orders. *"DROP THE GUN, DROP THE FUCK-ING GUN!!!"*

He doesn't do it. In an instant, he points the gun at you. You see the muzzle flash of his gun. You know he fired. You are too late. He has already fired. You realize you're firing. Time has slowed down, and you realize he is down. He has dropped the gun. You assess the situation, you scan and feel the threat is over. Shaking, you get him handcuffed.

You realize your partner has also shot at him, but you aren't sure how you know this. Things are in a dream state, but more real than you have ever experienced before. Colors are enhanced, and vision is so unbelievable sharp, more than ever before. Some sounds are muted, some sounds are louder. Your adrenaline is going through the roof. *FUCK*, someone just tried to kill you. But you are not hit. When he fired, he missed you. You just traveled somewhere else. You traveled not to another state, not to another country, not to another planet, not to another solar system, but you traveled to another universe.

It gets worse, much worse and you will read about those incidents this book. To get where someone is killing you, where you are getting shot and at the same time you are shooting and fighting for your life, ranks as one of the most horrifying things you can experience. That my friends is like going to another dimension…And it is where I am going to take you.

You'll read those accounts. But you do not have to be shot to become a victim.

There's another side. These are the incidents cops experience. It's the horror or the terror cops go through that little by little chip away at their life. There are approximately 900,000 peace officers in the United States. In relation to those numbers, there are a small number of cops who are shot. But every single cop who has been out in patrol has the stories, their stories of experiencing the horror or terror. They are also victims. You will read both accounts here. Those who were shot, and those who were victims by other means.

Hear their voices

They speak

Listen, and you will hear them…

They are the Victims' Voices

Chapter 1

Brain on the Badge

Account of Robert McCrary
Pomona Police Department

In February 1995, I was working a two-man car as a City of Pomona Police Officer. It was nighttime, and my partner and I were patrolling on the north side of the city in an area known as *The Islands*, an area heavily infested with a black gang, but still housing many Hispanics.

I heard pop, pop. I thought, "Oh it's probably fireworks." But in the back of my mind, I also wondered if they were gunshots. I didn't know where the pops had come from. We turned a corner, and I saw a huge melee in the middle of the street about ten houses or so up the block. Probably ten seconds had passed from the time I heard the two pops until the time we turned onto the street where the disturbance was happening.

I grabbed my microphone to put out a call for backup that there was a fight in the middle of the street. Before I could get the call out, we got a call of, "Shots fired, man with a gun." The address of the call was where we were, where the melee in the middle of the street was.

I thought, "Oh cool, okay we are already here."

We drove up to the fight and didn't see anyone with a gun, but there were a lot of people in the street, yelling, cursing and scrambling about. I bulldozed my way through the center of the crowd. My partner was also trying to get through the group from a different angle. As we were making our way through the crowd, all these people were yelling, "He's got a gun, he's got a gun! He just shot up a house!"

When I got through the crowd in the street, there in the middle, surrounded by this mob was a Hispanic man lying face up. A smaller Hispanic man was straddled on top of him. The Hispanic on the bottom was trying to get up. And the Hispanic on top had his right forearm across the other man's chest trying to keep him down. With his left hand, the small Hispanic was holding the other man's right hand down on the street pinning it to the ground.

Even though I heard the shots, and we received the call of, "a man with a gun, shots fired" it was still a shock when I saw his hand gripping a revolver. "OH SHIT! HE'S GOT A GUN!"

I recognized the man with the gun. He was a member of a Hispanic gang who had strong ties to the Mexican Mafia. I had dealt with him before. He had not been involved in anything too crazy I knew of. I had had several contacts with him such as car stops or as a passenger in a stolen car. I knew him, and I'm sure he remembered me.

He looked like he was dusted, (high on P.C.P., angel dust). He had that, "out of it" look in his eyes. The smaller Hispanic on top of him saw me and gave me that look on his face pleading for help. All of this was happening in fractions of a second.

I grabbed his hand and the gun with my left hand and pinned it to the street. Time instantly slowed to super slow speed. As I shoved the smaller Hispanic man off the suspect, I quickly worked my left hand to the revolver's cylinder. Now I was straddling the suspect and had a death grip on the gun. By grabbing the revolver's cylinder, the gun could not be fired. I intended to peel the gun out of his hand, but as hard as I tried, I could not get it away from him. My gun was out and in my right hand.

The suspect looked up at me, and he had those dead eyes like he didn't give a shit about anything, and he was hell-bent on what he was going to do, and no one was going to stop him.

As I held his gun, I was talking to him, trying to reason with him. I was trying to get the gun away from him as I said, "Dude, this is over, let it go, drop the gun, this is over."

Then I could feel the pressure. He was trying to turn the gun toward me. I started yelling at my partner, "GUN, GUN, GUN!"

Time was still in slow motion. This was going on forever. He was trying to get the gun turned toward me while not saying a word and staring at me with those dead eyes. I was trying to hold onto the cylinder so the gun wouldn't fire and I was trying to peel the gun out of his hand. I was yelling at my partner, primarily to come and shoot the suspect.

I looked up for a second and saw my partner bouncing all over the place. He was pointing his gun at the suspect, he was pointing his gun at me, and he was pointing his gun at the crowd. I had a dreadful feeling of hopelessness.

I could feel the suspect tensing. His torso, his shoulders, and arms were tensing up, and it seemed like every fiber of his being was focused on getting the gun pointed at me. I looked, and I could see the tendons in his wrist flexing. His finger was on the trigger, and I could feel the cylinder of the revolver trying to move as I held onto it trying to keep it from moving. He was relentless, and everything he had, every ounce of energy he spent was on trying to pull the trigger.

I thought for a second, "Okay, he can't-do anything, he can't shoot me because I've got the cylinder." Not too much time had gone by, but as soon as the above thought went through my mind, I realized I was getting fatigued. That was scary. I could feel my grip on the gun loosening. I looked at the gun. It looked like a .22 caliber gun. I thought, "Okay if he shoots me my bulletproof vest can handle that, I'm going to be okay." And I had this little discussion with myself, "Because of where I'm at, if he shoots me it will be a body shot and it will hit my vest. It's a little gun, I'll probably be okay, but I really don't want to get shot."

Then the idea of getting shot really pissed me off. I thought, "I don't want to get shot." I got really angry. I was trying to get the gun away, I was yelling at him in anger, "Motherfucker, let go of the gun!" and I pistol-whipped him in the head with my own gun as hard as I could. And I'm not kidding; I hit this guy really hard.

He had no, and I mean no reaction. Zero. When I pistol-whipped him, he still had those dead eyes looking at me. He didn't even flinch.

Nothing worked, nothing. The crowd had thinned out. There were now less than ten people standing around in front of me in a U-shape watching. My partner was in front of me with his gun out, pointing it at the suspect. He was yelling at me, "Get off of him, get off of him Rob, I got him."

I was thinking, "If I get off of him, he's going to shoot me!"

I could feel the palm of my hand start to sweat and my grip was now slipping from the cylinder. Of course, this was all happening super, super fast, but it seemed super, super, slow. I was having all these conversations with myself, and I had different thoughts going through my mind at the same time. The thoughts and conversations were like, "Why am I thinking about him shooting me in the vest? Why am I thinking of getting shot at all, like it's okay?" I was arguing with myself.

I was spent. Out of gas. My hand was slipping, and I didn't think I could hold on much longer. I had been in this life and death grip using every inch of my strength for maybe thirty or at the most forty-five seconds. I asked myself, "How can I be so tired and he's not?" It didn't make sense, and it scared the hell out of me.

I was out of options. I had done everything I could think to do. I was exhausted, and it had come down to either me or him. I thought, "If I can shove his hand up I can retreat off of him and buy myself a fraction of a second and maybe not get shot." I shoved the suspect's gun up and away from me as hard as I could. The position I shoved his hand was the same position as if a student was raising his hand to ask a teacher a question. As I shoved his gun hand up, I fell back toward his feet. He was coming up like he was doing a sit up. I knew I was going to shoot him but time was so slow I felt like I didn't have enough time to get the rounds off before he would shoot me. As he was sitting up, I quickly shot two rounds into his chest like pop, pop. Even while I was shooting him, I could not believe he was still moving to sit up. Now I was on my butt literally sitting on one of his feet. He was still getting up. I couldn't believe it. When he sat up his gun was still in his hand, and it was pointed it at me. I had just milliseconds before I shot him twice in the chest, but now his gun was pointed at me. I was like, *"WHAT THE FUCK? HOW IS THIS EVEN POSSIBLE?"* I could not believe it! He was going to shoot me. It seemed to take forever and ever, and things were so slow I was scared I couldn't get my rounds off fast enough, but in reality, it was really quick. I raised my gun a fraction, it took forever and slowly I squeezed. Pop, I shot him in the head. His head made a popping noise, and I saw it almost like deflate a little bit for a second, and then he was down. I saw all this steam coming out of his head like his head was smoking a cigarette. Simultaneously my partner started shooting.

All I could think of then was I was going to get shot by my partner. I rolled right, and one of my partner's rounds ricocheted off the pavement and hit me in the shin. It was probably shrapnel, and it didn't penetrate, but it hurt like hell. It felt like someone took a golf club and hit me in the shin with it.

Although I was going through hell, it was pretty funny because I saw the rest of the crowd run, yelling and screaming as they scattered in all directions. I guess they had seen enough.

So here is the backstory to this incident. The suspect and several of his homies tried to crash a backyard wedding. The family told them it was a family wedding and they had to leave. This suspect got angry and shot his gun into the reception in the backyard. By a miracle of God, no one was hit.

About a half hour later they transported me to the station. They had nowhere to put me, so I was sitting in a chair in the hallway outside of the watch commander's office for about an hour. Of course, everyone in the station knew what had happened. A records clerk came up to me and was staring at me. She didn't say anything to me but just stared at me. It made me angry; I mean why was she staring at me? Finally, I asked her, "What, why are you staring at me?!"

It kind of snapped her out of it, "Oh I'm so sorry, but what is that on your badge?"

I looked down, and I had a chunk of brain matter about the size of a thumbnail on my badge. It kind of looked like cauliflower. As soon as I saw it, I freaked out and jumped out of my chair and swatted it off. It grossed me out; I don't like gore. My immediate reaction was to swat it off. It must've landed on the floor. I ran to the bathroom and looked at myself in the mirror, and I was horrified to see my uniform shirt spattered with blood and little pieces of tissue and I guess brain matter.

I really didn't want to shoot the guy. I really thought I could get the gun out of his hand. That's why I didn't shoot him initially. But as hard as I tried I could not get the gun away from him. I really gave this guy every opportunity to surrender. But he just would not give up. When homicide did their investigation, they found out when the guy fired into the reception, he emptied his gun. He didn't know his gun was empty because during the struggle he was trying to kill me. When I found out his gun was empty, I was really angry I had killed a man who had an empty gun. There was no way for me to know it was empty at the time, but it was. It still pisses me off he made me shoot him and that he died.

I had been with the department four years when this happened. I did twenty-four more years with the department.

I had two good friends killed while on the department. In total, I was in five shootings. Once a suspect shot at me multiple times from about fifteen yards away from an elevated 2nd-floor landing. I was trying to talk to him when he started shooting at me. I had no time to react or draw my gun or anything. He just started shooting. He missed each shot. I mean he missed each shot! I was amazed he missed! I am still amazed! I think about it all the time. I never understood how I got to walk away from death and others didn't.

The nightmares come and go. They are mixed. Sometimes in my dreams, I live the scenes. I see gunshots being fired at me. I see the little chunk of brain matter on my badge and my uniform decorated with the death of another person. I see a man possessed, using every inch of his body to take my life. I am myself yelling in hopeless desperation, knowing my life is about to be taken from me, but no one can help me. I still see the smoke from the sizzling bullet in his brain. It's only part of what I relive. I've woken up and find I am putting my wife in a chokehold. A full career and five shootings…guess this is what I will live with for the rest of my life. The nightmares will never end…

Chapter 2

M&M

Account of Mike Willis
Whittier Police Department

Joel told me, "You need to talk to my dad. He's a genuine badass. He… is…the toughest guy I know. He is 70 years old, and I'm still afraid of him."

This was coming from a guy who'd been shot numerous times. Who'd faced multiple men shooting him with AK-47's trying to kill him. He who himself is a genuine badass.

But he was right. Dad too was a badass. It runs in the family.

* * * * *

I met Mike at his home and parked behind a truck with Vietnam Veteran decals on it. It turned out to be his. When I met him, I immediately thought of Paul Newman. At 70 he is trim with raw muscle running through him and a grip that could squeeze the life out of you if he wanted. Mike is gregarious in his speech leaving no doubt he is strong-willed, all the while looking at you with steel blue eyes that tell nothing and see everything. He is a great family man who brags about being married to a woman, who as he says, "She is the nicest woman I've ever met in this world. Everyone who has ever met her thinks she is the nicest woman in this world. It's because she is the nicest woman in this world." They have five children together, and he beams when talking about each one of them. As I said, he is a great family man.

Mike started talking, "I was born in northern California. We grew up very poor in Lodi, where my father owned and ran a chicken ranch. I had five brothers. My dad was an alcoholic, and he was a mean drunk. None of us brothers got along with him. He had lost an eye when he was nineteen as a logger, and he would never wear a patch. He would wear a bandage with two strips of tape over his eye," Mike laughed. "I was the third son after my oldest sister and two older brothers. My mom was an absolute saint. After we sort of booted my father out when I was about thirteen, my older brothers and I worked to support my mother and the other nine children."

"Yeah, there were nine other children; fourteen kids total. Seven boys and seven girls."

I was blown away. Mexicans have that many kids. But Mike is white.

"Yeah, all single births, no twins. We worked in the vineyards in the fields. We did a lot of pruning, irrigating, and during the harvest season we would move with the migrant workers and pick fruit, vegetables, cabbage, lettuce, tomatoes. We migrated with the Hispanic people. Of course, my best friend growing up was a Mexican kid."

I looked at Mike, maybe Mike was really Mexican.

"Oh yeah," he laughed with his eyes beaming, "We weren't nearly as good as them!"

Ok, maybe Mike wasn't a Mexican.

"Picking cherries, we got $1.10 a bucket. It took me a whole day to get one bucket. We'd go way up the ladders to get to the top of the trees. All day to pick a bucket. Of course, those braceros (The Spanish word for a farm laborer or farm hand) could pick a bucket in an hour. They were just, so fast, but us little white boys, we couldn't pick shit."

We were both laughing, and I was more than warming up to this man.

"I tell you the best thing was my mom. She would get a loaf of day-old bread, and she would make a whole loaf of baloney sandwiches. Bread, baloney, bread baloney, bread baloney. No food value. No mayonnaise, no cheese, no lettuce, no tomato. Just bread and baloney. We would swap those sandwiches with the Mexicans for burritos. And that's how I got to fall in love with Mexican food.

"When we got paid we would give our mom all the money for the rest of the kids and the family. We were really poor, but I think we were very rich as far as a childhood goes. I probably had one of the greatest childhoods of anyone. I mean we fought, we laughed. Me and my brothers, who are still alive are very close. I learned I never wanted to be that poor again. Not to have a penny in your pocket when every other kid around you could buy milk for school. They could buy lunch. There were times when we didn't have a penny. One day I looked at a cop and said, 'Wow, if I become a cop, I don't have to sit at a desk. I get to do something different every day.' I remember when I was in the eighth grade they wanted us to do a paper on a vocation we wanted to be when we grew up. I did my paper on being a cop. I really wanted to be a pilot, but my eyes were too bad."

Then he loudly and emphatically proclaimed, "I was legally blind."

"How could you have become a cop? You had to pass an eye test!" I said. I wondered if it was the baloney sandwiches.

His voice got all soft and low like. He squinted, leaned forward and looked at me out of the corner of his eyes from across the table and said, "I cheated."

Now I realized what kind of a character was in front of me. You, "CAN'T" be a cop if you are legally blind. I was on the edge of my seat knowing something great was going to come out of this man's mouth.

He smiled at me, "Then I got a little older and started getting into fights. The police would take me to jail. You know not a big deal. Just fighting. But my mom would have to get me out of jail. Thank God it all happened while I was under eighteen. This was in Lodi where we lived and worked. When I got out of high school, I went to a junior college for a little bit. In college, I majored in parking lot drinking 101 and parking lot drinking 102. One day I said, 'You better do something, or you're going to end up in prison.' Friends of mine were getting busted for crimes and going to jail. Always in the back of my mind, I said to myself, 'You can't do anything really bad because then you can't be a cop.' So, I decided on a brilliant move, I joined the army. It was 1965."

"Whoa," I said, just like you probably are now. "How about the eye cheating part?" I wanted to know how he eye cheated to become a cop.

He now had a hard glint in his eye, telling me to shut up. He ignored me. Obviously, he was in charge, "They were really nice until you signed on the line. Then their whole attitude changed. They ate me alive, beat my ass, yelled at me, worked me to death."

Of course, he was talking about the military, totally ignoring the cheating eyeball test thing.

"All I wanted was my mommy. I wondered what I had gotten myself into. After basic, I got into M.P. school (military police school). Of course, then I got orders for Vietnam and got there in February 1966. I came back home to the U.S. in February 1967. When I got back people I passed would say behind my back but loud enough for me to hear, 'Hey baby killer. Gestapo. Did you ever throw a baby under a truck?'

"And that round symbol, that peace symbol? I'd want to shove it up somebody's ass. I look at the citizens today, and I thank those people, God bless them for treating our troops right. It's about damn time."

I was still wondering about the cheating eyeball test, but it was fading. I trusted he was going to get there in his own sweet time. This was his time now. I was just along for the ride. And I was "on the boat."

He continued on, "I ended up in Southern California because I chased a skirt. She stopped. And I caught her. I think she let me catch her. And I'm still with her. I had to marry her…I'd been sending her all my money from Vietnam, I had to marry her. She had all my money!

"She is the nicest woman I've ever met. To this day she is the nicest woman I've ever met. I married her after returning to the United States. I married her when I still had another year and a half to do in the military. This year will be 50 years we've been married. When I got out of the military, I tested with the Downey and Whittier Police Departments. I actually was going to go with L.A.P.D. because there were L.A.P.D. recruiting posters in the day room in Vietnam. Motorcycle cop posters, you know, 'Be an L.A.P.D. Cop'. I thought, 'Yeah!' I would not test with the Sheriff's because I had worked in the stockade in Fort Dix and I said I would never put myself in that position again. Working the jails. That was almost as scary as Vietnam."

Mike looked directly at me and said, "I mean I don't know how you guys do it." I had been a Los Angeles County Deputy Sheriff, and I had to work in the county jail before hitting patrol.

"It's a constant 24 hour a day game. It's you against them. You couldn't carry a gun, no nightstick. You were always looking and thinking they would jump you. If you joined Los Angeles County Sheriffs, you had to do six months in the jail."

Mike was right. I came real close to getting killed while working in the jails. I've been scared two times in my career as a deputy. One of those times was when I was working in the jail. Another was when flames were shooting onto my windshield while driving on a surface street at 110 miles an hour, (I guess I don't want to burn to death. Thus I am not a fireman). I'm not saying I wasn't concerned a whole bunch of other times, but near-paralyzing fear only happened a couple of times.

"So, I drove to Parker Center and saw all the tall buildings in Los Angeles and said to myself, 'Nope, I'm not doing that.' Big city government was not for me."

"My eyesight was 20/400, 20/600 something like that?"

I'd been waiting for this part.

"The military took me, hell they would take anyone, as long as you were breathing. But I knew the police departments were different. They wouldn't take you if you had bad vision. I knew this, but I decided the departments were going to have to reject me. I was still going to apply. My wife had a family friend who was an optometrist. When I went in to see him, he knew what he was doing. He was getting me the right glasses, and I could see. He was real, reeeaal good. When I told him, I was applying to be a police officer he told me he might be able to help me. He said I had astigmatism, which is an oddly shaped eyeball. So, he gave me flat glass contacts. He told me to put the contacts in several days before the police department medical test, 'Leave the contacts in until the very last minute before the eye test. They are going to ask you if you have contacts. Tell them "Yes." They will have you remove them. Take them out right before the test. You should have about thirty minutes of good vision. The reason for this is the flat contact has reshaped your eye, your cornea for a little while. But after thirty minutes your eye will go back to its odd shape, and your vision will deteriorate.'

"So, when I went into my eye test, the doctor asked me if I had contacts. I told him, 'Yes.' He had me take them out. He had me read an eye chart at the end of the hallway, and I could read all the letters, except for the last one. He told me to hang on a second.

"He left the office, and I could hear him on the phone speaking to someone. 'He is very, very close; he can see everything on the eye chart except the last letter.' He came back to me and said, 'You are the last one on the list, and you are going to pass this. I've got some paperwork to do in my office, and when I come back, you better be able to tell me what that last letter is.' And he left. I ran to the end of the hallway and looked at the letter, and it was an, X. I will always remember it was an X, because, X, marks the spot. The doctor came back in a few minutes and asked me, 'Okay, what is it?'

"I said, 'It's an, X.

"He said, 'Okay, good you passed.'

"I walked out of there, and I knew I had to make a decision. 'You dumb fuck! What did you do? Now you've got to shit or get off the pot.' My eyes were the only thing that could have stopped me, and I had just passed, or uh, cheated the eye test. I was twenty-two years old. I was married with two boys. I decided I was going to be a cop.

"Whittier hired me. It was eight days before Downey offered me a job. So, I became a Whittier cop. I got hired in 1968. I worked at the station for nine months. I couldn't go in the field because I had no training. It's when I was working at the station where I met Mike. He was an explorer. He was a cadet with Whittier. I worked in the records bureau as a cop. I was treated very well. The guys were pumped the department had hired someone that had been somewhere and had done something. I was respected because I had been to Vietnam. I wasn't a college kid with no life experience. When I flew into Vietnam, I was in a tent next to a medevac pad. They were flying these GI's in, and they were strapped on the running boards outside of the helicopters. I saw all that. Of course, you spend a year in a country, and you see a lot of shit. So, I was treated well, except by these two old homicide detectives. They were just having fun with me. They took me to an autopsy thinking they were going to make me throw up. They thought they were going to show me something. Well, they did. The Los Angeles County Coroner's office was called the L.A. County Canoe Factory because they made canoes out of the dead bodies. They had this female who was killed by her husband. They were working on her. Then behind us, they brought in this 300-pound woman whose boyfriend beat her to death. They opened her up and pulled out a full term eight-month baby. They threw the intestines in this big bucket and in went the baby. I almost lost it. And I thought to myself, what did I just see? And I was like, 'Jesus!' That was an eye-opener. Then we went to Philippe's and had a French dip sandwich.

"I went to the Academy. The first day the drill instructors asked the class, 'Who was in the military?' Well, I knew why they wanted to know that. They wanted someone who knew the drills and commands to lead the class. I just wanted to blend in and get through the academy. So, I didn't raise my hand. Well, there were a few Whittier sergeants assigned as drill instructors. They knew me, and they knew my background because I had been working at the station. They yelled out, 'WILLIS!!!'

"'Sir yes sir!' I responded.

'WEREN'T YOU IN THE MILITARY?'

"'Oh, yes, sir, I forgot!'

"So, they got me in front of the class, and I had to lead the class through-out the academy. I did something right; I graduated number one in the class. I was the honor cadet. I got to patrol and worked dayshift for three months. I wanted to learn the reports. The next time I worked dayshift was 20 years later. After the first three months, Mike and I got together and worked sister cars, (this is best described as two separate radio cars which covered and backed each other on calls). We worked from 7 P.M. until 3 A.M. We had a nice competition on who could make the most 'obs,' arrests, (these are known as observation arrests, or arrests made from self-generated and initiated work, not from calls). I could not get enough. Had I not had a family, I would have done it for free. I loved it; I could not wait to go to work. It was exciting. I couldn't wait to get in there and see what the day was going to bring.

"Mike was the same way. In May 1974, I was asked if I wanted to go to this multiagency anti-burglary surveillance team coming up, named SEBIT. The acronym stood for, South East Burglary Investigations Team. It was to be a Federally funded operation. There were cops from Norwalk Sheriff's Station, Pico Rivera Sheriff's Station, Downey Police and Whittier Police Departments. We followed known burglars and bandits and watched them caper and took them when they came out of the victim's pads. They asked me if I wanted to go to the SEBIT team or be a motor cop.

"Give me a fucking break," he laughed and dismissively threw his arm and hand my way. "Write tickets or be a real cop!? Well, they offered it to Mike too. I don't have to tell you what Mike said. It was downhill from then on. We became known on the department as M&M, Mike, and Mike. We were inseparable. We were this close, (Mike crossed his fingers). It became the joke by some of the guys, 'Hey Mike I'm going to tell your wife I saw you without with your wife and you were cheating on her.'

"This SEBIT unit was brand new, and it was really exciting. After the team got tweaked here and there, it got really fun. We were on FIRE. We could find anyone. One of us would wake up in the middle of the night and call the other Mike, and then meet somewhere. We would go to the bad guy's pad at 2 A.M. We would verify he was there. We'd go back home, get some sleep, then at 8 A.M. we would get the team together and form our game plan. We never got paid for that. We did it because that's how we got information. It's how we operated. We did it because it was so much fun!

"In 1978, the federal funding for SEBIT ended, and Mike and I went to narcotics. I left SEBIT with over 200 hours of unpaid overtime. I just gave it away, never got paid for it. We started doing surveillances per our station detective's requests. We started doing dope buys. We earned a pretty good reputation. Anytime a detective needed someone followed or needed someone to do a buy, we were the guys. One of the sergeants approached Mike and me, 'You've got to get out of this business. You're going to get hurt. You've come too close. Something's going to happen to you.'

"We were having so much fun. The thought of stopping never entered our minds." The glint in his eyes momentarily left him.

"We were watching crimes go down and taking down the bad guys. We were getting guns, taking robbery suspects down while they were doing their robberies. We were in teller lines behind robbery suspects at the banks while they robbed them. I stood next to a guy in Von's supermarket while he did a robbery. I was pretending to read the back of a Wheaties box while he did it. This is how we did things. It was adrenaline pumping, very dangerous but also exciting stuff."

* * * * *

"December 12, 1979, I was here, and the kids were playing in the backyard. The call came in.

"'Can you come to the station? We need your and Mike's expertise.' It was Dave Butler, our auto theft detective. 'I've got a thing I need you and Mike to set up.'

"We were always getting those calls to help out, to set up special operations. We were the M&M boys. We had a reputation for doing undercover things. I remember we had been trying to solve a serial rapist case for about nine months. One day a girl got followed home in her car. She noticed it, and it happened when she got home her sister came out of the house, and they got a description of the car. We got the information and later spotted the car. We got the guy in the car and took him in for questioning. We got talking to the guy, and he was going to show us some of the locations where he did his crimes. While we were going to the locations in the car we got hungry; we hadn't eaten all day. So, we drove to a McDonald's. We asked the suspect, 'Hey do you want anything?'

"He was hungry too. He answered, 'A hamburger and a milkshake.'

"So, we bought him a hamburger and a milkshake. He thought we were the nicest guys in the world. We were his best friends. I remember later when I went to court on his case…Mike was dead by this time…"

Mike and I locked eyes, he quietly said, "…he was dead…

"…the rapist was in shackles in court. I was trying to put him in prison, and he knew it.

"As he passed me he leaned down and said to me…"

18

Mike swallowed hard as he squinted still locking eyes with me, "He said, 'Man I'm really sorry to hear about your partner.' He genuinely liked us."

Mike looked at me, "You know Robert, I'm getting better, a couple of years ago I would be sweating right now talking about this.

"When he said it, I got goosebumps thinking about my dead partner. And it was all over a hamburger and a milkshake.

"Robert, how'd we get sidetracked?"

"We're not."

"Robert, he was that guy. He was so much better than me about thinking his way through things. He was the…he was the guy who came up with the idea. He was a lot more than me. He was the guy who would figure things out. He was the consummate thinker. I was the bull in the china shop. So, either he pulled me back, or I pushed him forward. It's probably why he and I gelled so well together. To me, he was brilliant with the ideas.

"Anyway, getting back to December 12, 1979, when we went in to do this. Detective Dave Butler met us at the station. There was this biker guy named Igor, who was the president of the Cossacks motorcycle gang. He was the only member, and that made him the president. Someone had broken into his home in Pico Rivera and stolen all his guns. Well, he ends up getting a call from a Vagos motorcycle gang member named Harvey. He is now in Folsom Prison. So, Harvey calls Igor, he tells him 'Hey, we're just fucking with you. We are down at the Scavengers' Clubhouse (another motorcycle gang). You want your guns back just come down to the Scavengers' Clubhouse, and we'll give you your guns back.'

"So, he jumps on his motorcycle with his old lady on the back and goes down to the Scavengers Clubhouse. The guys at the clubhouse proceed to kick the living shit out of him. They put a gun to his head, they take his colors, (his jacket), they take his motorcycle and send him and his girlfriend walking.

"Of course, he's embarrassed now. He walks to the Whittier Police department and tells Dave everything that happened to him. After Igor gives his statement and gets home, Harvey called him, 'Hey you want your bike back it's going to cost you $500 bucks.'

"This is what they would do. They would do it to prospects especially. A prospect is a guy who wants to join the gang but has to prove himself first before they'll let him in. If the gang didn't like him, they'd steal his stuff, his bike, and then ransom it back to him. They would have you pay money to get back your own property. But they never gave you back your property. Now the guy would be out the money AND his property. And if you made too much noise your ass would be buried in the sand in the desert in a grave. Nice folks, huh?

"So, they want to do a meet with Igor to get his $500, and then they promise to give him back his bike.

"So, Igor called Dave, and that's when Dave called us to set this meeting up. Mike and I are just nasty looking, long hair, beards, I mean we would fit right in. In our job, we would switch off as the person doing the buy. That's what we considered a fun E-ticket ride buy. If it didn't scare the hell out of you, then what was the point? Now it was Mike's turn, and he insisted on taking it. It was already night and dark out."

* * * * *

For you babies, excuse me, my editor has a problem with me calling you readers, "babies," you young folks under forty reading this book, Disneyland used to sell ticket books to their rides. A-ticket book had different letters in them. To get on the Matterhorn, you had to have an E-ticket. To get on Mr. Toad's wild ride, you might have had to have a B-ticket. So, an E-ticket meant the ride with the utmost excitement.

* * * * *

"So, we figured this out, and Harvey called Igor. 'Hey, are you going to pay us the $500?'

"Igor told him, 'Yeah, but I need a driver because you have my bike. I found someone to drive me there.' Well, Mike was going to be the driver. The car was a little red Nissan pickup truck that belonged to Dave. We had dealt with the Vagos and the Scavengers, and they knew our undercover dope cars. So, we decided to use Dave's pickup. We got to Igor's place, and Mike went in. He was wearing a wire. Dave and I were sitting in a car outside of Igor's house. We had some other guys in other cars nearby. While Mike was in the house with Igor waiting for a call from Harvey, we picked up guys, bikers, doing counter surveillance. Bikers were driving by to see who was at his place, who was coming and going. They wanted to know if Igor had called the cops. About 45 minutes went by, and Mike turned on the wire. He said, 'Okay we're going to meet him at P.J.'s Bar at Whittier and Comstock.'

"Mike backed in an auto electric, auto repair shop parking lot at the northwest corner of Comstock and Whittier facing south. They were facing PJ's bar across the street. Mike was the driver, and Igor was the passenger. Mike had $500 of the city's money from their fund. We had three undercover cars and four black and whites within half a block of the bar. Dave and I were parked in the northeast corner parking lot of Whittier and Comstock.

"Igor went in the bar. A short time later he came back out and told Mike, 'They want you to go inside the bar.' Mike said, 'No, that ain't happening.' See, we already knew these guys would rip you off. Mike told him to go back inside and tell them when the bike is dropped off in front of the bar then they can send a guy over to get the money.

"Igor goes back in the bar and comes back out. 'Man, they're really pissed. They don't want to do it that way.'

"As we're sitting there listening to the wire and the conversation between Mike and Igor, we see Rocky, who is one of the Scavenger's gang members, come out of the bar. Harvey is also outside of the bar. Rocky looks over at Mike and flips him off. They then go back inside the bar.

"As I'm looking around just scanning the area, I hear the wire and Mike said, 'Oh, oh, go meet those guys and tell them only one.' He was talking to Igor in the truck. That's when I noticed both Rocky and Harvey walking across the street toward Mike and Igor. I saw Igor walking toward Rocky and Harvey, I guessed to head them off like Mike had just told him to, to tell them only one guy needed to come over. Mike stayed in the truck.

"I said to myself, 'this is fucked.' We were in trouble. I got out of the car and saw Dave was still in the car. He had never worked undercover stuff. So, as I'm getting out of the car, I tell Dave, "Call them in!" meaning all of our backup units. I don't know why he didn't. It could be I shut the door too quickly, and he didn't hear me, it could be the conversation on the wire coming into the recorder was too loud, but in any case, he didn't call for our backup. Dave later told me he thought I was going for a better look. It wasn't until he saw me leaving our parking lot he realized something was wrong.

"When I got to the parking lot where Mike was, Rocky and Harvey kind'a had their backs to me. Rocky was at the driver's door of the pickup and Harvey was at the driver's front left quarter panel. Harvey is kind of quarter turned toward me and kind of looking through the windshield. Rocky is talking to Mike. I can't hear what's being said, but I came up right behind them. I was walking quickly, I knew we were in trouble. At this time, I had no idea where Igor was.

"My badge was in one hand, and my gun was in the other. I was now ten feet away. Rocky stays put but Harvey started to move in front of the truck toward the passenger side of the truck. At the time I thought he was trying to get behind Mike, but in retrospect, I think he was going after Igor. In my thinking, Mike has to take Rocky because he's in front of him. Harvey is moving behind him, so Mike can't handle him; I have to take him. Neither Mike nor I can take them both. So, I have to take Harvey. When I get to within six feet, I yell, 'police freeze!' I actually shouted it twice because a guy who was working in the auto store heard me say it twice. He thought we were filming a movie.

"Harvey, whose back had been to me this whole time, understand we're talking just a few seconds, turns. As he turns, I saw he had a gun in his hand as he was spinning toward me. As soon as I saw the gun things went into super slow motion. Everything went from normal speed, like a normal humming sound going slower and slower."

Mike put his hands up in front of him, shoulder width and slowly brought them together slowly, indicating how time slowed.

"There was a gun in his hand, which he pointed at me. It turned out to be a .44 magnum. The barrel was huge. We were three feet away from each other.

"The only thing I could see was Harvey's hand and the gun. In slow motion, I watched as his finger ever so slowly squeezed the trigger. The gun was in my face. I wonder to this day how I could see his finger squeezing the trigger. At the time I thought to myself, 'Are you nuts? No one can see someone squeeze the trigger of a gun. You must be going crazy. Am I going nuts?' And everything got clear, clearer than ever before in my life. My vision got very clear, but I could only see his hand and the gun and the barrel. I don't remember seeing anything else but that. It got so clear, I could actually see him doing it, squeezing the trigger. It's crazy.

"I wasn't thinking anything but, *'SHOOT!!!'*

"He didn't shoot. His finger was squeezing the trigger, but nothing happened. The gun didn't go off. With the gun he was using if you didn't squeeze the trigger all the way, the hammer came back, the cylinder turned, but the hammer didn't fall. The hammer just went forward without firing the gun.

"As he was squeezing the trigger in slow motion I was shooting in slow motion. We were moving as he was squeezing and I was shooting. He was going backward toward the passenger side of the truck, and I was moving toward him, all in slow motion. And I could see was him squeezing as I was shooting him. I shot four times in very slow motion. I could see my bullets hitting him. It was cold that night. December 13, 1979. We were all wearing jackets. As my bullets hit him I would see his jacket moving in. It was like little puffs. The rounds would hit him, and his jacket would puff, and his body would shudder. I saw each round hit him, and he would shudder, and now I could see his face, and it looked like he wanted to cry. Each time he got hit, it looked like he wanted to cry. We were still moving; he was still squeezing, and I was still shooting. His jacket was still puffing and he was still shuddering, looking like he wanted to cry. The only thing I can hear is a little pop from my gun. That's it. I couldn't hear anything else.

"I know from past shootings the little pops didn't mean anything. In my first shooting when I heard the little pop, I thought my gun wasn't working, so the little pops this time didn't worry me. I knew the gun was working.

"He finally went down facing the rear of the truck, face down at the rear passenger tire. He actually bounced a little when he hit.

"Remember I couldn't hear anything but the little pops from my gun. As soon as Harvey went down, I got my hearing back, and I heard Rocky screaming. He was inside of the truck now. I didn't see how that happened. I was too busy with Harvey. He was lying face down on top of Mike. They were lying down on the bench seat. And Rocky was screaming, *'GO FOR IT MOTHERFUCKER, GO FOR IT!!!'*

"Things were now at normal speed, and I could hear again. I could see through the windshield and Rocky was on top of Mike, and he was screaming. I started shooting Rocky through the windshield. I was trying to get him off of Mike. Mike's head was almost to the passenger door. I know Mike was still alive then because I saw his knee come up.

And I thought to myself, 'Oh, my God, did I just shoot Mike?' That made me back off a little.

"Now while I'm at the front of the truck I catch a movement at the back of the truck. And it's Harvey popping his head up. I see he's got both hands on his gun. I know he's been hit at least four times. Now I hear Rocky again, *'GO FOR IT MOTHERFUCKER!!!'* And then from inside the cab, *BOOM BOOM!!!*

"And I shot into the cab boom, boom, boom. Now I see Harvey standing at the back of the truck with both hands on his gun, and the gun is pointed at me. Time slowed down again. And as I'm throwing myself down onto the hood of the car, and then trying to get to the ground, attempting to desperately get away from the front of his gun barrel, I see his barrel explode. *BOOOOOM!!!* And with the boom was a huge red and yellow ball of flame that came out of the barrel so slowly toward me. It slowly expanded then just as slowly contracted back, seeming to suck back into the barrel.

"Now, I am pissed off. I am no longer a police officer just doing my job. This is personal. I am completely enraged. Out of my mind enraged. Someone is trying to kill me. And someone is trying to kill my partner, my best friend. This is very personal. I could not understand why they wanted to kill me. When he fired that round, it was like he really wanted to kill me. I was now on the ground. And things were very slow. I thought 'This is not training. This is not a game. If I don't win this, I am going to die. I won't be going home. He is coming to kill me.' I didn't know if he was coming from the right or from the left, but I knew he was coming. I remember thinking 'This is for real and this is for keeps.'

"I was lying on the ground in the front of the truck, and all those distinct and separate thoughts went through my mind in no more than an eighth of a second. I was so fucking scared. And like a slap to my face, ANGER!!! I got *ANGRY!!!* I know I've never been that angry before.... it wasn't anger, it was rage. *RAGE!!!*

"And I stood up. I turned around. I had to see where these assholes were and I saw Harvey running back toward the businesses. As he was running, I stepped around the driver's side of the front of the truck and fired one or two rounds at him. Now I see Rocky on his feet, backing out of the driver's door of the truck. Throughout this whole thing, I never thought about the other cops. I didn't wonder about Dave or where he was, or what he was doing. I didn't see them, and they never entered my mind. To me, it was me, alone, against them.

"So Rocky was backing out of the truck. *'Fuck...does...this...ever... stop?'* I thought. I turned, and I started firing into Rocky. Rocky went down, and I got slide lock. My gun was empty. Now Robert as you know every good Narc always carries an extra gun magazine...in his attaché case...in his car. So now I've got to go across the street to my car and get more bullets. That's what I was thinking. I was so enraged I was willing to cross an open parking lot area. I was willing to cross the street to my car and either get the shotgun and my magazine or just my magazine and run back through the open parking lot back and finish this thing.

"And as I left the relative security of the front of the truck, as I was walking across the open parking lot, I turned my head toward the auto electronics store where Harvey had run to, and I was so enraged I screamed to him, *'I'M COMING FOR YOU MOTHER FUCKER!!! I'M GOING TO KILL YOU!!! I'M GONNA COME AND GET YOU!!!'* And I kept screaming, *'I'M COMING FOR YOU MOTHERFUCKER AND I'M GONNA KILL YOU!!!'* as I was walking to my car.

"I got about halfway to the middle of the parking lot, and I see Rocky lying face up in the parking lot at Dave's feet. Where Dave came from I have no idea. I didn't know where he was through this whole incident. Rocky had a revolver in hand, which is pointed toward the sky and he is trying to reload it. As you know this is impossible to do. You can't load a revolver with the barrel pointed at the sky, the bullets won't stay in.

"I didn't know until later that Dave had been to my right throughout this incident. The reason Harvey ran after shooting at me was Dave was also shooting at him.

"As I'm walking to my car and screaming at Harvey, he comes out with his hands up. He's almost crying, 'I give up, I give up! I've been shot, I've been shot.'

"I holstered my gun and took him to the ground, facedown and hand-cuffed him. Dave was at my side. A little panic set in, *'Where's Mike, I haven't seen Mike, where's Mike?'* And I ran back to the truck, to the driver's window. Mike was laying on the seat facing me with his back up against the passenger's window. And he was snoring like he was in a deep, tremendously deep, deep sleep. And he was wearing a beige stocking cap, and I could see the hole in his head. The bullet hole. His red dot.

"Rage and umbrage hit me like a freight train. Who were these people to shoot my partner? Mike was not part of my family, he was my family. He was always over my house. My kids called him Uncle Mike. He was as close to me as any of my brothers. I loved him. This garbage helped kill him. This garbage had the nerve to complain he was shot.

"I now was outside of myself. It was like I was watching another person. It wasn't me. I wasn't a cop anymore. Darkness and rage enveloped me and nothing else mattered to me except that he didn't deserve to live. It was a cold, ice-cold thought, 'I'm going to kill him.' Nothing, no force on earth could stop me now. I watched myself walk to Harvey. He was on the ground crying, 'I'm hurt I'm hurt I'm shot I'm shot.'

"I turned him over. He was now facing me. I reached for my gun. I said, *'You're not hurt, motherfucker; you're dead!'*

"My hand was on my gun, and I was pulling it out of the holster when I heard Dave screaming, *'GET AWAY FROM HIM MIKE GET AWAY FROM HIM!!!'*

"I froze. Time stood still. For an hour it seemed, I stared into Harvey's eyes. I saw his pain turn to fear. He knew, he understood. He knew what I was going to do and how close he was to death. He had no question I was going to do it. Dave was still screaming at me, and I awoke from my deep sleep. I was no longer a robot focused on revenge. Logic returned. I remembered, 'You're out of bullets. Your gun is empty... empty...empty. I realized my gun was empty. It was a hollow feeling.

"I went back to the truck and opened the passenger door, and Mike's upper body fell out onto me, and I held him until he died. Red and blue lights were now bouncing off of the buildings, and I knew the cavalry was there.

"Robert, ten years ago had I told you this story I'd have been sweating right now."

We sat for a little while in silence.

"What happened to Rocky?"

"He died at Dave's feet trying to reload his revolver. There were all kinds of live .38 caliber rounds on the ground around him. He was shot 12 times. Ten of those rounds were 9-millimeter rounds. The rounds I was carrying. Two were Dave's .357 caliber rounds. Out of the fifteen rounds, I shot that night ten were in Rocky, four were in Harvey, and one took Harvey's hat off.

"I remember going back to the station that night, it was about 10:30. It was a Thursday night. The night we got paid. And I was like 'Oh My God' and my head was spinning, and I was sitting at Mike's desk. I opened it up, and there was his check. It was 400 and some bucks. I looked at that thing, and I said to myself, 'Fuck he died for $435 bucks. And these fucking people don't care. Nobody cares.'

"And who do you call a hero? I remember thinking, these guys are running around playing basketball, and they're called heroes. Making all this money and risking nothing. And we walk into a locker room, just like they do, but when we strap on a uniform, we're risking our life. And for what? For $435. Fuck. It took me the longest time to get over that. Our society doesn't get it, I don't know if they even care. NO ONE CAN UNDERSTAND IT UNTIL THEY HAVE BEEN IN A SITUATION WHERE THEY MIGHT DIE. How do you get society to understand?

"I thought the shooting lasted half an hour. From the first bullet fired to the last was 12 seconds.

"How could so much happen that affected and changed so many lives in such a short period of time? 12 seconds."

* * * * *

This incident really played havoc with Mike's head, as it would with any normal human. He seriously thought of leaving the department. He took a little time off and visited his brothers. Mike came back to work and was placed in the what you would now call, the CSI unit. He became an expert in reading fingerprints. He learned how to photograph crime scenes, and gather evidence. He also taught at an academy and spoke of his shooting to the young cadets who wanted to become police officers. He worked as a background investigator. Mike promoted to sergeant, and became a field sergeant and eventually went back to narcotics. He worked another 18 years after this horrific event, holding the values of honor and integrity as he did so. He finally retired after completing 30 years with the Whittier Police Department.

For their actions on December 13, 1979, Detective David Butler and Detective Michael Willis received the Whittier Police Department's Medal of Valor, the highest award the department can bestow upon its officers.

For his actions on December 13, 1979, Detective Michael Lane posthumously received the Whittier Police Department's Medal of Valor, the highest award the department can bestow upon its officers.

Andrew Harvey was approved for parole in September 2016. California Governor Brown approved his parole, and Harvey was released on December 2, 2016.

Chapter 3

Realizations

Account of Robert Rangel
Los Angeles County Sheriff's Department

While going through the academy, you are hit with many realizations. You study tactics, law, driving, weaponless defense, and shooting. You march and drill and run in 107-degree weather.

The realizations are this is real, and you might face life and death situations. You slowly make the transition from a civilian to cop. Every person who goes through the transition has realizations throughout the process.

In 1983, I was working the Hall of Justice Jail in the juvenile section where all the juveniles housed there were being tried as adults. I had just graduated from the academy. For me, my full realization came when I spoke with a baby-faced 16-year-old gang member who was being tried as an adult due to the nature of his crime.

* * * * *

I asked him, "Why are you here?"

"I killed my homegirl," he answered.

"Why?"

"Because she told on my homeboy."

He was pretty matter of fact.

I asked him, "How did it happen?"

"We were in the park, and she went into the bathroom. I followed her in. After we were both in the bathroom, she heard me behind her, and she turned around. I grabbed her by the hair and chopped her in the neck with a hatchet."

"You chopped her in the neck? Did she scream?"

"No, she was silent."

"What happened next?"

"I still had her hair, so I chopped her in the neck again."

"Then what happened?"

"Her head came off."

"Her head came off? What did she do?" I asked.

"Her eyes opened real wide and her mouth opened wide too."

"Then what happened?"

"I dropped her head."

"Why," I asked.

He answered, "I ain't never seen no shit like that before."

That's when I had my full realization of the type of customers I would be dealing with.

This was no game

Chapter 4

If Only...

Account of Thom Bradstock
Los Angeles County Sheriff's Department

He still believes he could have done more as if anything he would have done differently would have changed things. On the morning of September 19, 1983, he put on his Superman suit and went to work. He jokingly said, "There is nothing I can't handle while I am wearing the Superman suit." He was referring to the uniform of the Los Angeles County Sheriff's Department. He was to learn even Superman is vulnerable. He is vulnerable to kryptonite. On this morning, his kryptonite was the deadly beauty of the Malibu Pacific Ocean. And it would never look the same to him again.

Thom told me this story in 2007, 24 years after it happened. On March 1st, 2017, I asked Thom if I could include his story in this book. He agreed to do it. He thought about the story for three days and had three sleepless nights. He cried through parts of the day on March 3rd reliving what he was to tell me when we met on March 4th.

Oh, by the way, if you think Thom is a wimp for crying here's something for you to think about. He played water polo in college, one of the hardest most cardio stressful and violent sports there is. After that, he joined the Marine Corps and went through Officer's Candidate School boot camp, one of the toughest boot camps in the world. He graduated and was a lieutenant in the Marine Corps during the Vietnam era. After serving in the Marine Corps, he joined the Los Angeles County Sheriff's Department and as he told me, "I kept waiting for the academy to get hard."

Well, I'll say this, I went through the Los Angeles County Sheriff's Department Academy, and I thought it was a real bitch. One-quarter of our cadets did not graduate. Some classes lost three-quarters of their cadets.

Here's his account.

* * * * *

There is a great surfing spot at the Leo Carillo Beach in Malibu, California and all the surfers used to park on the Pacific Coast Highway. Criminals realized the cars belonged to the surfers and the surfers kept their wallets locked in their cars. In September 1983 we had been having a rash of car burglaries with the wallets being stolen from the parked cars. At this area, the Pacific Coast Highway is high above and away from the ocean, and the cars parked on the highway are not visible from the ocean. To get to the ocean, you had to cross about one hundred and fifty yards of a semi-flat plateau with natural scrub and wild growing plants. When you got to the end of this plateau, you were on a bluff looking down about a twenty-foot rock cliff to the ocean below.

My regular shift started at eight in the morning, but on this morning, I was to work two hours of overtime, starting at six a.m. All the surfers were parked on the highway and were in the water. My special detail was to observe a car burglary in progress and to arrest whoever was committing the crime.

I drove up the coast and made a right on Mulholland Highway. Mulholland Highway goes inland or away from the coast. About two hundred feet up the Highway is a dirt road which leads to a hilltop overlooking the Coast Highway. There was plenty of brush to hide my patrol car. From my vantage point, I could see all the cars parked on the Pacific Coast Highway. I waited behind the brush and was observing the people coming and going.

I saw a young boy who was walking very fast across the plateau towards the parked cars. He looked to be about eight to ten years old. At first, I thought he was the burglar, but then I saw him go into the driver's side of a car and he started honking the horn. After honking the horn for a little bit, he got out of the car and looked up and down the highway. It was hard to read the details of his face because he was about two hundred yards away, but he was trying to get someone's attention. I knew something was wrong. I had the impression he was frantic.

After looking up and down the highway he went back to the driver's side of the car and started honking the horn again. I needed to get to him; I could tell he needed help, but I had no idea what was wrong. I got into my car and drove down the dirt road losing sight of the highway. In under a minute I was back on the highway. I stopped and looked at the car where I had last seen the boy, but he was nowhere in sight.

There was a locked gate to the entrance of an access road across the highway on the ocean side where the cars were parked. This road went through the plateau, and you had to cross it to get to the ocean. I had a key to the gate and thought I would drive down the road to see if the boy had crossed back over the plateau toward the ocean. I unlocked the gate and drove down the road but did not see the boy.

I turned around, and he ran up to the passenger side of my patrol car. He was scared and frantic and sobbing. "My dad's hurt! He fell and hit his head trying to get a fish! He fell off the cliff, and he's hurt." He pointed toward the ocean. It was in his eyes and the catching sobs of his words, he was pleading with me to save him. The ocean was about a hundred yards away, but the water's edge was not visible because we were back so far and we were about twenty feet above it.

I grabbed the microphone and put out that I needed backup and to send the fire department and the lifeguards, there was probably a man in the water.

I opened the trunk and took off my Sam Browne, (his gun belt), and threw it inside. Slamming the trunk closed I told the boy, "Stay with the police car. Help is coming. Stay with the police car because when help gets here, they will see the police car. You tell them where I am."

After the boy acknowledged, he understood I took off at a sprint. It was about a hundred yards. When I got to the rock cliff, I looked into the ocean, and I saw the boy's dad about twenty-five yards off the shore in the water. He was face down and submerged just below the surface of the water. I was at the top of a twenty-foot rock cliff. It was the same rock cliff the boy's father had gone down to try and grab a fish. It was the same rock cliff he had fallen off of and hit his head on the rocks below. I thought about it for a second. How could I face the boy and tell him I didn't try to get his father out of the water? I had to go down.

I started climbing down the face of the cliff. I could see where my hands needed to go, but I had to feel my way down with my feet. I got down about ten feet, and I got stuck. When I tried to look down, I couldn't see past my body to the face of the cliff. I could not see where to put my feet. I felt around as well as I could and worked my way down just another foot or two, and then I was stuck again. I may have had one foot on a toehold and the other dangling and searching for a hold. To move further down I would have to let go with one hand, and I was afraid I might slip. There was water and a whole lot of rocks below me. I thought the man who had just climbed this cliff had fallen and was lying face down submerged in the water. I knew one false hold would be a slip and could mean my death. I said to myself, "Are you some kind of fucking idiot? The guy who just tried this is lying face down in the ocean." I thought of climbing back up but then thought, "How could I face the boy?"

It was better to let go and jump than to slip and fall. I let go and thank God it was only about a three-foot drop from where I was to the rocks below. I landed on some rocks, and they were hard, but I didn't get hurt.

I started swimming out to the ocean not just in the water, but amongst a sea of rocks. I was wearing my shoes, a wool uniform, and a bullet-proof vest. Hurricane Manuel, which was centered six hundred miles south of San Diego was just winding down, but it had created a substantial surf that was still hitting the Malibu Coast. The first wave hit me and knocked me on my ass onto a rock. It hurt, but I was not injured. I got up and started making my way out again. When I got to about neck level deep in the water, another wave hit me and knocked my head onto some submerged rocks. That really hurt me but not enough to knock me out or make me swim back to the cliff. I was now swimming. My clothes were weighing me down. My bulletproof vest was very heavy, and I was sorry I didn't take it and my shoes off before getting in the water. I could not move my arms except in a breaststroke movement because of the way the bulletproof vest was riding around my body. I got out to where I thought I had last seen the boy's father, but I couldn't find him. I could not see over the swells because my head was just above the water. As I swam around some, I kept turning in 360-degree circles, straining to find him. I didn't see him.

I was growing weary, not tired, but weary. I had been in the water for over five minutes now. It seemed an eternity with the weight of my clothes. I got over to some submerged rocks where I could stand in the water up to my chin and take a break. I looked around and tried to catch my breath. After a little bit, I decided to swim out again. My clothes were like lead threatening to take me under.

I swam out another ten yards along the coast when I saw a lifeguard carrying a surfboard running. He was descending down the cliff, and although I could not see them, I could tell he was running down some stairs. They were about thirty yards away from the cliff I climbed down. I thought if I had just looked around I would have taken the stairs instead of climbing down the cliff. I yelled to the lifeguard that I thought the man was near me. He paddled out to the ocean and called out to someone on the bluff who yelled back and pointed to the boy's father in the water.

The lifeguard got on his knees and spotted the man. He was just yards away from me. Neither the lifeguard nor I had seen the man. It struck me hard that if I had just let the boy follow me to the bluff, he could have directed me to his father from above. I could have gotten to him sooner, and maybe saved his life. It was this thought that has haunted me my entire life and will continue to haunt me for the rest of my days.

The lifeguard got him to the shore. I swam about thirty yards to shore and joined the lifeguard. I was exhausted.

The paramedics were performing C.P.R. on the man. One of them looked at me and said, "We're going to take him to the hospital because his body temperature is high, but he won't make it because he's been in the water too long."

I got to the top of the stairs. I walked another hundred yards or more to my radio car. The boy was waiting. I got on the radio and updated them that the paramedics were going to transport the man to the hospital. There were no other deputies there. I was alone with the boy. I was instructed over the radio to drive the boy back to the station. It was a thirty-minute drive.

I didn't want to take him. I didn't want to be with the boy because I knew his dad was dead and I felt guilty. I didn't want to have that conversation with him. On the drive back, the boy was doing his best not to sob. But he did. He sobbed all the way back. I will never forget it. I had nothing to tell him. I couldn't lie. I couldn't tell him everything was going to be okay because it wasn't. I said one thing to him on the drive back. I said, "The paramedics took your dad to the hospital and let's pray he's okay." It was still a lie. But it was the only thing I could think of to say.

Neither of us said anything else. The car was silent, except for the heart-wrenching sobbing of the boy.

* * * * *

I got to the station, and someone took the boy. I was soaked.

One of my bosses asked me what happened. I told the story. Their question was, "How long were you in the water?"

I told him 10 or 15 minutes. Several days later I was told I was being considered for one of the department's awards for heroism. One of my bosses said, "You know you're not going to get an award because you are a great swimmer."

I thought, "I just went down a cliff that killed another man."

I was asked if I had another uniform. I told them I did. I was instructed to get showered and suited up because I still had my shift to complete.

I did as I was instructed.

After cleaning up and leaving the Sheriff's Station, I stopped at the central lifeguard station, which was about four miles from the scene of the accident. I wanted to see what had happened to the man. He was dead. The lifeguard captain looked down and then at me and said, "I won't allow my men to go into the area you were swimming in, even in normal circumstance because the waters are so treacherous."

I looked at him questioningly. He said, "We are at the tail end of Hurricane Manuel. The waters are extra treacherous right now. I can't believe you were in there in full uniform."

I went back to patrol and finished my shift.

* * * * *

As far as I know, no one from the Sheriff's Department ever went to the location to see where everything happened.

* * * * *

I had a hard time for the next several days. Anytime I got a radio call I started crying. I couldn't pick up the radio and speak because I was crying. After the call would come out I had to wait to calm down until I could talk and then I answered my radio.

A sergeant noticed I wasn't doing so well. He talked to me.

He told me I had been through a traumatic experience. He told me I was not a robot, but a human being. He said it was natural in a circumstance such as mine to recreate the scenario and to second-guess my actions. It was normal to question every action I did and to think if I had only done this or that thing differently I could have saved him.

It's exactly what I had been doing, thinking I should have used the boy as my spotter. His talk helped, but it didn't stop me from second-guessing myself. I still do. To this day. Thirty-four years later. I must have second-guessed myself now about a hundred trillion times.

Sometimes I can talk about this…most times I cannot. It rears its ugly head less now than it did. Occasionally something will trigger the memory, and I second-guess myself.

If only I had…if only I had…

* * * * *

Thom Bradstock received the Los Angeles County Sheriff's Department Meritorious Service Award for his actions on September 19, 1983.

He had a full career and retired from the Sheriff's Department at the rank of lieutenant.

* * * * *

In preparation for this account, Thom agreed to go back to the location of this incident with me. It was the first time he had been back there in thirty-three and a half years.

As we stood above the ocean to the right of the State Park Rangers lifeguard tower number three, looking down the cliff he descended, I thought to myself there was probably less than a fifty-fifty chance of getting down without falling

We drove back to the old Malibu Sheriff's Station where we had met earlier. From there Thom had driven us to the scene. It was indeed a thirty-minute drive back to the old Malibu Station. The drive he took alone with the sobbing boy.

Thom had been saying maybe if he could have gotten to the man sooner, he might have saved him. I was incredulous. I thought of the cliff and told this brave man, "Thom if there were twenty playboy bunnies naked waiting for me at the bottom of the cliff, and if all I had to do to get to them was to climb down the cliff, I would not have done it." In traumatic situations, the mind works differently. My comment was not to diminish the situation. I wanted so desperately to offer this brave man solace, some sort of comfort, but no words would be strong enough. Comedic relief helps but only for a second. Like the waves of an ocean, they recede quickly, exposing the bareness of the sand, of the deep wound. It happens all the time in the line of duty. It is how the mind copes with dire, drastic situations that 99% of people will never experience.

* * * * *

Thom belly laughed, then abruptly stopped and looked at me. In an instant he was serious. "Robert, if you had to face that boy and tell him you didn't try to save his dad you would have climbed down.

I stopped laughing also. The full weight of the seriousness of the situation Thom had been in hit me. He was right, I would have climbed down, I know I would have, but I would have probably drowned.

Chapter 5

Badass...It Runs in the Family

Account of Joel Willis
Downey Police Department

The teacher got a book from the student. Now the student was the teacher. The student was taking a Criminal Justice class in high school and had just finished reading, *The Red Dot Club*. He asked his teacher, "Have you read this book?"

The teacher answered, "No."

The student was not pleased. Through furrowed eyebrows, he told his teacher, "How can you teach this class without reading this book?"

Joel Willis smiled and took the book. He read it per the instructions and order of the student.

I didn't know Joel, but I had heard about his shooting, and I had been trying to find someone to put me in touch with him.

It ended up Joel contacted me. He told me about the student, and how the book changed him. It seemed the student didn't like cops too much. They had harassed him; they were always after him. After he read the book that changed. He changed. He is moving forward in a positive way. He now wants to be a cop and is living his life with that career in mind.

I had to meet this seventeen-year-old kid, soon to be an adult. He is a very likable guy. He told me, "The book helped me develop my mindset into someone who sees rules and authority for their worth, and the necessity for people of law enforcement." He is smart.

I wish him Godspeed in his quest to help his fellow man.

* * * * *

Joel found himself in front of the academy class. He was basically dragged out of his dad's car by the Los Angeles County Sheriff's Academy drill instructors after they found out he was on the academy grounds.

I asked Joel how they knew he was there. He still doesn't know, but he thinks his dad, Mike, who you read about in the chapter titled M&M might have told them. The drill instructors told Joel he needed to talk to the academy class because they were too cocky. They knew Joel's story would sober them up. Joel had no choice but to go.

Several months earlier the back of his right leg had been blown apart and ripped open, exposing hanging tendons behind his kneecap. He had been shot in the hip. Also, the triceps muscles in his right arm had been shot through and through with an AK-47 round. Joel was a member of The Red Dot Club.

As Joel stood in front of the class, the recruits looked at him and thought, "What the Fuck?"

Joel stared the class down with his steel blue eyes. He was on crutches; his arm was in a sling. He started, "Eight months ago I was sitting where you are now..."

* * * * *

Joel sat across from me in the cool morning breeze of his backyard.

"I had an intense welcome to patrol. Two days after I got off of training with my Field Training Officer, I was riding a one-man radio car. It was three thirty or so in the afternoon, and the call came over the radio, 'Units we have an officer down at Lindell and Telegraph. Shots fired.' I was a half-mile away. The hair stood up on the back of my neck. Everyone was accounted for, and I was trying to figure out who was down. I was there within a minute. When I got there, I saw Hispanics running everywhere.

"Two longhaired, bearded dudes wearing police raid jackets were manhandling two Hispanics trying to get them handcuffed. They saw me and started yelling, 'GO TO ARRINGTON!' This was the street just east of where we were. I get to Arrington, which is a cul-de-sac, and I literally see 12 to 15 Hispanics running everywhere. They were in the street, jumping fences, just going everywhere.

"And I see two cops pumping on the chest of another guy, and there was blood everywhere. I asked them what they wanted me to do and no one could tell me what to do. The next thing I knew our helicopter landed in the middle of the cul-de-sac. Three or four undercover cops lifted Fullerton Undercover Officer Tommy De La Rosa into the helicopter and off they went. It was Tommy's chest who the cops had been pumping on and who they were trying to save. He had been shot numerous times by numerous people, ambushed. He had been doing a reverse drug sting, (selling dope instead of buying dope). Tommy managed to kill one of the guys in the shootout before he died. It was June 21, 1990.

"This was my indoctrination into police work.

"From my earliest recollections of my father, he was a longhaired, longbearded hippie looking man, who spent my younger years working as an undercover cop. He was flat out the scariest man I knew. My friends would say to me, 'How do you go home? Aren't you afraid of your dad?'

"I would tell them, 'Hell yeah, I'm afraid of my dad! Aren't you afraid of your dad?' He was a strict disciplinarian and very intense.

"I have four brothers and sisters; I am the oldest. We would have dinner at my grandma's house, and on the way, home dad would drive by a crook's house to see if he was there before he would go out to follow them. We would drive by like at ten o'clock at night with the whole family in the car.

"We were always at Uncle Mike's house, (Mike Lane who you read about in M&M who was killed), on the weekends, or his wife and kids would be at our house. Until I was twelve years old when Uncle Mike got killed, I grew up wrestling with him or playing with his kids.

"At ten thirty at night, the night Uncle Mike was killed, I was asleep. It was a school night. My aunt came in and woke me up. She was crying, the house was abuzz with people. My mom was in the kitchen, and she was crying. A lot of the people in the house were crying. I couldn't wrap my head around it. I was twelve years old. I went back to sleep.

"I got up the next morning and went to school. We were doing some Christmas game involving the radio. It was like any other day. Then while we were playing this game a news flash came out over the radio, 'Officer Mike Lane was killed last night in an undercover shooting. He was with Officer Mike Willis.' Everyone in the class turned and looked at me…and I started crying.

"There was a picture in the newspaper of my dad crying. I'd never seen my dad cry. He is the toughest guy I have ever known. It still gets me to remember him crying. When he spoke at Mike's funeral, he cried then too. It's almost too much for me, even now to handle. It was an intense time, an unbelievable time of sadness in our house.

"I had some natural talents playing baseball. I was a star in high school. My high school coach was kind of new and didn't know how to get scouts out to see me play. I played a little in junior college, but I wasn't going anywhere. I got frustrated. I thought I was good, but no one was picking me up. I got disgruntled and quit. Dave Butler, (the other officer in M&M who was in the shooting with Mike), bought a gas station. I started working there.

"One day while working at the gas station, I was wearing my high school baseball jacket with my name on it. This guy came in to get gas. He turned out to be a scout with a professional baseball team, the Royals. He had tried to come out to see me play against Mater Dei high school but he missed the two games. I told him, 'It's too bad you missed the game. I went nine for eleven, with two home runs, two triples and a double and eight RBI's.'

"He asked me if I was playing.

"I answered, 'Nope I just quit two weeks ago.'

"He asked, 'Do you still want to play?'

"I answered, 'Yeah I do, kind of.'

"He said, 'Okay, meet me at St. Paul High School.'

"I did, and we had two or three workouts. Afterward, he said, 'Okay meet me at Yucaipa High School Saturday morning at eight.'

"So, dad and I loaded up and went to Yucaipa High School. Dude, it was a cattle call tryout. There were six hundred guys there. I was one of eight guys they kept. They put me in the instructional leagues.

"I played for nine months when I got my girlfriend pregnant. Now I needed a job. A real paying job. I had a baby on the way, and I was going to meet my responsibilities. My girlfriend didn't want to get married, but I still had obligations.

"I went to see my dad at the station, 'Dad, can I be a cop. Do you think I can be a cop?' I was twenty-one. That's how it happened. I couldn't be a cop at Whittier where my dad worked, they would not allow relatives to work in the same department. My dad knew someone at the Downey Police Department, and he called him. Downey was hiring, and I applied. The next thing I knew I was in the Los Angeles County Sheriff's Academy, class 259. It was October 10, 1989, Black Monday."

Black Monday is the first day of the academy and is like the first day of boot camp. The drill instructors yell and scream at everyone for the most minor infractions. They are trying to weed out the weak and get the class to learn to pay attention to instructions.

Joel went through the same academy class as Angel Jaimes and Javier Valencia, (their shooting is depicted in Chapter 10 in book one of *The Red Dot Club* series).

"My dad had prepared me. He told me they were going to yell at me, but on the first day of the academy, on Black Monday (look up Los Angeles County Sheriff's Academy Black Monday on YouTube) I was going, 'What the fuck, what the fuck did I just get myself into. I was terrified. They stripped me down from this weak-minded kid, who thought he was better than anybody else, and then built me back up. They took this cocky kid, who pretended to the world and to himself to have self-confidence and they built me up to have true self-confidence. My measure of a man was my dad, and I could never be who he was or is."

Joel had a serious look.

"Maybe I didn't do so bad," he said in an undertone voice.

He continued. "I entered the academy with doubts I had what it took to do the job. I did well in shooting. I did well in driving. I excelled. By the time the academy was over, I knew I could do the job, and do it well. I thought the training was top notch and first class. I was cocky, but it was now a humble, cockiness with self-confidence, and I was ready to start.

"When I got to Downey P.D. I got pulled aside by some of the officers who told me to stop being so cocky. I'm opinionated and don't have a filter. What I think, I say, I had no idea the guys looked at me as being cocky. The truth was I was terrified. I didn't worry about getting killed; I just wanted to get off of probation. I learned to shut up, and things went smoothly after that.

"I made it off probation. It was now Friday night October 5, 1990, about one thirty in the morning. A Cadillac had been stolen at gunpoint. We now call them carjackings. I slowly drove eastbound on Imperial Highway, and sure as shit, it drove past me. I made a U-turn, and it took off. I told myself to remain calm. I told myself to breathe. I was so excited I needed a little time to calm down. I grabbed the mic, '16 can you repeat the plate?' The dispatcher was irritated with me because he supposed I hadn't copied the license of the stolen vehicle when he first put out the call. The reality was I had the plate, but I was trying to calm myself down before I started broadcasting the pursuit. I hadn't even engaged my red lights and siren yet.

"Dispatch came back with a pissed off voice, 'COPY…The plate is…' His voice was telling me I was an idiot for not writing down the information.

"I replied I was in pursuit of the stolen car, and I gave my location.

"Now dispatch puts it out, and all the fellas are coming to back me. The suspect had a gun, and he threw it out of the window. The metal sparked when the gun hit the asphalt. I thought. 'Oh shit, he's shooting at me.' But it didn't happen again and I sort of dismissed it. The Los Angeles County Sheriff's helicopter caught up with me and came on the air they would call the pursuit. I was so relieved because now I only had to drive. I was hitting the steering wheel, 'This is so bitchen!!!'

"Other agencies were blocking off intersections. We were doing 100 miles an hour. On the freeway then off the freeway. We covered 26 miles. He ran until he ran out of gas. He was a Kelly Park crip, and he ran out of gas in the rolling 60's neighborhood, (another set of crips). These rolling 60's crips were outside at one forty-five in the morning, and they were cheering us on. They were on their porches, and they were yelling, 'KICK HIS ASS KICK HIS ASS!!!'

"This guy wouldn't get out of the car. Our K-9 unit runs up to the car, smashes the window and opens the door. The police dog goes in and latches onto this guy's inner thigh and rips him out of the car.

"The next night on Saturday, October 6, my partner and I got a domestic violence call. It was on the second floor of an apartment complex. When the door opened a huge Hispanic guy rushed us, and the fight was on. He went to hit my partner, and we grabbed his arms. He was shoving us against the second-floor railing and then the walls and doors of the apartment building. We were pinging back and forth off the wall and railing like pinballs. He got my partner's back against the railing and was bending him backward to push him over the railing. My partner was flailing his arms trying not to get thrown two stories into the patio area. I was hitting the guy and pulled him and my partner back away from the railing to the landing. I got my arm around his neck. I was trying to choke him out. I couldn't get the hold on right, and he wouldn't go out. We kept bouncing around for a couple of minutes with neither side winning. I finally got him tripped up, and we went to the ground. My partner and I struggled to get his arms behind his back to handcuff him because he had his arms locked in front of him. I kidney punched him and felt his arms twitch and loosen up. We finally got the handcuffs on. My partner and I were both exhausted and banged up, but we won.

"Then the next night, on Sunday, October 7th, I got into another car pursuit of a stolen vehicle.

"It was a helluva weekend. I was like, 'THIS IS FUCKIN' AWESOME!!! They're actually paying me to do this stuff.' I had a ball.

"My shifts went from nine thirty at night until seven thirty the next morning. On my way to work on Monday, October 8, 1990, I went by the girl's house I was courting, who is now my wife. I put a note on her car windshield with a snickers bar. Then I went to work that night, Columbus Day, the day Chris discovered America. The bastard. If he hadn't discovered America, then there wouldn't have been manifest destiny, and this whole area would still be Indians and Mexicans. I would be drinking scotch on some Irish Highland wearing a kilt playing the bagpipes. Then I wouldn't have gone to work at Downey P.D. having all that fun. Hell, there'd be no Downy P.D...well you get the picture. One thing leads to another, and this didn't lead to anything but lead. Bullet lead.

"Two and half hours into my shift, Monday, October 8 turned into Tuesday, October 9, 1990. I was working a one-man car. I met Ewing who was working another one-man unit in a secluded parking lot. We talked, caught up on our paperwork, wrote reports, caught up on our logs, the usual stuff guys do after everyone, including the bad guys, go to bed.

"After about an hour of trying to finish reports, trying to stay awake, the call came out. It was five in the morning. The call came out as a possible robbery at the Pace Warehouse, 11111 Florence Ave, in Downey.

(Folks a robbery is a dangerous crime. It means someone is taking someone else's property from them using force or fear. The potential for violence is strong.)

"It wasn't even our call. We said, 'Let's roll.' The handling unit, Bruner, got on the radio and acknowledged he was rolling to the warehouse. The assisting unit also got on the air acknowledging he was rolling. So, we had four one-man units rolling to the call, all the cars on duty that night for the City of Downey were going. The units were 11, manned by Bruner, 12 manned by me, 13 manned by Ewing, and 14 manned by Biarneson.

"Ewing and I saw Biarneson on the street rolling to the call. We all parked on Florence Ave. under the 605 freeway about 50 yards from the large Pace Warehouse parking lot. There was a gas station in the corner of the lot. Look, man, it was five in the morning. The Pace Warehouse was closed. If it was a robbery, it was at the gas station, which was open.

"If someone called 911 from the parking lot pay phone, it would have shown as coming from the Pace Warehouse, but we knew it was probably the gas station. I was actually thinking if this was real, someone probably pumped some gas into their car and then ran without paying.

"Ewing, Biarneson, and I were out of sight of the parking lot under the freeway. All three of us were west of the parking lot. We got out of our cars to approach on foot when Bruner drove up. He had just arrived and told us he was going to the parking lot east of the Warehouse and have himself a look-see.

"The rest of us walked to the parking lot to check on the gas station. There was a lady inside at the booth. Thinking there was a possible robbery in progress we cautiously approached. She assured us there was no crime going on and everything was okay. We checked out the place and made sure ourselves everything was okay, and there was not a hostage situation. It took us several minutes to clear the gas station.

"While this was going on Bruner was doing what he said he was going to do, having himself a look-see. The front of the Pace Warehouse had four pillars holding up a façade. He parked his radio car on the east side of the Pace Warehouse. He got out on foot, and half walked, and half crouched alongside some shopping carts lined up in the front of the building. He got to the front of the store and looked inside. And there they were, masked people with AK 47 rifles. And they were herding the unmasked people into an area. None of us could see this though or knew what was going on, we were all busy at the gas station.

"After clearing the gas station, the three us started making our way to the front of the Pace Warehouse. As I was walking through the parking lot and as I got closer to the store, I noticed several things. When the warehouse was closed, it usually had a corrugated steel gate that rolled down in front of the doors. But it was up. The lights inside the warehouse were on. But it was five in the morning. There were about 25 cars in the parking lot. I was thinking this was really strange. There are no customers at the Pace Warehouse at five in the morning. Why are the lights on and why are there cars in the lot?

"Ewing was behind me with the shotgun as we made our way across the parking lot. I had not seen Bruner since he arrived but I assumed he was where he said he was going to be.

"I heard Bruner on the radio. I can't see him, but he was panicked. He was clearly in trouble. But I couldn't understand what he was saying. So, I started sprinting east across the parking lot, toward him. He needed help. I could hear it in his voice. He was scared, and I had to get to him. I was still in the parking lot about 25 feet away from the front of the store in the driving lane. I then understood Bruner, and I could now see him at the rear of his radio car.

"He had the radio in one hand, and he's yelling into the radio as he's motioning toward me, *'GET BACK!!! GET BACK!!!'*

"I knew something was wrong. I could see he was alright and did not need me physically with him to help him. What was he yelling about?

"It hit me, it was a good robbery.

"I stopped in the middle of the parking lot and realized I had to get to cover. I was near the second pillar in front of the store just off to the side of the front doors. I needed cover, and I remember thinking, 'If I get to that pillar we can mow them down as they come out if they decide to fight.' I was still in the driving lane that goes in front of the store. Ewing was behind me.

"I started sprinting my way to the pillar. I had my gun in my hand and as I took my first step, *BAM*, I got hit in the leg with a fucking sledgehammer. I didn't know it, but I knew it. I'd been shot.

"From the time Bruner was yelling at me, 'Get back, get back' to the time I got shot was maybe a second.

".... And time slowed to a crawl. Now time seemed as if it was a dream, but it was more real than anything I had ever experienced.

"The AK 47 round went in the back of my right leg, just where the cheek of my ass and my leg meet. The round spun down the back of my hamstring, shredding muscle downward toward the back of my knee. It blew out portions of muscle, tendon, sinew, and my hamstring, and opened and exposed a huge gap of tendons and the leg bone, open to the outside world…

"…And I thought, *'Who the fuck just shot me?'*

"Time was so slow. Things were moving in slow motion. I slowly turned around, the turn taking a minute…And twenty feet away is this black dude. He was standing outside of a van with a rifle in his hands. Unbeknownst to me, inside of the van is another guy with a rifle. He is slowly, lazily shooting at Bruner. I saw Ewing to my right. He was ten feet away from me.

"We were in front of the van, exposed in the open parking lot. Exposed to two guys shooting at us.

"I looked at Ewing as the left front of his lower guts slowly blew out onto the parking lot. His feet went forward from under him, slowly taking their time. It looked like a cartoon character slipping on a banana peel with his feet sliding forward and his head and upper torso going back. But it was no cartoon, and it was not funny. It was very real. More real than anything I had ever seen before. Horror mixed with the mind-numbing chill that this was real. I was bewildered and shocked, how could this be happening? Horror and terror seized me and squeezed my heart like a steel fist of ice. A huge spray of blood and gore blew out of him, onto the parking lot, ten feet away from me. The suspect was ten feet behind him. And Ewing was down.

"Now the guy outside of the van was pointing the rifle at me. And ever so slowly the muzzle flashes are reaching out to me. Fire coming out of the end of the rifle, snaking out of the rifle, slowly reaching out to me, to kill me. And it went on and on…and on…and on….and the horror and the terror continued forever.

"Ewing was dead. I knew it because of what I saw. No one could live through that. I later learned he took two rounds to his lower right back by his Sam Browne, (gun belt) and they exited out his left front lower stomach.

54

"I turned ever so slowly and looked at the pillar. I had to get to the pillar. It was my only safety. I knew the rifle was still shooting at me because I could hear the muffled slow reports of the shots. The bullets were whizzing by my head now. I could feel the air being displaced by the bullets as they passed me. The concussion of the bullets and the terror continued. On and on and on. I was waiting for them, for the bullets, to do to me what they did to Ewing. I could see in my mind's eye, the front of my face coming apart, blowing outward, just like Ewing's guts, with the gore of my brains all over the parking lot...and me dead. I could not shake the terror, and revulsion chilled me.

"From the time, I first got shot to this time it seemed like ten minutes had gone by. An eternity.

"And I was still trying to figure it out. '*WHAT THE FUCK?* They're supposed to be in the store, in front of me, not behind me. It was like, 'Did someone accidentally fire their gun? What the fuck?'

"Now I was running to the pillar in front of me. And I could see it. The pillar was chipping away from the bullets aimed at my back. They are whizzing by every part of my body. I could feel them passing my head, my body, my legs, and even my feet. And the bullets were hitting the building and the pillar in front of me, and I could see chunks of the building coming apart, actually exploding. Sparks were coming off the ground around me. I was running in slow motion as fast as I could to the pillar, where it was coming apart, where the blue sparks were. And I knew it was over. I had nowhere to go but to the place where the bullets were hitting, where the building was exploding, and where the blue sparks were. I was running in slow motion, running to my death.

"The next thing I knew I woke up and I was behind the pillar. I can't tell you how I got there.... I don't know.

"I came to, and I was sitting on the ground. I couldn't believe I was alive. But I was. And the building behind me was still exploding and coming apart. Sparks were coming off the ground. And I was terrified. I knew I was going to die. I was thinking of my son, my dad, my mom, my sisters, my brothers and I thought I would never get to see them again. I was profoundly sad. I was a twenty-two-year-old man. A kid. I was alone. I had seen Ewing blown outward. I was alone and sad, and they were going to kill me…

"And…the aloneness and the sadness overcame me. And…I…I think I started crying. I think I was, no I was, I think I was blubbering. I was sitting behind the pillar, and I was blubbering, like a little fucking baby. And it was all going on, and it seemed like forever."

Joel looked away from me, his eyes were no longer on mine.

"By now it felt like 30 minutes had gone by. Like it would never end, ever.

"I got on the radio, '12, I'm hit, I'm hit,' and it knocked me back into reality. I looked down, and there it was, right there in my hand, my gun. My fucking gun was in my hand. I forgot I had my fucking gun in my hand. It was out the whole time.

"The second I saw my gun in my hand a core of fire lit and welled up inside me. There's no other way to explain it. The fucking rage, all the sadness, being scared, disappeared in an instant. Gone. And I was transformed. I became this enraged pissed off motherfucker. Un-recognizable to me or anyone who knew me. And without thinking, my head screamed inside me, *'THERE'S NO WAY THIS MOTHER-FUCKER IS GOING TO KILL ME!!!'*

"From a sitting position, I rolled over onto my belly, out into the open, out from the safety of the pillar. The fucker was standing there still shooting at me. And I started firing. Behind him was a Cadillac deal-ership. And the lights were on. He made a perfect silhouette, and I started banging away. As soon as my first shot went off, he took off running. And I thought, 'You fucking pussy when the bullets are com-ing your way you don't want to fight.'

"Boom, boom, boom, boom. I saw him clench up and hit the ground. He got back up and took off.

"Time was going so slow that I had all the time in the world to aim and shoot. Up until now the slowed down time had been my enemy. Now it was my friend. I could see him in my sights with each shot I made. I was so full of rage that I wanted to go and rip his larynx out. It was so weird how I turned into this person I didn't know, this crazy rage filled person. Seconds before I was this guy crying behind the pillar. Who had I become?

I was like, *'Let's go, motherfucker, you want to fight? Let's go!'*

"He was gone. I don't know where he went. I realized I was now twenty feet into the lot. I don't have any idea how I got there, how I had moved away from the pillar.

"Bruner told me I was in this gun battle, mano-a-mano for twenty seconds. I don't think it was twenty seconds, but Bruner said the suspect and I were shooting at each other, exchanging shots, banging away at each other for twenty seconds.

"There were two times I blacked out. I don't know how I got behind the pillar and I don't know how I got twenty feet away from the pillar after the shooting ended.

"It felt like ten or twenty minutes that I was laying in the parking lot. And just like they taught you at the range in the academy, 'Clear and holster an empty weapon, that's what I did.' I dropped my magazine, which still had a bullet in it, and holstered an empty weapon. And I said to myself, 'Oh, shit, there are still bad guys in the store behind me! What the fuck are you doing? This thing isn't over.' I reloaded my gun.

"Time was back to normal, and I got scared again, 'They're going to come out from behind me and execute me.'

"The next thing I remember was these two paramedics belly crawling to me. I don't know how much time I had been laying there. I didn't know where everyone was. Ewing was dead. I felt alone. I was bewildered. The paramedics got to Ewing and I. They dragged us out of there.

"I was in the ambulance and the goddam paramedic or whatever he was, was so nervous he couldn't get the IV in my arm. He kept missing. I said, 'Goddammit get it in the vein, I'd rather get shot than go through what you're doing.' And I was conscious, and not conscious; I was in a semi-fog. I was in the ambulance, and they were cutting my uniform off, and pieces of bullets, and shrapnel, and whole deformed bullets were falling out of my clothing. It was ricochet shit, from the pillar and the wall that had gone into my uniform. That's when I learned I took a bullet through my right triceps. The bullet went through my arm and into my vest on the right side of my chest and entered my skin by my chest muscle. The vest saved my life. Had I not been wearing it the bullet would have torn through my chest. I had four bullet fragments come out, and one full bullet come out of my pants. I got shot in the hip by a shotgun pellet. They figured the driver of the van, a guy I haven't mentioned, had a shotgun and it was probably him who shot me. It was probably a ricochet.

"Ewing didn't die. Amazing. He came back to work on the desk, but sadly he had to medically retire.

"I lived. But if it weren't for the anger, I wouldn't have survived.

"I still struggle. I don't like that I was scared. I don't like that I cried. I don't like that. That is not me. I don't like it. I struggle with it."

* * * * *

"The guys in the warehouse saw the cops at the front of the store shooting it out and said, 'Fuck this!' They ran to the back of the warehouse and met with a locked exit door. They shot the door open and ran out of the back of the store to the freeway fence. They jumped the fence but in their haste to get away they dropped over one hundred thousand dollars in cash. They also left all their body armor and guns at the fence and ran across the 605 freeway.

"One guy got captured at the freeway carrying a cone. He was pretending to be a Cal Trans worker. But he had tar all over his body from going through the roof of the Pace Warehouse. That's how they got in, they cut a hole in the roof and broke into the store at two in the morning. They broke into the warehouse knowing it was the Columbus holiday weekend. The banks were closed, and they figured there would be a lot of cash in the office. When the alarm company called the manager at two in the morning, he told them, 'Don't worry about it, the alarm goes off all the time.' He then went back to bed. So, we were never called and told there was an alarm.

"The wannabe Cal Trans suspect guy identified all the robbers by name.

"It turned out these guys were all members of the Black Guerilla Family, a well-known prison gang. From what I understand they were all on parole, at least two of them were on parole for murder. There was six in total. Three went through the roof at two in the morning and waited for the employees to arrive. Three waited in the parking lot.

"The guy I traded bullets with was found dead two weeks later. He was stabbed to death in Gardena. The story I got was he was screwing a woman who had a boyfriend who killed him. He had two .45-caliber bullet holes in him, from me.

"The driver with the shotgun was a crack head, and the Black Guerilla Family was worried he would rat everyone out. So, he was killed in a drive-by in south central Los Angeles.

"The guy who was shooting at Bruner, and probably me too, was arrested in Downey for selling dope. This was around February 1991. He gave a false name when he was arrested. Several days after his arrest, another Downey officer and I transported him to the Los Angeles Sheriff's County Jail. After I got off shift and had gone home, they identified the guy. A detective called me and told me that I had transported the guy who was shooting at Bruner and probably me also. He was the guy shooting from inside the van.

"I could not believe it. I remembered one of the guys had been eye fucking me. It was him. I guess I'm glad I didn't know.

"Two of the other guys inside the store were identified, but no one could put them at the scene. They got away with the crime.

"Bruner could not return fire during the gunfight. Ewing was between him and the criminals. But as they left and he had a clear shot, he did engage."

* * * * *

Officer Willis eventually transferred to the Anaheim Police Department. It is advertised as a "Sun-splashed Southern California city." It is known as a city with, "world-famous theme parks and attractions, celebrated restaurants, award-winning local craft breweries, specialty shops, pro sports, cultural museums, top entertainment and unlimited outdoor recreation."

In other words, it's different than the City of Downey. Or is it?

Joel continued with more horror.

* * * * *

"I was a brand-new Anaheim cop. I was working patrol. A call went out of a car-jacking that just occurred. The suspect was armed with a shotgun, and he was inside the Embassy Suites at Frontera St. and the 91 freeway.

"Again, in front of the hotel are two pillars that hold up an overhang which shade the cars pulling up to unload. I went to the right pillar, and my partner went to the east side of the hotel. A panicked patron met him there. He said there was a guy inside of the lobby/bar area and he had been chasing another guy around with a shotgun. He now had a security guard and a clerk hostage.

"I was behind the right pillar about fifteen feet from the front doors. The upper half of the doors were glass, and the lower half was wood. So, when I looked into the hotel, I could only see through the top half of the doors.

"I was behind the pillar peeking my head around the pillar, looking into the hotel when the door quickly opened. The suspect had been crouched down behind the bottom half of the door, and now I was fifteen feet away from him. He stood up and screamed at me and scared the shit out of me. It was like someone sneaking up behind you and screaming at you. Well, I jumped, but I jumped the wrong way. Instead of jumping behind the pillar, I jumped the wrong way. I knew I jumped the wrong way. I jumped away from the pillar, away from cover. I was in the open. As I was jumping, I saw the barrel of the shotgun pointed at me. At my face. Time slowed down now. I stared down the barrel of the shotgun, and it was huge.

"I had all the time in the world again, but I didn't. Things were so slow, and I was waiting for the shotgun pellets to take off my head, but my gun was up at him too. It was a furious race in slow motion. I knew I was going to get shot, I knew it wasn't going to hurt. I remember thinking, 'Don't shoot me in the face or the dick.' I could handle getting shot in the legs or the chest. Our guns were five feet away from each other face to face, again, mano-a-mano.

"I squeezed the trigger, click. Nothing, nothing happened. I thought, 'I better have a round in the chamber of my gun because if I get killed, it's going to look really bad that I had an empty gun.'

"And then it happened, I heard his gun go click. He had fired. Both of our guns went click. Now we were back in the race. A slow-motion race. I had beat him the first time, but now we were back to square one. Who could get their gun to work first?

"I closed my eyes, waiting to be killed. I hit the bottom of my gun magazine to make sure it was seated properly inside the gun all the way. I opened my eyes and pulled back the slide, and as I did so, a round came out of the gun in slow motion. I could see it slowly flying and tumbling through the air. There had been a round in the chamber, so the gun should have fired. Our guns were still pointed at each other. I thought, 'Okay I have a new bullet in my gun.'

"I got my gun back on target, pointed at him, and he has now taken his shotgun and tried to get it under his chin. And he's screaming at me, *'KILL ME MOTHER FUCKER!'*

"I was screaming at him, *'PUT THE GUN DOWN!'*

"He yelled back, *'FUCK YOU, FUCK YOU, KILL ME!'*

" *'PUT THE GUN DOWN, PUT THE GUN DOWN!'* And he brought the barrel of the shotgun from under his chin, and as he ever so slowly pointed it at me, I shot. And in slow motion, I could see my rounds hitting him, poof, poof, poof, poof. His clothing was opening and closing, and moving as my bullets hit him. I heard a barrage of shots being fired to my left. It was my partner. He fired twenty-three rounds from twenty-five feet away and missed every shot. I kept shooting as he fell back and he was no longer a threat. I shot nine times and hit him seven times. I don't know if the suspect lived or died. I never followed up on it. I never went to court. I won the gunfight, and so I didn't care to know what happened to him.

"I was scared, but not like at the Pace Warehouse shooting. Not being hit makes a big difference. Shooting someone when you think you are dying or you think you are going to die is desperate. It's touch and go, and there are no promises you will survive. Nothing is more intense than that.

"I could've shot ten other people in my career, and I decided not to. It wasn't necessary. And I'm glad I didn't. I could have. They would have been justified, but I didn't shoot. It just wasn't necessary. I'm not a killer, and I don't have to shoot someone to prove to anyone I'm a badass."

THAT ladies and gentlemen is what makes Joel Willis a true badass, and a hero.

It turned out the ammunition from the batch Joel was using was defective. The seal around the primer where the gunpowder is held did not seal properly. After the shooting, an investigation was conducted, and gun oil was found in the gunpowder. When the pin on Joel's gun hit the primer, the gunpowder did not ignite, and the bullet would not fire.

* * * * *

Joel Willis, son of Michael Willis and informally adopted nephew of Michael Lane, went on to complete 25 years as a peace officer. He knows all too well each, and every time an officer puts on that uniform they risk it all.

After retiring, Joel obtained a job teaching Criminal Justice to high school students. He is still making a positive difference in society; this time to our nation's youth.

He loves his children and loves his wife who has stood by and supported him through all the tough times.

* * * * *

Joel Willis was awarded the Medal of Valor from the Downey Police Department for his actions on the early morning October 9, 1990. It is the highest award that can be bestowed upon its peace officers. As far as we know Joel Willis and his father, Mike Willis, are the only father and son who have each received the Medal of Valor from their respective departments.

I told you badass runs in the family.

Chapter 6

Innocence Lost

Account of Craig Worden
Gardena Police Department

Around 1975, I was working patrol as a City of Gardena Police officer. My partner and I got a call to respond to a local junior high school. We were to meet one of the school administrators.

When we got there, we were told a thirteen-year-old female student had been having sex in the schoolyard behind the handball court. She had been charging the boys whatever amount of money they were carrying.

My partner and I interviewed the girl, and she confessed she had been having sex on the orders of her parents. She told us her parents told her to charge to have sex with the boys, take their money, and to bring the money home to them. She said her parents were heroin addicts and needed the money to buy drugs.

We called the Juvenile Detectives, who then came to the school and took charge of the investigation. We got the residence address where the girl lived and went to the apartment.

We knocked on the door repeatedly and got no answer. We finally tried the doorknob, and the door opened. Mom and dad were right there in the living room semi-conscious. Right on the table were hypodermic syringes, spoons (spoons are used to heat heroin with water in preparation to injecting it), and cotton balls (these are used as a filter when drawing up the heroin into the syringe).

We arrested the couple and took them to the hospital. Of course, they were under the influence of heroin.

I had already been on the job for several years, but this hit me really hard. To think a thirteen-year-old girl would be prostituting herself at the order of her parents to support their drug habit was mind-boggling. It was gut-wrenching to know some mothers and fathers would do that to their own children.

It really makes you realize what drug addiction can do to someone. Of course, we all know how damaging drug addiction is in people's lives but seeing it in real life drives it home. It really turns you against the belief some might have that it is a harmless recreational activity."

Chapter 7

Injured and Dead Friends

Account of Abel Morales
Long Beach Police Department

Long Beach officers Abel Morales and Rick Delfin are friends. They worked the anti-gang detective unit together. He was also the friend and former partner of Daryle Black, the officer who was killed on April 29, 2000, in the same incident where Rick was shot.

Abel was one of the first officers to arrive at the scene of the shooting.

* * * * *

Abel and I were sitting across from each other at a TGIF restaurant laughing and telling war stories. His were so much better than mine. You could tell he understood the streets and gangs and the frustration with the courts and the politicians. He was again, like Rick, another Cop's Cop.

When I asked Abel to tell me what he went through that night, he instantly went from a huge smile to seriously somber, and tears filled his eyes.

* * * * *

"I had been longtime partners with both Rick and Daryle and had just recently been moved to work with another partner.

"On April 29th, I was working the gang unit. I was working a three-man car, and our mission was to arrest as many gang members as we could. We had arrested a juvenile and just finished dropping him off at Juvenile Hall. I was driving back to the City of Long Beach when a gang sergeant put out radio traffic he was in the area of Pacific Coast Highway and Martin Luther King Boulevard, and he had heard multiple gunshots. We were on the 710 freeway about two to three miles away.

"Several seconds went by, and more radio traffic came out. It was Rick. He said he had been shot. You could tell he was scared. You could tell he was hurt and in pain. He was begging for help, but he didn't know where he was. I said out loud, 'That's Rick.'

"I looked at the radio and turned the volume all the way up. I stomped on the gas and took off toward where the sergeant said he had heard the gunshots. When I got off the freeway at the Pacific Coast Highway, I saw a lot of police units rolling with lights and sirens, so I followed them.

"When I got to the location, officers were there, and they were holding some people at gunpoint. Rick's car was there also, and there were a bunch of officers around it.

"I figured the ambulance had already taken Rick and Daryle to the hospital. I jumped out of my car and went to the passenger side of Rick's car. Daryle was in the passenger seat...and he was missing the back of his head. I didn't see Rick. The car was riddled with bullet holes. Glass was everywhere especially on the passenger side. The dash was destroyed with bullet holes, and the windshield was cracked all over the place."

We stopped while Abel composed himself.

He continued, "So, I was thinking, 'Okay, Daryle is gone, they must have taken Rick to the hospital.' I started walking around to the driver's door, and I was looking at the officers holding the people at gunpoint when I realized two officers were at the driver's door talking to someone.

"It was Rick."

Again, we had to stop. We took a drink of our strawberry lemonades, and Abel took a deep breath.

"He was a mess. I couldn't believe it. I was wondering why he was still there with all these officers around talking to him. Rick had both of his hands locked on the steering wheel in a death grip. The officers were trying to talk to Rick, like, 'C'mon Rick, we've got to get you to the hospital.'

"I went over there, 'Rick, we gotta go, we gotta go, we gotta go!' He looked so bad with his knee blown out, I thought he was going to bleed to death. Rick was saying, 'No!'

"I said to myself, 'Fuck this,' and I bent the driver's door back as far as I could to give me room to get him out. I moved some of the officers out of the way. I grabbed him and pulled him out. Rick was screaming in pain. He turned and looked at me. He had a bullet hole in his forehead.

"I thought to myself, 'He's got seconds until he dies.'

"I didn't want him to go into shock, so I told him, 'Keep talking, keep talking.'

"When we got him out of the car we were asking each other where we should put him, there was no ambulance there. I said, 'Lay him down in the backseat of the radio car!'

"Rick wouldn't fit in the back seat lying down, so I busted out the rear passenger window of a radio car with the butt of my gun. When I busted out the window, someone thought shots were being fired at us and put it out on the radio. I didn't know they put out the call because I had busted out the window and I believed we were taking shots. Now we were on high alert.

"I intended to put Rick's leg and foot out of the window after we got him in the car. Rick was screaming, and in such agony, there was no way we could have gotten his leg up to the window. So, two officers got in the backseat with Rick, and I got in the front passenger seat. Rick's feet were hanging out of the rear passenger door. Rick couldn't bend his leg, and we could not close the door, so I leaned my upper torso out of the front window and held the rear door open by the rear door window frame. Because of the radio traffic of shots being fired, my gun was in my left hand as I held the rear door open with my right hand. Radio cars were blocking us, so I told the driver, 'Go over the curb.' And that's how we drove to the hospital.

"When we drove a couple of blocks, I saw the fire departments and paramedics, and I was thinking you guys are in the wrong place.

"Because Rick and I were friends, I got assigned to go and get his wife and get her to the hospital. I called her and told her I was coming over and to get herself ready to go to the hospital. Of course, she asked me what was going on. I had to tell her Rick was hurt. Of course, she assumed that but she wanted to know what happened. I had to tell her Rick had been shot but he was okay.

"When we picked her up we were sitting in the backseat of a radio car. I was crying, and instead of me helping her, she ended up comforting me."

* * * * *

"I relived this incident over and over again. It wouldn't stop. Often I would be driving alone, and I would look over at the passenger seat, and Daryle would be sitting there not saying a word. Nightmares were pretty frequent, but they have pretty much disappeared now."

How ironic that I had interviewed Abel Morales on April 28, 2017, and I am sitting here writing this on April 29, 2017, seventeen years later to the day this incident happened.

* * * * *

Some years later another partner of Abel's was shot, and Abel was at the scene. Homicide detectives were there and told other officers to watch him. Abel wondered why he needed to be watched. The officers asked why they should watch him; Abel was a solid officer and detective.

They said, "This is the second time a partner of his has been shot."

Abel had been fine until he heard this. Then he started shaking and couldn't stop.

* * * * *

I had turned off the digital recorder. Abel and I were laughing and eating sliders when he got serious again.

He said as tears again welled up in his eyes, "Let me tell you the kind of guy Daryle was. About three months ago I was at a gas station. An Asian man was looking at me. We kind of acknowledged each other and the man told me I looked familiar. I thought maybe he was a cop who I had met sometime in my career somewhere. I asked the man, 'Are you a cop?'

"The man answered he wasn't, but then he recognized me. 'You're Morales, I remember you. You are a cop.' The man got serious, 'I was really sorry to hear about Daryle.' We spoke for twenty minutes, and he recalled how Daryle and I had stopped him with other gang members many years back when he was a teenager, and how we treated him with respect and didn't belittle him. About every five minutes during the conversation he thanked me and mentioned how Daryle and I had actually made a positive difference in his life. He said he has straightened out his life and was now married. He fully realizes what Daryle and I said about life, values, and family was true."

* * * * *

Abel Morales is a highly respected Long Beach Police Officer and detective. He knows the communities, and the streets as very few others do.

Abel Morales has given to the community in many ways. He has put his life on the line countless times. He has been in four different officer-involved shootings, all justified, faithfully protecting the citizens of the City of Long Beach for twenty-five years.

He is a hero.

* * * * *

You can read the details of Rick's shooting in his own words in the first book in this series, *The Red Dot Club*.

Chapter 8

Fighting a Naked Man, Hang On To It

Account of Eve Irvine
Inglewood Police Department

She is a small cop who is full of energy. She is feisty, tenacious, smart and caring. She is also tough and strong-willed. And just like the Royal Canadian Mounted Police, her motto should be, "I always get my man."

You'll see.

* * * * *

"I was hired by the Inglewood Police Department as a police officer in 1984. By the spring of 1985, I had graduated the Los Angeles County Sheriff's Academy and had been working patrol for several months.

"On this particular evening, my training officer was off. I was working with a male partner, Mike, who I did not usually work with. About midnight or so, we got a call of a naked man in the middle of the street at Hardy and Myrtle Ave. Even though I had only been working the streets for several months, I had already dealt with numerous dusters, (people under the influence of P.C.P.). It was rampant. It seemed like when someone was acting bizarre, especially if they were naked, they were probably on P.C.P.

"Unless we handled these suspects exactly right it could easily turn into a fight. Knowing this, and thinking I did not want to handle a naked man without wearing my gloves, I put them on.

"We pulled up to the intersection, and there he was. A naked man in the middle of the intersection with clenched fists. Oh, joy. Even from a distance, he had the telltale signs of being under the influence of P.C.P. He was sweaty, he had a blank stare, his body was rigid, and he was unresponsive to commands…all the telltale signs were there. I knew after we confirmed what we supposed was true, he was probably going to go to jail for being under the influence of Phencyclidine, P.C.P.

"In those days, the patrol units did not carry Tasers. Only the sergeants had them.

"Mike wore really thick glasses. After we got out of the car and got up to the suspect, Mike got punched in the face, and his glasses flew off. I think Mike really needed his glasses because when they flew off his face, he went to his hands and knees and was looking for them.

"Right after Mike got punched I got on the handheld radio and put out we needed some backup. I knew this was not going to go well.

"I looked at the suspect, and he looked through me with a thousand-yard blank stare that goes right through you, and I thought with a sinking feeling, 'Oh man,' and before I knew it, the fight was on. Time slowed down to a crawl. He was punching me in the face and in the chest. I was punching him, and I was trying to get control of him and block his punches. I looked down at my partner, and I was thinking, 'He's not going to be able to help me, I'm on my own.' When I tried to grab the suspect, he was so sweaty that he was slippery and I could not get a grip on him. It was a full-on fight, and he was swinging at me with everything he had.

"Here I was fighting a naked sweaty man in the middle of the street.

"I knew help was coming and I thought to myself, 'Help is coming, DON'T LET HIM KNOCK YOU OUT!!! STAY CONSCIOUS!!! If you get knocked out, he is going to take your gun and kill you!'

"Somehow I ended up in the middle of the street on my back with the suspect on top of me. I leaned over to my left just a little to lie on my gun so he couldn't get it. He was still hitting me in the face and chest. I tried to knee him, I tried to punch him, but nothing was working. Try as I might, nothing I did hurt him or slowed him down, that is, until I reached down and grabbed his crotch. I mean I grabbed it hard. That seemed to slow him down a bit. But then he started punching me again. So, while still holding onto his penis and testicles, or maybe it was one testicle, I'm not sure, I pulled back and punched. He felt it and grunted. It slowed him down, and I felt him shiver a bit. But in the next instant, he started punching me again.

"These seconds were like hours. He was frothing at the mouth and dripping sweat onto me. I can't tell you how disgusted I was. I was also repulsed that I had a hold of his privates, but it was all I could hold onto, and it was the only thing that stopped him from momentarily hitting me. I wasn't letting go. I was afraid he would knock me out and kill me. Secondly, he had hit my partner and me, and I had decided he was NOT getting away and he was going to jail. Every hit I gave him made him stop hitting me. Even though we were face to face, I don't even know if he realized I was a police officer. He was looking through me. These slight respites I got when I hit him, were just enough for me to catch my breath and for me to re-grip his crotch. I was twisting, yanking, and pulling at his groin every chance I had to try to get him to stop hitting me. It was hard to get the leverage because of my position and him being right on top of me.

"At some point, my partner was back in the fight and was helping me, but I couldn't tell what he was doing because the suspect was on top of me. I was seriously worried and was thinking, 'I don't want to die like this in the middle of the street.'

"After what seemed like an eternity, but was probably no more than several minutes, backup arrived. No one could get the guy off of me, and I was still getting punched. One of the officers tried to hit the suspect in the head with the yawara handle of the baton, (this is the side handle for the baton used in those days) but along with the suspect, he was hitting me in the face too. I started yelling, 'STOP, STOP, YOU'RE HITTING ME IN THE FACE!!!'

"Finally, enough officers got there and pulled the suspect off of me. But I wouldn't let go of him. I yelled out, 'Hey guys the only thing that stopped this guy is when I hit him in the crotch!'

"I finally let go, and they got him handcuffed. We all looked down, and nothing between his legs looked right. His penis and testicles had road rash, they were purple and swollen. I really did a number on him."

Eve looked at me, "It's really embarrassing, but it's what I needed to do to survive."

"We took him to the hospital. He was so whacked out, (high on P.C.P.) they had to tie him down in the emergency room.

"The doctor finally asked us officers, 'Okay, who caused the damage?' I had to raise my hand, 'I did, that would be me.'

"I explained how he got the injury.

"During the fight, I had scraped my knuckles raw on the asphalt through my leather gloves, and the hospital treated them. Even now I can still feel his sweat and the froth from his mouth on my skin. After the fight, and for days afterward, this thought, and the memory of grabbing and punching his groin to survive revolted me so much, all I could think of was I needed to take a shower.

"For the next couple of days when I went to briefing, I was met with the drawing someone had made on the chalkboard of a swollen set of testicles.

"I was twenty-one years old."

* * * * *

I told you her motto should be, "I always get my man."

* * * * *

Eve Irvine attained the rank of Captain with the Inglewood Police Department. In May 2011, she was appointed as the Chief of the Manhattan Beach Police Department in which capacity she has been honorably serving ever since.

Chapter 9

Trading Bullets With A Killer

Account of Robert Kolenda
Overland Police Department

"I thought I spit the bullet out. I was wrong."

* * * * *

Bob grew up in Kansas City, Missouri. He was recruited right out of high school to go work for the Federal Bureau of Investigation (F.B.I.). It was a dynamic shift for him.

* * * * *

I grew up playing baseball. I ran track and played football in high school. I was too aggressive, so I didn't make the cut for basketball. I guess I would have been considered a jock.

While in high school I was one of the head cooks at the local Sizzler restaurant. They were going to put me in the program to be the assistant manager. I saw the money. As a high school kid, I thought it was pretty good. So, I was planning to go into the restaurant management business when I got out of high school. My dad worked in the retail business, and he didn't want me to go into anything related to that field. He knew the long hours did not equate to good pay.

My dad had a friend who worked for the F.B.I. He heard I was going to graduate soon and I didn't have plans to go to college. He told me about a deal if you worked for the F.B.I. for three years as a Clerk

Agent, and got your degree, they would let you test for the position of F.B.I. Agent. Prior to this, they would only let you test if you had your law or accounting degree. I thought it sounded like fun, so I applied for a job as a Clerk Agent with the Washington D.C. field office. I ended up getting the job but not in Washington D.C. I got the job in the Kansas City F.B.I. Field Office. I started going to night school, majoring in criminal justice.

I was an F.B.I. Clerk, filing papers and inputting information into the National Crime Information Center. I was shooting photography for the agents and doing general clerical stuff. It was the closest thing to police work I had ever seen or been around. I had never considered doing anything law enforcement related, and this was a quantum leap in experience for me.

While attending college at night, I ended up being around a lot of Kansas City Missouri police officers. Of course, they always had a lot of stories. For a young man to hear all the adventures of the officers, it made up my mind. I wanted to be in law enforcement. I decided I wanted to be an F.B.I. Agent. After some time, an F.B.I. Agent approached me. "You know Bob, this Clerk Agent program isn't working. We have a lot of guys who have been in the program for years. They have their degrees and are not being given the opportunity to test. You ought to start looking around and testing to get into a local police agency as a police officer. Finish your degree then re-apply as an F.B.I. Agent." He suggested I look into the Overland Park Police Department as he thought they were a great department.

I applied with the Overland Police Department in the State of Kansas in April 1977. I was hired as a police officer in October. I was 21 years old.

I spent 10 years as a patrol officer. I then was promoted to sergeant and worked for about 12 years in that capacity. So, I had 22 years of pushing around a police car. Throughout those years I was on the S.W.A.T. team. I was also the firearms instructor; a training officer and I was the range master throughout various times in my career.

I then went to the Criminal Investigations Division in March 2001. I was in charge of two guys that worked computer crimes in the Fugitive Task Force. I also had two guys who were on assignment with the Drug Enforcement Agency.

Four months before I got shot I almost had to shoot someone. It was the first time in my career I was pulling the trigger ready to shoot. There was a bar that was having an increasing number of drunks causing disturbances and fights in the rear parking lot. Cars were also getting broken into. My partner and I were sitting in my unmarked car in the back parking lot along with two other detectives who were in a separate car in the parking lot. Without any noise or yelling, or arguing or any other warning, a guy in the parking lot starts shooting his gun into a car. The car was squealing tires trying to get away and drive off into the street. It was nighttime, and my partner and I saw the muzzle flashes of the gun as the guy was firing into the car. We bailed out of the car and ran toward the suspect. As we were yelling at him to drop the gun, he started turning toward my partner. My partner didn't have a shot because of the patrons coming out of the bar and was behind the suspect, in her line of fire. I was at a different angle and did have a shot. Whereas seconds before I had seen him shoot into the car, now, due to where I was, and where he was holding his gun, I could not see the gun. I was yelling at him, *"Drop the gun, and get on the ground, drop the gun!!!"*

He was still turning toward my partner. I heard his gun hit the ground and he dropped to the asphalt belly down. He ended up lying on top of the gun.

If he had turned just a few more inches toward my partner, I would have shot him. I later learned he was out of bullets. I didn't know. I don't think he knew it either.

* * * * *

On December 4, 2001, I got paged at home at 7:43 P.M. Another sergeant who worked financial crimes had served a search warrant at an apartment complex earlier in the day. The background to the search warrant was a woman who worked at a kiosk at our local mall was taking credit card numbers and customer information from people. Then she and some other people were taking the information and making fraudulent credit cards.

The sergeant who paged me said she and her team had searched the apartment, obtained a lot of evidence and had arrested several people but there was still an outstanding guy they were waiting for. They knew he was staying at the apartment and they were staking out the apartment, waiting for him to return. His name was Brown. The suspects they arrested told the detectives that Brown was very athletic and would probably resist arrest. Brown was working as a security guard at a bakery. Further information from the suspects was there was a guy hanging around Brown named Peterson. After working up Peterson's background information, the detectives learned he was wanted for a murder he had just committed in the state of Washington several days before. Peterson was considered armed and dangerous.

The sergeant wanted us to relieve a couple of their detectives who were conducting surveillance on the apartment and arrest Brown when he arrived there after work. We knew Brown got off work from the bakery at 10:00 p.m. and he would probably show up shortly after that. The information we had was Peterson had been tipped off, and he was likely headed out of town.

So, myself and another detective got to the apartment around nine thirty and relieved the other detectives. Everyone, all the patrol units, and the station knew where we were and where we were set up. We were wearing a police raid jacket with a bright gold sewn on badge, and we had our hard badges around our chest hanging by a chain from our neck. The apartment address was 6542 W. 91st Street in Overland Park. We were sitting in a car, north of the apartment building backed into a parking space. We were facing the doors of the target apartment building.

We had a description of the car Brown was driving and a picture of Brown and Peterson. We were set. We knew Brown's apartment keys would not open the door because when the detectives had served the search warrant earlier in the day, they had damaged the lock to his apartment door and had replaced it. The apartment complex was a three-story unit. There were two subterranean units downstairs, two units on the first ground floor, and two units on the second floor. His unit was on the second floor. The entrance to the apartment complex was an unlocked door. To the left side of this door were three glass windows. They run from the top to halfway down the door. As soon as you open this door, you are at the landing, and the stairs are to the left. Brown's apartment unit was on the second floor at the top of the stairs. You could see his upstairs apartment door from the apartment complex's entrance door.

We knew when Brown went up to his apartment door, he would be stuck. He would not be able to get into his apartment, and there were no other stairs for him to exit out of the building. We decided we would let him get in the building and get to his apartment door. We would then breach the apartment complex's door and confront him. If he was going to fight, my partner was going to use his O.C. (pepper spray) gas spray, and I was going to use my asp (a type of collapsible baton).

After sitting in the car for about an hour, a brown Ford Explorer showed up and parked about 100 feet away from us. It was the car Brown was supposed to be driving. Two guys got out. And there he was, Brown, we recognized him right away. The other guy was wearing a hoodie, and we couldn't see his face.

I thought, "That might be Peterson."

I later learned my partner picked up on the fact it wasn't that cold out. He wondered why he was wearing the hoodie. The other thing he noticed was the guy had both his hands in his sweatshirt pouch. He was thinking he might have a gun. He didn't tell me what he was thinking...we were in motion.

My partner had a portable radio. I told him, "Go to the car and get the tag numbers and call it in. Get us some backup. I'll go to the building."

We took off. When I got to the door, I could see through the glass window on the side of the door into the landing and stairs. Both of the guys were upstairs standing at the apartment door and trying to get the key to work. In an instant, the guy in the hoodie turned. It was almost like he knew I was there and I can't tell you why, but I had the feeling I had been seen.

Without hesitation, he ran down the stairs. From the time he turned to the time he was down the stairs was no more than two seconds. In those two seconds, I got my gun out of my holster and in my hand, and I was ready to challenge him. I was seven feet from the door. The door swung out toward me. I saw his arms come out....and then I don't remember anything. Nothing. There is a blank spot in my memory. I don't know if I blacked out a part of the time, or if I blacked out due to the fact I saw a pistol. Psychologists call it, Trauma-Induced Amnesia.

I think I said, "POLICE!" Anyway, the next thing I remember is a loud bang and felt a tremendous impact in my lower right jaw. But I was shooting at the same time.

I don't know who shot first. I know I saw the gun, but I don't remember seeing it. The reason I know I saw his gun is my first bullet went through his right wrist, the wrist that was holding the gun. The bullet then went through his left wrist then into the wall. Even though I don't remember seeing the gun I know I saw it. Remember I was a firearms instructor. We are trained to focus on the threat. The threat was the gun, and that is what I hit, the wrist that was holding the gun. I have no doubt when I shot I was looking at and focusing on the threat, the gun.

I felt my gun bucking in my hand as much as heard it. It was incredibly loud. So loud my ears were still ringing two days later.

Because of the impact to my jaw, I knew I had been hit. I used to compete in full contact karate. I had been kicked in the face before. The impact was less than being kicked in the face. I think the reason for this was the bullet was cutting through me on its journey, thereby lessening the full impact of the force of the bullet. I shot three times, and in a millisecond of assessing if the threat was still there, I shot three more times. It was an almost instantaneous three shot follow-up. I was still standing. On my last shot, I saw him go to the ground and the door shut behind him.

I thought I spit out the bullet. I was wrong. The round hit me just below my mouth and maybe even touching my lower right lip. You can't even see the scar on my lip today. It went into my lower right jaw. It shattered my jaw. Then the force of the bullet embedded one of my teeth into the roof of my mouth, the soft pallet. Another tooth flew so hard it embedded in the bottom of my mouth. A third tooth embedded into the bottom of my tongue. A fourth tooth had to later be pulled. At the back and base of your tongue is a bone. That bone was fractured by the force of the bullet. The bullet misaligned the cartilage in my Adam's apple.

I don't know what I spit out. Was it teeth fragments? Splinters of jawbone? Gristle and tendon? I don't know. I thought it was the bullet. The reason I know I didn't spit out the bullet was it tore down my throat. Somewhere along the way as it was tearing through my mouth, the bullet separated from the bullet jacket, (a piece of metal housing of the bullet), thus becoming two different pieces of metal. As the bullet and the bullet casing tore down my throat, it ripped my right vocal cord. The bullet and bullet jacket went down my trachea, and I inhaled it into my left lung.

He had shot me one time.

I was still standing when the suspect fell to the ground. I now started looking for the other guy; the guy I assumed was Brown. While looking through the side door window, I saw him running down the stairs to my gunfight. There was no question to me that he was a threat. There was a gun somewhere where he was running to. I shot one round through the side door window. He fell down the last two stairs and crumpled to the landing. I missed him.

My partner who was just finishing putting out the radio transmission saw me shoot all seven times.

From the first shot to the last was about four seconds.

I went to one knee. I was pointing my gun at the door, covering any threat that might come out. My partner was now at my side.

He asked, "Are you okay?"

"No, I don't think I am."

Because of the damage to my vocal cord and mouth in general, I now sounded like Marlon Brando in the movie *The Godfather*. My partner thought I was whispering when I replied.

I was bleeding and drooling. When I went to my knee, a significant amount of blood splattered on the ground and down my shirt. Pieces and fragments of bone, teeth, and gristle, were drooling out of my mouth. It was flowing out. I was surprised I could halfway speak.

My partner did something extremely brave…he opened the door. He had no idea what was waiting for him when he did so. From his angle, he could see Brown lying at the base of the steps, but he could not see the second guy, Peterson. The guy who shot me. The sight of me bleeding and drooling should have been enough to make anyone second-guess the idea of going through that door. Pointing his gun in front of him he opened the door. Peterson was lying about ten feet away from the door on the landing. He held them at gunpoint until help got there.

While we were waiting for backup, I was trying to figure out how badly I was hurt. I was still covering my partner with my gun pointed forward as I self-evaluated myself. I went through the A.B.C.s. Airway. Breathing. Circulation. I could breathe, and my airway was clear, that was a positive. Because I was bleeding, I knew my heart was still circulating. I knew I was hurt, but I didn't know how badly and I was scared. I could hear the sirens coming, and I knew the cavalry was coming. To hear them coming was so very comforting.

I was thinking I might be dying. I was worried and scared. I was thinking about leaving my family and not seeing my kids grow up. I started praying.

"God, I don't want to die tonight, I still want time to spend with my family."

I had accepted Christ as my personal savior many years before. As I prayed a realization and a calm came over me that if I died my salvation was secure, and I really didn't have anything to worry about.

People came to me later and told me I was very calm. It was because I knew if I died, I didn't have anything to fear. I knew where I was going.

When you listen to my partner's second transmission for backup, which he put out after I'd been shot, you can hear my last shot being fired. That's how fast these things happen.

The first two officers who arrived at the scene were medically trained. One had been a medic in the military, and the other had worked for an ambulance company. I knew they were medics. Only the hand of God could have sent the only two medically trained officers to my shooting. This calmed me even more. It was as if God was telling me he was taking care of me. These were the only two trained medical guys in our department. What were the chances they were the first two guys to show up? I am convinced God was looking out for me.

When I got to the hospital, it took about two and a half hours for the pain to really kick in, and it was bad. While I was in the hospital, I had a nurse who was trying to start an I.V. on me. After her second miss, I turned to her and said, "I've got good veins, find one." I was still drooling blood down my now shirtless chest.

I was in the hospital for 12 days. I went back to work in a month with my jaw wired shut. I did not want the bad guy to beat me, and I thought if I stayed home, he would have won. I was on limited duty for a year. My jaw was wired shut, and I carried around a pair of scissors in case I choked someone could cut the wires. I ended up having numerous reconstructive surgeries. They put a titanium plate in my jaw. I had a bone graft from my hip to rebuild my jaw. I have a bridge from my lower wisdom teeth to hold in four teeth that were replaced. They ran a stitch from my Adam's apple to my vocal cord to reattach it until it healed so I could speak normally. They had to realign the cartilage in my Adam's apple. Of course, I had to have a tracheotomy while they did various procedures.

* * * * *

Peterson had committed a murder in King County in the state of Washington just prior to going to Kansas and shooting Sergeant Robert Kolenda.

During the commission of the Washington murder, he shot the victim in the head four times. After killing him, he removed the four empty shell casings out of the gun and never reloaded them with live rounds. After removing the casings, the suspect closed the cylinder. He had two live rounds in the gun left.

The gun he used in the murder was the same gun he used in the shooting of Sergeant Robert Kolenda. At the time of shooting Sergeant Robert Kolenda, he only had two bullets in the gun. After the shooting, he told detectives he shot Sergeant Kolenda two times when he had only shot him once. It was surmised in Washington after he removed the empty casings, he lined up the cylinder wrong so when he fired it skipped the first bullet and the gun only fired once.

Peterson had just purchased drugs prior to the shooting. He claimed he shot Sergeant Kolenda because he thought Sergeant Kolenda was going to rip him off. This is despite the fact Sergeant Kolenda was wearing a police jacket, and his badge was plainly visible. Peterson did have drugs and cash on him at the time of the shooting. Peterson got 22 ½ years for the attempted murder of Sergeant Robert Kolenda. He was then extradited back to the State of Washington and stood trial for the murder he committed there. At the time of the murder he committed in Washington, he was already a twice-convicted felon, a two striker. If he was arrested for the Washington murder and convicted, he was going to be a three-time convicted felon, a three-striker and would be going to prison for life. This is most likely why he shot Sergeant Kolenda.

* * * * *

The district attorney's office could not prove Brown was involved in the attempted murder of Sergeant Robert Kolenda and he was charged with a property crime in connection with the credit card forgeries. He got probation.

* * * * *

Sergeant Kolenda has been promoted to the rank of captain. At the time, this book was published he will be retired with 39 years and 5 months on the job.

He has a strong faith in God and in his will. I asked him how he could reconcile his beliefs with the possibility of having to take someone's life.

He said, "Just to let everyone know how I reconcile maybe having to take a life and my belief in God: I am very comfortable in maybe having to take a life. There are several places in the Bible that talks about the fact evil needs to be dealt with, about having to take a life. I am very cognizant of the sanctity of life, and I believe God created everyone, but some people earn the privilege. One of my favorite verses is, 'Blessed are the peacemakers for they shall be called the children of God.' That's what we are, we are the peacemakers."

* * * * *

This is an excerpt from a scrapbook Robert Kolenda's wife, Cindy Kolenda made for him after his shooting:

December 4, 2001

December 4, 2001, started out like any other day. We went to work, came home and went to work out at Prairie Life. After we were done, we went home to get dinner started. In the process of making dinner, you got a phone call from the police department. They called to see if you could get 2 people to relieve the officers on surveillance all day. You started making phone calls immediately and were only able to get one volunteer, Terry Schmidt. At that point, you decided to volunteer yourself. Of course, I was not happy, you had already worked all day and then had to leave again. However, I understood, this is what your job was all about.

Later that evening, I decided I was in a movie-watching mood. I went upstairs to watch Home Alone Part 1. For some reason, I could not sleep that night, which was very unusual for me since it was a work night. After the movie was over, I put home Alone Part 2 in the VCR and started watching it. It was getting even later at that point. I decided if you were not home by 12:00, I was going to call you to see what was going on. This was around 11:40. At approximately 11:50 the doorbell rang. This startled me, and I was not going to answer it since you were not home. I decided I would look out our bedroom window to see if I could see anything. I saw an OPPD patrol car parked next to our mailboxes. At first, I thought maybe you were stopping by the house to pick something up. Then I realized you would not be ringing our doorbell. At that point, I knew something was wrong. I ran down the stairs and looked out the side windows and saw two police officers standing there. Then I really knew something was wrong. I opened the door and immediately asked what had happened to you. Everything started moving in slow motion, it seemed like it took them forever to tell me you had been shot. I remember asking them the question, is he okay, is he alive? Again, the answers seemed slow in coming. At that point, I sat down on the stairs and started screaming for Justin. Justin did not hear me, so I ran upstairs, threw open his door and told him you had been shot, we needed to go to the hospital. I did the same thing with Bethany. I am afraid I was not very diplomatic about it. At that point, we quickly got dressed and flew out the door so we could get to the hospital. I was shaking all the way there. I simply could not believe this was happening.

Once we arrived at the hospital, I ran through the ER doors and frantically started looking for you. I saw several people and police officers outside of your room. When I entered your room, I could not believe what I saw. I was still having a difficult time processing everything and tears filled my eyes. I do remember I was so thankful you were alive. I could not believe you were not in any pain, based on what I saw.

Approximately one hour or so after I arrived at the hospital, they took you to surgery. Everyone who was waiting there went with me to the surgery waiting room. I had a lot of love & support that night. Family, friends and police officers surrounded me, and it was a very comforting feeling. The surgery seemed to take forever. Once the surgery was over, Dr. Tanner came out to visit with me. He let me know up front this was a severe injury and he did the best he could for now. It was going to take more surgeries down the road to correct the damage done to your jaw. From surgery, they moved you to the ICU for a few days. While in the ICU, they had to perform a procedure to remove the bullet fragments you had aspirated into your lungs. It was not until later we found out these fragments had damaged your vocal chords.

Here we are, two years later and you are still facing more surgeries. This has been an incredible journey for you and our family. I want you to know I am incredibly proud of you and your job. Never once throughout the whole ordeal did I ever see you complain or feel sorry for yourself. Even though this was a difficult time in our lives, many good things have come out of it. Friends and family continue to love and support us, your faith in God has grown stronger, and our love for each other has grown deeper. You have been an OUTSTANDING example to our children and me. For that I thank you. You are my HERO!

I hope you enjoy this scrapbook, as much as I enjoyed making it for you.

I love you,

Cindy

* * * * *

Captain Robert Kolenda received the Gold Award for Valor for his actions on the evening of December 4, 2001. This is the highest award the Overland Police Department bestows upon its members.

Additionally, Captain Robert Kolenda received the Purple Heart for the wounds he received on the evening of December 4, 2001.

Captain Robert Kolenda also received the Combat Ribbon for his actions on the evening of December 4, 2001.

Chapter 10

A Tough Night

Account of Robert Rangel
Los Angeles County Sheriff's Department

I'm a wife beater.

No, I'm not.

Yes, I am.

You decide.

Here's what happened.

I was in uniform, and I was chasing a gang member. I was struggling to keep up with him as in every foot pursuit, with the weight of my gun and baton slapping at my side. He had a tattoo of a spider web on his neck and two teardrops on the corner of his right eye. He was just running and running, and I was running and running. It was dark, darker than a moonless night. Over fences, we went. Through front yards and backyards. Street after street we huffed. Yard after yard. The knowledge I was alone weighed heavily on me. It was never good to chase someone alone. As tough as you thought you were, these guys grew up fighting on the streets, and you never knew what would happen when you caught them. It was desperate sprinting, and I was running out of steam.

I cornered him. In a cul-de-sac, he stopped running. I thought he was tired. He wasn't. It turned out he cornered me because when I went to arrest him, ten or twelve of his friends surrounded me. They put their hands on me. Strong gripping iron fingers tore at my uniform. It was like a pack of lions, each wanting to be the first to take a bite. I knew it was not to beat me but to kill me.

I was fighting, elbowing, screaming, biting, kicking, punching, twisting violently so they couldn't hold onto me. A knife came up. Then down, down, I watched, helplessly, ever so slowly it sank into my shoulder. Again, I screamed. The pain was excruciating, and I couldn't move. Sharp, my shoulder coming out its socket with my arm falling off in pain. Screaming, twisting, fighting...getting punched, someone yelling at me... "Wake up!!! WAKE UP!!!"

A slow realization hit me as I woke up. I'd been dreaming. It was a week after I'd been shot. My wife was hitting me and yelling at me to wake up. It was a nightmare. And in that vivid horror of senses, while I slept, I was hitting her.

The pain in my dream of being stabbed was the pain of my bullet being thrashed around in my shoulder socket.

This event happened a week after I was shot. This shooting is recounted in *The Red Dot Club*.

Chapter 11

Boiled

Account of Brian Hawksley
Los Angeles County Sheriff's Department

It was my call, but Bobby Rangel, the author of this book, was my assisting unit. It was a "check on the welfare," call we got on a Monday afternoon. These calls mean someone was not able to get a hold of someone else, and they wanted an officer to try and make contact with the person and see if they were okay.

In this instance, it was the neighbors who had called. Rangel and I got there at the same time. The neighbors were waiting for us outside of the guy's house.

The story we got was their neighbor had been very sick. They had seen him get home from work on Friday as was his normal routine. But they didn't see him the whole weekend. This was not normal. Usually, they saw the man come and go throughout the weekend. His car was still parked in the driveway, and they were pretty sure he hadn't left. They had tried calling him, but there was no answer, and he wouldn't answer his door.

One of the neighbors had the key. Rangel and I spoke, and we decided we needed to go in.

We opened the door and knew. Now, we had both seen and smelled dead bodies before. It is the most unpleasant thing you will ever smell. This was the worst I had ever smelled.

What struck me first was the stench, then the humidity. The house had wood paneling, and water was beaded up on the walls and then running down to the floor. The smell was so overwhelming it was tough not to throw up.

Bob and I went into the house, and we could hear water running. The house was really like a little bungalow. To the right was the living room and behind it was the bedroom. To the left was the kitchen and behind it was the bathroom.

I went right, and Rangel went left.

Twenty seconds later Rangel yelled to me, "B-Hawk, I got him!"

I was trying really hard to not throw up. Rangel was in the bathroom standing sideways to me. His face was ashen, and I could see he also was trying to not throw up. He gasped, "He's in the bathtub."

The bathtub was to the right, and both sliding frosted shower glass doors were both slid open, side by side, and you could not see through them. The bathtub had water slowly running into it. It was enough, so the water was running into the overflow without going over the sides of the tub. The bath was steaming hot. It was creating the humidity in the house.

Rangel was gulping as he was breathing.

Since I couldn't see into the tub, I edged forward, and there were his feet. He was a black guy. As I crept forward, I could see his legs were unbelievably swollen. I got just past his thighs, and I was disgusted. His head was lying face down at his crotch with his black hair floating in the water, and his head was swollen to the size of a basketball. I couldn't help but wonder how his head could be so swollen. I crept forward and saw his stomach all swollen. I wondered, how could I see his head at his crotch and not see his back but I could see his stomach? The horror then hit me as I kept creeping forward, he was laying with his back against the rear of the tub. His head was tilted back.

96

OH, MY, GOD!!! What I had believed was his head was swollen to the size of a basketball was actually his testicles.

I was fighting desperately to not throw up. Rangel was gone. I left the bathroom and met Rangel outside. He had already told the neighbors what they already knew. Their neighbor and friend were dead.

We stepped away from the neighbors. I asked him the question I knew the answer to, "Buddy boy, did you see the guy's balls?"

"Yeah, B, I thought it was his head," he answered.

"Me too, me too. Oh, my GOD!"

Bobby went to get some cigars. I had to stay with the body. It turned out the poor guy had died on Friday with the hot water trickling in the tub. It was running slow enough the water heater was constantly on and keeping the super-hot water going. At some point, he died and slowly and partially boiled himself until we got there on Monday afternoon.

When I spoke to the neighbors, they told me he was a one-hundred and sixty-pound white guy. I thought he was a 280-pound black guy. He had died of AIDS, which was killing so many people in those days.

The mortuary got there, and as they were getting him into the body bag, parts of him were coming off due to him cooking in the bathtub for three days. I thought of a chicken boiling and coming apart in a boiling pot.

Bobby later told me he gulped down a bunch of air while in the place. The next day he burped up the dead smell and again almost threw up.

Those cigars did not help one bit.

Chapter 12

Ambushed

Account of Vern Jefferson
Marshalltown Police Department

Vern is an American Indian from the Meskwaki Indian tribe. They are connected to the Sauk (Sac) and Fox people, or tribe. The name is derived from the term, "a rigorous people." Their culture believes the creator molded a person from the red earth.

In 1851, the Iowa legislature passed an act which allowed the Meskwaki to purchase land. Prior to this, they could not do so because the United States government had declared tribal Indians were not legal citizens. In the mid-1800's a farmer in present-day Tama County, Iowa, allowed the Meskwaki Indians to buy some of his land, 80 acres to be precise. Tama County is named after a Meskwaki Chief, Tiamah, of the early 19th century. Over the years many Meskwaki moved to the Meskwaki Settlement in present-day Tama. They have now expanded the settlement to probably more than 1500 acres. This settlement is different than a reservation where the government owns the land. The Meskwaki people own their own land, not the government. It is interesting to note how some of the men of the Meskwaki tribe, served a critical role in the Second World War as code talkers.

This Meskwaki settlement is where Vern grew up.

* * * * *

During the time I grew up on the settlement there were about 700 to 800 people living there. It was great. Everyone knew everyone, and it was a close-knit community. If someone saw someone doing something wrong, and this relates primarily to kids, the adults would come over and counsel them. No one took it in a bad way. It was a way to keep us on the straight path. There was a lot of respect for the elders in the community and what they had to say.

In those days, the parents would back up the other elders in the community. Things have changed. In today's climate, it is different. As a current police officer if I were to give a citation to a juvenile, their parents, just like anywhere else in the country, blame me and ask why I am picking on their child. Parents don't hold their children responsible for their actions like they used to. I don't think this helps the structure of society where children are not held accountable for their actions.

While I was growing up, I never thought about whether we had money or not. Looking at what I have now, I guess we were poor. But breaking off a stick and going to play war with my friends, or buying a plastic gun at Wal-Mart and going off to play war was the same thing. We were still having fun.

I thought I was a good kid. I didn't get in trouble. I didn't have a lot of fights. One time someone wanted to fight me, so I didn't go to school that day. My parents told me not to fight other people because someone loved the other person. They taught me someone cared about the other person and it was wrong to want to hurt them. Now I tell my kids the same thing.

At the time, I was in high school, my older brothers were drinking a lot. They were getting in trouble. They were getting arrested, or sometimes an officer would bring them home instead of arresting them. They were alcoholics. Because of the situation, my mom and dad were really stressed out. I didn't want to put them through that. I wanted to do something different. I wanted to be better.

My dad was a veteran, and my mom had this tremendous respect for veterans. In referring to the soldiers and veterans, she would say, "Those are all my kids out there, those are all my sons and daughters fighting for us." She would say things like, "Oh, look at my sons and daughters fighting for us."

When I was in the 11th grade, I was behind in school. I wasn't caught up on my credits, and I wasn't going to graduate. I wasn't getting into trouble, but it was easy for me to not go to school. Sometimes I stayed at home and didn't have to worry about anything.

One day we had a career day at school. Some military recruiters came and gave a speech. I thought, "Well, that's kind of cool." I spoke with them afterward.

They asked me, "Do you graduate next year?"

I said, "No, I'm behind in credits."

He answered, "We only take high school graduates."

Two impactful life-changing events happened to me while I was in the 11th grade. One was the meeting with the military recruiter at school who told me the military only took high school graduates. The other thing that happened was one day I was sitting in a car in a parking lot in the city of Tama when an officer came up to me. He said, 'What are you going to do with your life, Vern?'

I don't know how he knew me, but he did.

I answered, "I don't know."

He said, "I'll tell you what you're going to do. You're not going to graduate high school. You're going to be a drunk. You're going to find odd jobs here and there. You're going to get your checks, and you're going to drink with the money from the checks. And you're going to do it again and again. You're never going to amount to anything, and you're never going to be anybody, and that's what you're going to do."

He looked at me and waited for a response.

I looked at him and smiled. I said, "No, I'm going to join the Marines, then I'm going to come back here and be a cop."

He looked at me and started laughing. He said, "Yeah, find me when you do Vern because that will be a first. You're going to be a lifer. You're going to drink yourself to death."

I said, "You'll see."

Looking back, I kind of get what he saw. I mean I had long hair down to the middle of my back. I was wearing this cut-off Metallica t-shirt. I don't know if he really meant it or if he was tricking me to get me motivated.

But it did motivate me. Was it reverse psychology he was using on me? To this day I don't know.

I graduated high school and went into the Marine Corps boot camp. It was here where I grew up. Nothing against my parents but while in boot camp I learned I had to do things I didn't necessarily want to do. I learned responsibility. They refined this character of responsibility throughout my military career. I was at Camp Pendleton for about a year, and then I went to Camp Lejeune in North Carolina. I got out of the Marine Corps in October 1996.

When I got out of the Marine Corps and went back to Tama, I got a job working security at the Indian Casino. I was also working as a janitor for some office buildings. In between cleaning toilets, I was doing a lot of cage fighting. They were putting me in with guys who were tough. It was like this guy won the state championship in wrestling, or this guy you're going to fight is a golden glove boxer. I was also running marathons. I was in great shape and was doing a lot of mixed martial arts fighting against some tough guys. Most of the guys I fought ended up going to the U.F.C., the Ultimate Fighting Championship, the top mixed martial arts league in the world. From what I understand if someone wanted to get to the U.F.C. I was one of the guys they had to beat. I fought in Illinois, Iowa, Minnesota, and Nebraska.

I got a call one Wednesday from a U.F.C. official. They told me they wanted me to try out for the U.F.C. fights on Saturday. I thought it was a joke. After we hung up, I called them back and asked, "Who put you up to this? Who is this?"

They said, "This is not a joke. We want you to come down here to try out for the fights."

I bought an airline ticket, and on Saturday I was at the tryouts. I beat two guys, but for some reason, they did not choose me to continue to the next round. That was my U.F.C. career. My fight record ended up being something like 24 wins and 14 losses.

One day, while I was at home with my mom, a car crashed and rolled over in front of the house. A guy came out of the car and asked me for help. We called the cops, but he was gone when I finished the call. He had run off. When the deputy arrived, I told him the guy who was driving ran off just before he arrived. The deputy told me to call the station when the guy came back.

After the deputy left, the driver came back. I told my mom to call the sheriff again. When the deputy was arriving the driver said, "Here come the cops again." He went to run off, but I managed to get him in a bear-hug. "Sorry, I'm supposed to hold you until the cops figure out what's going on."

When the deputy arrived, he arrested the guy and said to me, "Thanks."

I got talking to him and told him about my interest in law enforcement. He told me they were currently hiring reserves and it would be a great way for me to learn how things worked. In November 1997, I got hired on with the Tama County Sheriff's Department as a reserve deputy sheriff. In January 1999 I got hired as a full-time deputy sheriff with the Tama County Sheriff's Department. While I was working with the Sheriff's Department, I kept seeing all this action happening in the City of Tama. That's where I wanted to be, where the action was.

I applied with the Tama Police Department, and they hired me as a police officer in 2000.

I wanted to go west, somewhere warmer. So, I applied with the Las Vegas Metropolitan Corrections Department. Simultaneously, I applied with the Marshalltown Police Department in Iowa. The Las Vegas Metropolitan Corrections Department hired me in January 2004. I moved my wife and kids out to Las Vegas in July 2004. One day the kids wanted to go outside to play. Well if you've never been to Vegas, it is in the middle of the desert. Hot is an understatement. On this super-hot day, the Marshalltown Police Department called me and gave me a job offer. I asked the family if they wanted to go home, and the kids jumped up and down and said, "YAY, it's too hot here to play outside!"

In August 2004, I was back in Iowa as a Marshalltown Police Officer. I applied for a position as the defensive tactics instructor. I went through their course and got the spot. I'm sure my background as a mixed martial arts fighter helped me get the position.

On November 2, 2012, I was working patrol in Marshalltown. I was working day shift, from seven in the morning until three in the afternoon. I was a rover. I was the guy who backed up other patrol cars on their calls.

The call came out around nine thirty in the morning. "Any available officers, bank robbery at the Lennox Credit Union, 1004 East Main Street." I started driving in the direction of the credit union. The dispatcher put out additional information. The suspects took off on foot, two men with guns, one in a white shirt and one in a black shirt, last seen running west behind the Kum & Go. (The Kum & Go was a little convenience store located at the corner of 10th St. and East Main Street just across the street from the credit union. It is no longer there).

They were running west. I was west of them at Center and Ferner Street. I drove north on Center Street. When I got to East Anson Street, I made a right turn heading east. I made a left turn and went north on South 3rd Avenue. When I got to Nevada, I went east. Now I was about six blocks from where the robbery happened at Nevada and 8th Avenue. The last broadcast I heard was they were still running west from the Casey's General Store on 9th Avenue. So, they were close to either 8th or 9th Street. I drove up 8th Street hunting for them.

When I got to Main Street, I looked right and saw a patrol car coming toward me. I continued north on 8th Avenue, and two guys popped out in front of me running on the sidewalk north on 8th. They were on the sidewalk for about three seconds then cut back east between some houses. I got on the radio and transmitted that I had two guys running north on 8th Avenue just north of Bromley. I gave the description how one guy was wearing a black shirt, and the other was wearing a white sweater. I drove up a few houses and pulled east into a driveway just south of 207 North 8th Avenue between two houses. I stopped my radio car about ten feet into the driveway and got out of my car. Eleven seconds later I saw the man in the white sweatshirt running north, right to left, about 40 feet in front of me. Following right behind him was the man in the black shirt.

The description of the two suspects had been broadcast. These guys were running, and they matched the description. I knew it was them. I knew they had just robbed the credit union. And the last information I had was they were armed.

I ran toward the two suspects. I yelled "STOP, STOP, STOP. GET ON THE GROUND RIGHT NOW!!!" They kept running. As I chased them, the man in the black shirt looked at me, and I briefly made eye contact with him. He had big brown eyes. As I ran I was thinking, "Pace yourself, they're not going to shoot at me. They're going to keep running, and I'm going to have to run them down and catch them. I'm going to need all the energy I can keep, I might have to fight two men until help gets to me. I need to have the energy to arrest them after I catch them." I was giving out the location on my radio as they were running so the other officers could set up a perimeter.

They had already been running about eight blocks, and I thought they must be getting tired.

When they ran in front of me, they continued behind a garage at the back of 207 N. 8th Avenue, and I lost sight of them. The garage was not connected to the house and to get to the garage you had to pass an open yard area. I was putting out their direction as I was following them. My gun was in my hand pointed in front of me. I cut wide around the garage, and as I got past the building, there was the suspect in the white shirt. He was about thirty feet away. He had stopped running, and he was facing me. In his hand was a gun and it was pointed right at my head.

I was ambushed!

Time slowed down to a crawl. The barrel of the gun was huge. My vision became acute and not acute at the same time. To explain, most of everything was blurred. I couldn't see the suspect. He was blurry. The suspect's arms were blurry. I couldn't see my surroundings. They were blurry. Everything was blurry except one thing, the barrel of the gun. I could see the silver of the inside of the barrel of the gun…clearly. How clearly? Well, I can tell you the inside of the barrel of the gun was dirty. But not the whole circumference. Just part of the barrel was dirty. If you took the barrel of the gun and made it into a clock, as in looking down the circle of the barrel, and divided it into a clock, the barrel was dirty from the three o'clock to the five o'clock position. The rest of the barrel was clean. It was surreal. I questioned what was happening. I could not believe I could see the inside of the gun barrel so clearly from 30 feet away and I asked myself, "Is this really happening? Is he pointing a gun at me?" Then I said to myself again, "Is he really pointing a gun at me?" Forcing myself into reality, I said to myself, "He really is pointing a gun at me."

I was taught in training when faced with a gun to say, "Gun, Gun, Gun." That's way too long. It should just be, "Gun!" After all, this happened, I knew what I had to do. I had to shoot him before he shot me. He was going to try to kill me. But I wasn't ready to shoot. Even though my gun was out and pointed at him, I couldn't shoot because my finger wasn't on the trigger. It was alongside the barrel pointing straight ahead to prevent any accidental discharge. It is the way we train, "Finger off the trigger until you are ready to shoot." But I needed to fire now. Not in the few milliseconds, it would take for me to get my finger on the trigger. I needed to fire, NOW! I knew if I didn't fire first and accurate, he was going to kill me and take me away from my family.

I had trained for this since the Marine Corps and since I'd been a police officer. But when actually faced with it, it was unbelievable anyone would actually try to kill me. I was still coming to grips with the fact he had the nerve to do this, that it was real. I guess I never expected anything like this to actually happen. I was in disbelief and offended that he actually wanted to kill me. All these thoughts went through my head as I was desperately trying to get my finger on the trigger. It was taking forever and ever. It was an eternity. Not milliseconds, not minutes, but hours and hours. The thoughts kept jumbling through my head as I tried to get my finger on the trigger and I could not make my finger go any faster than all these separate thoughts running through my mind so clearly and distinctly and so slowly. I was waiting for him to shoot me and kill me and take me away from my family and there was nothing I could do about it. I was too slow.

Then it happened. I don't even know who shot first. I could not hear anything. I was in an *"OH, SHIT"* factor. Without consciously thinking about it, or maybe I did, I don't know, things were confusing; I was jumping out of the way. But there was nowhere to jump to. There was no cover. Nothing to hide behind. I was firing my gun. He was firing his gun. I was jumping to the side and pointing my gun at him and firing. I was trying to get back to where I had just been, it seemed hours ago…just three little steps behind the safety of the wall of the garage and I could not get there faster than the bullets were coming at me. I was exposed and helpless. Bullets were hitting the dirt around me. Things were taking forever and time was a snail moving through the grass.

Something brushed past my trousers. It was like walking through brush, and a twig caught my pants leg. It was a super slow brush. I thought, *"OH, CRAP, THAT WAS CLOSE!"* But then I felt this warm water running down my leg. I thought, *"OH, CRAP, I'M HIT!"*

Now, the blurry figure of the man I was shooting at faded from the view of the top of my gun. I didn't know if I hit him. He faded and fell backward and down to the ground. I was still shooting.

I had been running marathons and super marathons that were 31 miles. After I realized I was shot I thought, "Oh great now I can't run a marathon."

I was now behind the cover of the garage. But I was wondering, "Where's the second suspect?"

I was at the back of the garage, but the garage and the house were not attached. There was an open yard area between the house and the garage. As I was making my way back toward my radio car, I had to cross an open yard.

My gun was still out in front of me, and as I got to the area between the garage and the house, there was the second suspect. There was a fence which separated 207 North 8th Avenue and 205 North 8th Avenue. He had apparently been trying to run away north from me through the yards, but he was now at the fence. He turned toward me and raised his arm and pointed it at me. I saw a flash. Ever so slowly, as time was still slowed down, I fired several times. He ran west toward the street, toward North 8th Avenue.

So far five seconds had gone by from the first shot to my last.

I was alone. I couldn't decide in the next millisecond where to go. Should I return to the first guy who shot me or chase after the guy who ran to the street? Time returned back to normal. I thought I should go to the street because the first guy is done. I had seen him fade away. So, I wanted to see where the second guy was headed so I could let the other officers know.

I ran past my radio car toward North 8th Avenue and transmitted on the air with my portable radio, "I'm hit; a man is running north in a black t-shirt."

When I got to the street, a squad car was passing me. I later learned he had seen the suspect running down the sidewalk. He later apologized and told me it was so hard for him to drive past me because he heard my transmission that I had been hit, but he had seen the suspect and felt he needed to go after him.

When I got to the sidewalk, I couldn't see the suspect, so I made my way back to the back of the garage. By now about thirty seconds had gone by since I fired my first shot.

A radio transmission came out over the air. They were asking for my location. I couldn't answer them. I was at the rear of the garage and probably near the suspect. I didn't want him to know I was nearby. I felt awful because when I didn't answer the radio, I knew all the other units would think I was either too hurt to respond or I was dead.

I was limping now. My leg was cramping up. It felt like a "Charlie Horse." I had another officer with me now. As I rounded the corner of the garage for the second time, there was the suspect. He was on the ground, and he was trying to crawl away. He had left the money, which was in a bag, and his gun in one area, and he was crawling away from them.

I yelled at him, *"Get your hands out to the side, get your hands out to the side!"*

As other assisting officers were arriving and moving in to handcuff the suspect he was yelling, *"I've been shot! I've been shot!"* The officers hand-cuffed him.

The officers started asking me if I'm okay, and I told them, "No, I've been shot." My leg was cramping up really good by this time, and it was hard to walk. One of the guys draped my left arm over his shoulder. As we were limping back, I told him, "Get me to my car, I want to get the other guy."

He chuckled, "Let the other guys get him, Vern."

I learned after the second suspect was arrested I had missed him when I shot at him.

* * * * *

I was sitting in the back of the ambulance, and they were cutting off my trousers. I was angry. "That guy...that guy tried to kill me." I looked down at my thigh, and there was a red dot.

Once the ambulance started driving off, I don't remember any part of the next minute or so. I didn't pass out, but I don't remember anything. I don't know why. I guess it was the adrenaline.

* * * * *

A supervisor called my wife, "Vern's been shot, we're going to the hospital, you need to come up here."

She said, *"WHAT???"*

He replied, "Vern's been shot, you need to get up here."

My wife was at work. When she hung up the phone, a co-worker must have seen the look on her face and asked her, "What's wrong?"

She answered, "They just told me Vern's been shot. I've got to go to the hospital."

She didn't believe it. She said it felt like a dream. That it wasn't real.

Her co-worker said, "Let's go I'll take you right now."

She said, "I think I can drive myself, I'll be okay."

She got in the car and drove herself to the hospital, which was about twenty minutes away.

This has all changed, now we send an officer out to drive the spouse to the hospital. When I got to the hospital, it was full of officers. At some point, I told my wife she needed to get a hold of my brothers and tell them I was shot.

My older brother arrived. He asked me in Meskwaki where the suspect was. I told him he had been transported to another hospital. The suspect was actually in another room. I had to tell my brother he was gone because I was afraid what he would do to him.

I spent several hours in the hospital, and they sent me home.

I took three months off to heal up and then I was back to work.

The suspects had stolen $13,000. We recovered all the money.

"The guy who shot me was a 22-year-old who had robbed a grocery store with a gun the year before. His punishment for that crime was they took his gun and put him on probation.

"The shooter was sentenced 25 years in federal prison after pleading guilty to armed bank robbery and possession of a firearm in relation to a crime of violence. He got another 25 years for attempted murder on a police officer. He is going to serve the time concurrently. If he is a good boy, he will be out in seventeen and a half years.

The second suspect, who was also 22 years old, got 25 years for first-degree armed robbery.

Both of these guys were neighbors and lived right up the street. They almost got home.

One of the victims from the credit union made this statement in court, "I think of the words bravery and cowardice. I think of Officer Jefferson's bravery and your cowardice in threatening ten unarmed women with guns."

* * * * *

I am ready for the next one. I am prepared physically and mentally. And I hope when it happens it happens to me. Not because I want it, but because I've been through it and I know what to expect. People don't realize how difficult it is to go through, but I'm more ready than the guys who haven't been in a shooting or been shot. I know I can handle it. I don't want anyone else to have to go through what I went through.

* * * * *

Officer Vern Jefferson of the Marshalltown Police Department received the Medal of Valor from his department for his actions on November 2, 2012. It is the highest honor its department can bestow on its officers.

He also received the Iowa Police Chief's Association Officer of the Year Award.

He also received the Congressional Badge of Bravery for his actions.

Chapter 13

El Mengachi

Account of Paul Adams
California Highway Patrol

It was November 10, 1960. It was a perfect autumn afternoon in southern California. I was parked in the parking lot at 183rd St. and Pioneer Blvd in my marked black and white California Highway Patrol car. It was about 3:45 p.m. and I was catching up on some paperwork when a Plymouth came racing straight toward me, heading straight for my driver's door where I was sitting.

There wasn't a lot of time to react, and I only had time to think "OH, MAN, HE'S GOING TO HIT ME AND TAKE ME OUT!"

At the last possible second, he turned and almost threw the car into a left-hand skid. He just narrowly missed me. He jumped out. Near hysteria and in a high-pitched voice, only barely understandable, he told me a berserk man who was running loose had shot two people. He then told me the man was on Alburtis Street near South Street. This was less than a mile from where I was.

Without a pause, I told him to get in my car and take me to the shooter. I asked the guy's name, and he told me it was Efrain. The vibes I was getting from Efrain were so real, and he was in such distress we left his car right there in the parking lot, parked semi sideways. There was not a second to lose.

With red lights and sirens, I followed his directions south on Pioneer to west on South St. to north on Alburtis Ave. While I was driving, I was broadcasting the information Efrain was giving me.

Making a right on Alburtis St. I was now driving north and could see people running in the neighborhood. This was a mixed residential and business neighborhood at the time.

I slowed down, and as I continued on, I could see a woman on the west side of the street. She was lying on the front porch of a house, and I could see she was injured. Efrain told me she had been shot. Several Mexican women were attending to her on the porch.

I parked facing north on the west side of the street next to the house where the woman was shot. I told Efrain, "Get away from here, get away from this police car, and get to safety. I'll get you a ride back to your car later."

I stepped out of my car, not paying attention to Efrain any longer and started walking west toward the women on the porch. I had taken a few steps when one of the women yelled at me and pointed south, *"HERE HE COMES, NOW!"*

I was now on the sidewalk, my left side was to the south, the way the woman was pointing. As I turned to face him, I saw he had a rifle in his hands. It turned out to be an under/over .22 caliber rifle shotgun.

My gun was out in my right hand, and I yelled to him, *"HOLD IT!"*

He turned and faced me as he started raising his rifle.

I was raising my gun.

It was now a battle to see who could get their guns up first.

Time slowed down to a crawl. Things were more real than they had ever been, and slower, but also faster than they had ever been. It's tough to describe unless you've ever experienced it.

In this slowed down time I realized several things. One was I wasn't that good of a shot, and the guy was far away from me. He had a rifle which is much more accurate from a distance. It turned out the guy was 77 feet away. I knew I had one shot and it had to be right.

To make the shot I decided it had to be a single action shot. For you non-shooters, a single action shot is where you pull the hammer back, known as cocking the hammer, before firing. This lessens the trigger pull, or the length of time pulling the trigger. The longer the trigger pull, the more chance you have of moving the gun, the barrel. The lesser the trigger pull, you have less of a chance of coming off of your target during the time you are shooting. When making a long shot, any movement of the gun at all can make you miss your target very easily.

I turned at a 45-degree angle to the suspect as we had trained to do in those days and I cocked the hammer. I held the gun in a one-handed shooting stance as we had been trained in those days. He was facing me with his rifle pointed right at me. I remember thinking he was giving me his front, which was a wide target. I was going to shoot at the large target of his chest, and I knew if I missed I would be in real trouble. I had to hit him.

Things were still in slow motion, and it seemed like many minutes had gone by but in reality, only seconds had passed. All the above thoughts went through my head as I was cocking my gun and aiming. My shot finally went off, and my .357 caliber six-shooter was unbelievably loud, just like a canon.

The next thing that happened was I saw the suspect raise up in slow motion, kind of almost on his tippy toes. He then fell down face up. All this happened in super slow motion.

I was almost in a dreamlike state. I was numbly walking in slow motion toward him, and one of the Mexican women from the porch ran past me toward the guy. She was crying.

"Oh, my GOD," I thought, "I shot the wrong guy!" I was thinking the guy was a Good Samaritan trying to stop the bad guy. In all the confusion, I could not process he had just seconds ago aimed his rifle at me. I was second-guessing myself.

When the woman got to the guy, she spits on him. Relief hit me; I had shot the right guy.

He was dead, but his heart was still pumping. Blood was shooting out of his forehead with every heartbeat, about a foot in the air right between the eyes where I had hit him.

* * * * *

The follow-up investigation by the Los Angeles County Sheriff's Department revealed the suspect was a crazy man. He had been institutionalized before.

The suspect lived behind the El Mengachi Bar on Alburtis. On the day of this shooting, prior to Paul's arrival on Alburtis St., the suspect had walked into the rear of the El Mengachi bar. He then forced a woman who worked there out of the front door and pushed her to the ground. He then shot her in the leg with a revolver. This woman's 13-year-old son was sweeping the front of the bar and saw this. After the man shot his mother, the boy threw his broom at the suspect and took off running. The suspect shot at him several times, putting one bullet through the kid's shirt but missing his body. He then walked across the street to a store named the Trading Post. A man outside heard three shots coming from inside the Trading Post. When the suspect came out, the man yelled at him to stop.

The suspect said to the man, "I'll show you, you son of a bitch." The suspect then fired his revolver and shot the man in the left knee.

The suspect then left the Trading Post and walked across the street to the rear of the El Mengachi Bar. Shortly after that, the suspect came out between the El Mengachi Bar and a pool hall carrying a rifle. He approached another neighbor and shot the man in the foot.

Paul arrived pretty soon after that. Witnesses said just as Paul told the guy to "hold it," the suspect was pointing his rifle at some kids across the street.

Paul never saw the kids, but nonetheless, he probably saved those kids from being shot. The suspect had his pockets full of .38 caliber bullets for his revolver and .22 caliber bullets and shotgun shells for his over/under rifle. He also had two knives on him.

Who knows how many lives Paul saved that day?

* * * * *

Over an hour after the incident, Paul was interviewed. After the interview was over, he took out a cigarette and couldn't find a lighter or a match. The coroner was nearby, and he asked him if he had a light. The coroner pulled out a lighter, and as Paul held the cigarette to be lit, Paul's hands were shaking so bad the coroner could not get the flame to the end of the cigarette. Paul said he felt perfectly normal, at least he thought he did.

The coroner looked at him and said, "Hey man you're shaking a little bit. Are you okay?"

Paul said, "Geez, look at that."

The Highway Patrol and the Sheriff's Department were done questioning him around eight p.m. that night. He was off at eleven p.m. They gave him the rest of the night off.

He was back at work in his radio car the next afternoon at 3:15 p.m.

* * * * *

Paul Adams received the Medal of Valor for his actions on the afternoon of November 9, 1960, from the California Highway Patrol for the heroism he displayed. It is the highest award that can be bestowed upon its members.

Chapter 14

Paralyzed

Account of Peter Galassi
Gardena Police Department

He's my fan? Seriously?

He shuns the limelight. Craig Knapp became my fan after reading my second book *The Red Dot Club*. It's utterly ridiculous because as a Marine, he is one of the most decorated soldiers from the Vietnam War.

* * * * *

"Bob," he has said to me on more than one occasion, "I don't consider myself a hero. I am not anywhere near where you are. You guys got shot. I never got shot."

This statement is coming from a man who has been involved in countless operations and excursions during the Vietnam War. He has been in ten shootings after the war, both as a police officer and as a civilian where his life or his family's lives were threatened. Those who find out who he is and what he has done can't believe their ears. They can't believe such people actually exist. Craig explains, "They are like people at a circus. They want to be entertained. But then the stories are too much for them. They look at you like you did not do that. You become an oddity. I avoid letting anyone know what I did. I won't talk about it. I am not their entertainment. But after all I went through, I never got shot, but my body is marked with shrapnel, both as a result of battles in the military and as a police officer. I have an assortment of medals. Some of them I don't even know what they are for. I got another box of assorted medals 28 years after the war. Apparently, a review was conducted of my military record, and they sent them to me. But I never got shot. Guys are missing arms, legs, they are paralyzed; they have bullets in them, like you. And I am the hero? It's bullcrap. Pure bullcrap. Those guys, you guys are the heroes. All of you that have been shot paid much more dearly than I ever did."

What's astounding is he's completely sincere. He believes in the messages portrayed in *The Red Dot Club* book series. Craig says the public needs to know police work is not a game; it is serious, deadly serious. Cops hunt really bad people, and it is dangerous. He compares going through the experiences such as those depicted in, *The Red Dot Club* books, as running through barbed wire. People don't understand the depths of the cuts, and they are easily reopened. And the scars, just as if you had run through barbed wire, are everlasting.

I couldn't say it any better.

Craig told me to get a hold of Pete Galassi.

* * * * *

I sent Pete a copy of *The Red Dot Club*.

Pete texted me, "I received the book today. Thanks."

Two days later he texted me again, "Hi Robert… great book. I'm in."

I was genuinely impressed when I met Pete. I am a big guy, but I think Pete is bigger. He has a huge, easy smile and bear paw hands that dwarf mine with a grip of iron. When you meet him, it's as if you've been his best friend a thousand years and he could not be happier to see you again. He is likable as soon as you meet him.

We were sitting outside on his patio in the shade in the middle of January. It was 72 degrees out, a cool winter afternoon in Southern California.

* * * * *

"Craig told me I could trust you. I love your book. My son is a cop and thinks every cop should read your book.

"Craig saved my life. He taught me more about officer survival than anyone. This is how good he was. I was riding patrol with him one night when an oncoming car passed us. There were two guys in the front seat. As the car passed us, Craig saw the rear passenger door was unlocked. He saw the pushbutton lock was up. Craig knew someone was laying down in the back seat. We made a U-Turn and pulled the car over. Of course, there was someone in the back seat. They were gangsters. The stop turned into an arrest, the guys were capering (looking to commit a crime).

"He was phenomenal. I'd never worked with a guy that good, a cop that good, before or since. What he taught me saved my life, without a doubt.

* * * * *

"My dad emigrated from Italy. He ended up in New York, in Hell's Kitchen, and worked as a short-order cook. He met my mom, and they got married. One day they got tired of the cold and got out a map of the United States. They threw a dart, and it landed in California," laughed Pete heartily. "They moved to Gardena. I grew up in Gardena. Both of my parents worked so my brother and sister, and I could have a better life. Dad worked on the railroads and mom worked at Bank of America. They were big on making sure we had a good education. We didn't have a lot of money, but all three of us kids went to private schools throughout our whole lives. We never went on family vacations; there was no money for that.

"My whole passion since I was a kid was to be a cop. Since I can remember it's all I wanted to do. I loved putting on the cop's uniform. I loved the little cop cars you could peddle around in. I don't know why; it's just what I wanted to do.

"I played little league; I played basketball. When I got to be around 10 years old, or so I began to understand if I wanted to be a cop, I couldn't screw it up. I had to live right, not get in trouble. I knew the police agencies wouldn't hire you if you had any type of problems with your background.

"Around 1972 or 1973, when I was 14 or 15 I became a police explorer for the Gardena Police Department. I went through the Los Angeles County Sheriff's Academy every Saturday for six months. Now I knew all the cops at Gardena, and I had worked a number of various events. I knew I was put on this earth to be a cop. I was at the station as an explorer until I was 18 and it just reinforced I wanted to be a police officer. I wanted to be a Gardena Police Officer and protect the people I grew up with. I thought this from the time I wanted to be a cop when I was ten years old.

"At 18 I went to El Camino Community College. When I was 19, I was working at Gemco (this was an American chain of membership markets, they are now out of business), and started dating the woman who is now my wife. At 21 years old I got my associates degree in Criminal Justice, and simultaneously I became a reserve police officer at the Redondo Beach Police Department. This was in 1977, and it was hard to get hired as a cop. No one was hiring. You might have two openings and a thousand guys applying for those two spots. In March 1978 I got married. I knew I had to get a better job than stocking toys on the shelf at Gemco and I needed a flexible schedule so I could take time off for the different testing processes with the various departments. I took a job at a construction company. I was walking across joists, and boards and planks thirty feet off the ground. I used to carry planks and boards on my shoulders. When I got home from work, my wife and I had to peel off my t-shirt from my shoulders because of the dried blood from carrying the boards. I learned mental toughness.

"I had now been working as a reserve with the Redondo Beach Police Department for about a year to a year and a half, and I started testing everywhere. I remember testing for the Seal Beach Police Department. I took the written test in the morning. You had to have a 90% to pass, and I did. The next week we had to show up for the physical agility test. It was in the ocean. You had to swim out 100 yards, then swim parallel to the coast for 300 yards, then you had to swim back to shore. After getting to shore, you had to sprint so many yards back. Hundreds of people showed up. I recall them telling me only 50 passed. People were having trouble and had to be brought in by lifeguards with paddleboards. They were picking up people who were floundering in the ocean. Meanwhile, the cops, the testers, were on the shore drinking coffee and eating donuts. I thought, 'That's not right! Hahaha!'

"While I was testing everywhere, an opening came up in Gardena. The Gardena Police Department finally hired me in September 1979. I was 23 years old. So, there I went again, I had to go through another academy. I had been through the explorer academy with the Los Angeles County Sheriff, a reserve academy with the El Camino College and now the Rio Hondo Police Academy. My first day at the academy we were on the grinder, (the grinder is an asphalt or concrete area where you are drilled by the drill instructors or where you conduct calisthenics) at attention. It was hot, and we were all sweating. I did the thing we are all told not to do. I locked my knees. Anyone who has been in the military or in an academy and who has stood at attention knows you do not lock your knees. It can cause you to pass out. Well, I did, and I did. I passed out. It was the first day. Of course, the instructors were all over me, they were yelling at me, 'You don't belong here. You're never going to make it. You don't have what it takes.'

"It was a tough mental game. You just had to get in the mental attitude that you were not going to quit. We had to eat our lunch standing up. Whatever we didn't eat, we had to give it to the person standing next to us. This one day, the person behind me, I don't know what happened because we ate while looking straight ahead, almost at attention, threw up. He threw up on the back of the cadet near me. I didn't feel like eating after that.

"But there was nothing they could do to make me quit. And I made it.

* * * * *

"I immediately went to graveyards, (9:00 p.m. to 7:00 a.m.). I loved it. We were a group of young aggressive and smart cops. Our group took a lot of people to jail. These guys were criminals. We were known as the A-Team. Dale Pierce was a Gardena homicide detective who had been promoted to Sergeant who was on graveyard. He was the best guy to work for, and besides Craig, he was the best street cop I ever knew. He was smart and backed us up. For about a year and a half our shift would get off work and go to the Spanish Inn on Gardena Blvd. and Vermont Ave., and have chorizo and eggs and Coors Light for breakfast. We would decompress. We would lighten up and laugh. We were a tight group who trusted each other and who backed each other up. It was truly a brotherhood that few understand. The north end was the place to work. At the time we were the only city that had the casinos and the card clubs. All the gangsters from south central Los Angeles, from Compton, and Watts went there to rip people off who won in the parking lot or to follow them home and do home invasion robberies. We were very, very busy, and I loved it.

"It was during this time I got to work with Craig. As I said before he was an amazing street cop. I learned so much from him including officer survival. I owe him my life. He had a routine. He went to McDonald's, and he would buy three or four cheeseburgers, and he would stuff them in the sun visors in the car. The next stop would be to the liquor store to get his smokes. After that, he was good for the shift. McDonald's cheeseburgers and smokes.

"I had been off probation about six months, and I was partnered up with Craig. It was about 2:30 A.M. and I was driving. At 135th and Van Ness Blvd was Rowley Park. We had nothing but problems at that park. Gangsters always hung out there. Craig saw two guys, gangsters walking down the sidewalk. Craig told me to cut them off at a driveway. So, I took my radio car and pulled into a driveway and cut them off. When I pulled into the driveway, one guy took off running. I chased him through some apartment buildings. The back of the apartment building led into an alley. Before the second guy could take off Craig was out of the radio car and grabbed him. Craig handcuffed the guy to the bumper of the radio car.

"I was now out of sight chasing the guy through the apartment buildings. When I got to the back of the apartment building and turned in the alley, the guy, who was about 10 yards in front of me, turned and pointed a gun at me. Time instantly slowed to a crawl."

Pete was smiling. But the smile was not reaching the corners of his eyes.

"I don't remember drawing my gun. As I pointed my gun at him, I thought I was probably going to get shot. I knew my surroundings. There was no cover, none. I was in the middle of an alley. Even though I knew there was no cover, my mind was working on my situation, and I was trying to figure out if there was anything I could get behind, a car, a garbage dumpster, but I knew there was nothing there but open space. I was in the middle of an alley. I wanted to dig a hole in the asphalt, and I was thinking I was going to get shot. While all these thoughts were going through my head, I was desperately trying to get my gun on target, pointed at his body. I thought through the confusion and mixed thoughts, 'I cannot miss. I have to hit him, or I will be shot.' I was trained to shoot in two shot bursts. I fired. My muzzle flash lit up the darkness of the night and the darkness of the alley, and the fire from the barrel of the gun blinded me. I knew he was right in front of me and although I was blind, I did as I was trained and I pulled the trigger for the second time. My mind was screaming, *'DON'T MISS!!!'*

"Time was so slow, things were taking forever. My plan was to dive to the asphalt and continue shooting from a prone position. I thought I needed to change positions, to change where I was shooting from, so when he fired I would not be where I had been a second before. Maybe he would miss me. I finished pulling the trigger the second time…and nothing. Nothing happened. My gun didn't go off. It didn't fire. Time was still slow. I could not believe, my mind was numb, how I could be in a gunfight with a gun that would not fire. Fear numbing realization hit me. My gun was jammed. I could not fight. What should I do now? What options did I have? Through the blindness of the muzzle flash of my shot, I could now see the suspect running away. Running away down the alley. And time returned to normal.

"I got back to the radio car, and Craig was standing there. His suspect was handcuffed to the push bar of the car. Craig was smoking a cigarette. Calm as can be. It looked like he had not a care in the world. I lost it. I started yelling at him. *'You don't ever leave your partner, you never leave your partner!'*

"Craig looked at me, took a puff, and said as smoothly and quietly as could be, 'Stay…calm, calm…down.'

"The way he looked at me. The way he puffed his cigarette and paused before he spoke. His voice so quiet, just above a whisper. I half expected him to reach under the sun visor, grab a McDonald's cheeseburger and take a bite and start munching. I learned something in those seconds. His voice echoed and steeled me, 'Stay calm.' I got it, no matter what, 'Stay calm.' It had to be all his Vietnam incidents. I never saw Craig get excited. This one incident and the lesson learned from Craig, years later saved my life.

"Craig had heard the gunshot and had already broadcast there was an officer-involved shooting. He had units responding to set up a perimeter to box the suspect in.

"I later learned the reason Craig wanted to stop these guys was he recognized the suspect who ran from me as a very bad actor. He knew the suspect's background. This guy had been in prison for killing either his mother or grandmother for bashing her head in with a ball-peen hammer and was now out.

"The weapon I had that night was a Smith and Wesson Model 59. It is a semi-automatic 9-millimeter pistol. They are no longer in production. The pistol had a plastic ejection port. This is the part of the gun where after the bullet leaves the gun, where the empty shell or bullet casing is ejected. Well under the pressure of the gunshot, the plastic port broke. Parts of the plastic port went into the inner mechanism of the gun, (probably the slide), and jammed the gun, making it inoperable. As they say in life, timing is everything.

"The suspect was found hours later hiding in a neighbor's backyard. A Hawthorne Police Department K-9 dog found him. He kicked at the dog. He lost. He was arrested. The homeowner found the gun hanging from his backyard tree the next day.

"I absolutely believe in pro-active police work. Stopping persons involved in suspicious activity without a doubt stops crime. Of course, you need reasonable suspicion and probable cause to do that stuff, but pro-active police work prevents crime. Our goal was to get the word out to the criminals, that if you came into the City of Gardena looking to commit a crime, you were going to get caught and go to jail.

* * * * *

"On July 7, 1984, I was working a one-man car in the north end of Gardena. We handled a call of a loud and disturbing party at 149th St. and Budlong Ave. We knew this house as a place where a notorious Mexican gang hung out. There were always gang members there. We had been there over the years numerous times. On this night, multiple radio cars had gone to handle the call. I ended up taking two gang members to jail for being under the influence of P.C.P. (Angel Dust). After booking the two suspects at the station, I had to go back to 149th St. and Budlong Ave. to get another neighboring address to finish up my report.

"I left the station and headed back to the arrest site. It was now about 3:00 A.M. I was driving south on Budlong Ave. and as I got to 149th St. I noticed there was a police car parked on the opposite side of the street, the north side, of 149th St., facing Budlong Ave. A man was leaning into the driver's window of the police car. The officer in the car turned out to be my shift sergeant. I later learned the sergeant could smell ether, a telltale sign he was on P.C.P.

"As I drove past, I heard the sergeant yell out, 'Hey come back here!'

"I backed up my unit, and before I could park, I saw the man at the sergeant's radio car door run south to the front yard of the house at the southeast corner of 149th St. and Budlong Ave. I shoved the car in park. I stopped on Budlong Ave., and was facing south with the rear of the radio car partially in the street on 149th St. My shift sergeant was running after the suspect and caught him in the front yard of a house at the southeast corner of 149th St and Budlong Ave. As I got out of my radio car, my sergeant and the suspect were in a life and death fight. They were about thirty feet away from me. Running at a full sprint, I raised my baton and hit the suspect as hard as I could across his left shoulder blade. I hit him so hard I knew I had caved in his back...the suspect didn't flinch...he didn't yell...he didn't grunt, he just took a pause and with a blank stare looked right through me. At the least, I knew I had to have broken his shoulder blade.

"He was still fighting with the sergeant. It was all out hard fighting. The scary kind where he wasn't just trying to get away, but he was trying to kill someone. I hadn't even slowed him down. I knew he was dusted (on P.C.P.). It was the only way someone could have taken a hit that hard and still keep fighting. The angel dust had anesthetized him to where he could not feel any pain. I had to get him unconscious. It was the only way. I had already hit him as hard as I could with a metal baton, I had to choke him out. I threw my useless baton to the ground and got my arm around his neck. He was throwing both my sergeant and I around like we were rag dolls. It was probably a combined weight of over 400 pounds he was fighting with, and to him, it was like a pit bull shaking a puppy toy like we were nothing. With all the fighting, and as hard as I tried, I could not get my arm in the right position around his neck to choke him out. But I did have a hold of him. I yelled to my sergeant, *'GO GET THE TASER!'*

"The sergeant ran to get the Taser, and while I was still holding onto him. I heard two gunshots. I knew it was the suspect who had fired. I thought, 'He has my gun and is shooting at the sergeant.' This was really scary to realize he was shooting the sergeant with my gun, and both the sergeant and I fighting together could not control him. How could I control him, if both my sergeant and I could not, and now I didn't have my gun? I had lost sight of the sergeant. I thought he might be dead. I didn't know.

"After the shots went off, and all those thoughts went through my head, he threw me off his back like I was a butterfly. Immediately… *BAM, BAM, BAM*, I got shot three times.

"The first two shots hit the right side of my hip and right leg, the third shot hit my left hip. Hot, like fire hot hit my body. It was like I was on fire inside. Simultaneously I felt warm liquid flooding my left leg. He had hit my femoral artery. At least that's what I was thinking. There was no way I could have that much blood pouring down my leg so quickly unless he hit my artery. I pushed the thought away. I knew you could die within minutes after getting hit in the femoral artery. I felt myself passing out. How could it be within seconds of getting shot I was passing out?

"I had to get out of the way. He was going to kill me. Understand he was right next to me. Close enough to touch me and I knew he was going to finish me off, kill me. I went to move, to get up, and my legs, both legs were paralyzed. I could not move my legs at all.

"I don't know why, but he moved around me and walked toward the sidewalk about ten feet away. I knew he had my gun. I remembered Craig's words: 'Stay calm…calm down…' I thought and knew I had to do something. I was fighting passing out, I was ready to pass out, but I knew if I did he would kill me. I had my backup gun. It was a little five shot .380 caliber I kept in a holster on my left ankle. I pulled it out and fired at the suspect from about ten feet away. I fired a burst of two shots. Fighting to stay awake I fired two more shots. The suspect grunted. The fire in my hips and legs was intense. I was in excruciating pain, and I still could not move my legs. The suspect turned toward me and pointed his gun at me.

"The suspect looked at me and said, 'Well you're dead now, I'm going to kill you.' He pulled the trigger. Click, his gun didn't fire.

"The suspect went to one knee and moved his gun, which was in his right hand, to his left hand. He opened the cylinder and was either checking to see if he had more live bullets or he was reloading the gun.

"It was not over. He wanted to kill my sergeant and me if he wasn't already dead. I thought of the people in the house whose yard we had been fighting in. I thought after killing me, he was going to go in the house and take everyone hostage and maybe kill them. I wanted to protect them, but I was passing out. I was fighting it so hard, and I was losing. I was bleeding to death.

"Craig's voice returned to me, 'Stay calm.'

"Now time slowed down. It almost stopped. I thought of my whole life. It did not flash before my eyes, I relived it. I relived my life in a millisecond. I thought of my family. I thought of my wife and of my four-year-old son who I loved so dearly. I thought of family river trips we had taken. And I thought of them without me.

"Again, I thought of the people in the house. I knew I was going to die, but before I died, I had to stop this guy. I had to protect the people in the house. I had one shot left. I had to make it count. My legs were paralyzed, I was numb from the waist down, I was copiously pouring blood from my leg, fighting with every fiber of my body to not pass out, and I knew I was going to die, but I still had to stop him.

"Time was still so slow. I had to get a good shot. I had to stop him. I couldn't do it from ten feet away. I had to get closer. I thought of my family and started crawling. I thought of them never seeing me again. I crawled on and on, and it was forever. Each movement was so scary because I couldn't feel my legs, but I could feel the burning, the pain was excruciating, I was trying to not pass out. I thought with great sadness, 'You're never going to walk again. You're paralyzed forever.' I crawled on and on, and it was taking forever. He was still messing with the gun. I thought he was reloading it or looking for a live round to finish me off with. He had told me he was going to kill me. I crawled on. I crawled on my belly like some poor, beaten, run over dog. It took every ounce of energy I had to keep going. Finally, after an eternity, I got to within a foot of him. He was still on one knee. I raised my gun with one hand. Time slowed down even more. It took forever, the squeezing of the trigger. I kept squeezing, and it took a long, long time until the gun went off. My shot hit him in the head, and he collapsed...and I collapsed. I was done. I was ready to die.

"But I wasn't done. I couldn't move, but I still had my mind. I could feel hot blood running out of my body, but I thought of my family and my four-year-old son. The love of my life. I thought of Craig and his words, and I thought, 'I'm not going to die, I'm not going to die.'

"I thought if I could calm down maybe I could slow the bleeding. I thought of all the great things my wife and I had done and the things we had seen. I thought of my son and his walk and how cute he was when he spoke, and I relived the feeling of holding him. In the back of my mind, I was thinking we had just broken up the party at the house an hour before, and I was wondering if one of the suspect's friends was going to come and kill me. I wondered if my sergeant was dead.

"I found out later my sergeant while running to get the Taser had been shot several times. He took cover behind a car. He got to his radio car and dispatched he had been shot. When the first unit arrived at the scene, the sergeant told him to roll him code three to the hospital because he had been shot. While they were in-route to the hospital, he told the officer I was at the scene and had also been shot.

"When help finally arrived I told the paramedics I was dying. I told the first officer on the scene, I wanted Dale Pierce to notify my wife I'd been shot. I wanted someone who she personally knew to tell her. I'm convinced if I had lost consciousness, I would have died that night.

"Kim, a buddy of mine used to listen to the Gardena Police Department radio-calls on his scanner. It so happened he heard my shooting. He called my wife at 3:15 A.M. Well, I used to call my wife every morning about 3:00 A.M. or so to tell her everything was alright. It was our routine. So, when he called her, she thought it was me. My wife is always concerned with other people, and when she heard Kim's voice, she was immediately worried something happened to him. He asked her if she was okay. She said she was and responded, 'Why?'

"Pete's been shot," he answered. That's how she found out.

"When they got me to the hospital they put a coil in my femoral artery to stop the bleeding. I was still on fire, but I was also in pain right at the top of my penis where it meets the pelvis. Kim drove from Gardena to Garden Grove and picked up my wife and son. He then drove them back to Gardena to my in-law's house so my wife's father could take her to the hospital. She came into the room bordered by my two best friends who were also my patrol buddies. Cops have the sickest sense of humor. They can find humor in anything. The bullet that hit my right hip went all the way through and almost blew off my penis. The nurse pulled back the sheets and there it was. It was black with blood, it was shriveled up to nothing. It didn't even look like a penis. One of the cops looked at my wife and said, 'Don't worry Debbie, we'll take care of you!'"

Pete cracked up and couldn't stop laughing. He said, "Cop humor!"

When he finally stopped laughing, he continued, "It took me a year to learn how to walk again. You use your hips for everything. I had problems for the next ten years. I was 28 years old. I developed blood clots in my legs. The coil caused my artery and a vein to join together and caused a lack of circulation in my leg. I had back surgery. It was ten years of hell.

"I will never forget while I was in the hospital, the kids in a grade school around the corner made up these get-well cards and sent them to me. That was so cool. I still have them all. Cops from the A-team and several members of the Hawthorne Police Department were there anytime I needed anything, anytime, day or night. They would even come by and pick me up and sit me on the toilet. The brotherhood was unbelievable. I'll never forget it.

"I was told I would never have any more children. I proved them wrong, I fathered two children with my wife after the incident.

"The suspect had an interesting story. He was a hardcore gang member, who seven years before had shot and killed my neighbor's nephew. And as I understand it, when I shot him, I hit him all five times. My last shot killed him.

"It turned out I had my gun the whole time. I had been shot with my sergeant's gun."

* * * * *

A little follow-up to this story will be interesting to everyone. The suspect in the shooting in the alley, depicted in this chapter, had already killed his mother or grandmother with a ball-peen hammer and been to prison. He then pulled a gun on Pete in the alley and went to prison again. Craig later heard an unconfirmed report that sometime after getting out of prison again, he went to Magic Mountain in Valencia and committed a robbery. Some police units tried to stop him in his getaway car. A police pursuit occurred and he ended up crashing and dying in the crash.

Regarding the suspect who shot Pete, Craig had contact with him about a year before the shooting. Craig was walking up to the car where the suspect was the driver. The suspect was stuffing a gun under the seat. Craig didn't shoot him. It just wasn't the right circumstances to justify using deadly force. He holds a bit of regret he couldn't shoot him because the suspect ended up shooting the sergeant and Pete a year later. It turned out before these encounters, the suspect had been in the Marine Corps and had received a Section 8 dishonorable discharge. The word was he was stealing military rifles and selling them.

* * * * *

A citation was written up recommending Pete Galassi for the Medal of Valor. I have included the citation but removed the sergeant's name and the address of the location. It reads as follows:

At approximately 0335 hours on 7-7-84, Officer Galassi, working a one-man unit, had driven his police unit to the vicinity of --- S. Budlong on a follow-up to an arrest made one hour earlier where an officer had responded to the location on a loud party radio-call. The location in question was well known to officers working late evenings and early morning shifts due to the numerous narcotic usage arrests had been made in and around this residence. As the officer drove past the address northbound, he received a message over the police radio requesting him to come back. The officer looked to his rear and saw his watch sergeant, Sergeant -----, parked on 149th St. just East of the intersection of Budlong Ave. 149th Street is an East/West street which dead-ends at Budlong and is squarely aimed at the -----S. Budlong residence. Officer Galassi backed his police unit and observed Sergeant ----- attempting to talk to a male Mexican adult. As the officer stopped his unit, he saw the male subject run Southbound across 149th St. with the sergeant in foot pursuit. Sergeant---- caught the subject on the front lawn of ----- W. 149th Street where a struggle ensued. Officer Galassi went to Sergeant ------ aid, and all three ended up on the ground. At one point, Officer Galassi shouted to ------to "get the taser as they were having great difficulty in subduing the subject. As the sergeant pulled away to obtain the Taser weapon stored in his police unit, the subject broke loose of Galassi's grip, got to his feet, and ran around Galassi toward the residence driveway and Sergeant -----. Almost instantly after this maneuver Galassi heard two to three shots and heard ---- yell he had been shot. A split second later Galassi felt himself being hit twice in the lower back and buttocks area. The officer went down feeling a searing heat in the lower back and buttocks area. The officer rolled over and discovered the subject aiming a weapon at him, standing approximately ten (10) to twelve (12) feet from him, and beginning to walk towards the sidewalk. Galassi, at this time, had no idea where Sergeant -----was but was convinced he had been hit and both ---- and himself were going to be finished by the shooter. The officer also felt it possible the subject had obtained his service revolver during the struggle. At this point, the officer drew a .380 cal semi-automatic pistol from an ankle holster and checked on the subject's progress. Observing him to be even closer to the sidewalk and the shelter of automobiles parked there, Officer Galassi fired two rounds in his direction. The officer was unable to tell by the subject's actions whether he had been struck, so he fired two additional rounds. The officer knew by a grunting noise that at least one round had struck. The shooter then turned toward Galassi, went to one knee, pointed his weapon at the officer, and pulled the trigger. The hammer fell on an expended round and made a clicking sound.

The subject pulled the weapon to his chest with his left hand and placed his right hand around the cylinder. Galassi, feeling himself growing faint, believed the shooter was either checking the weapon for live rounds or was intent on reloading. The officer had no idea what or whose weapon the subject was using, but was convinced he was going to reload the weapon and kill both he and ----- if, in fact, ----- was not already deceased. Galassi further believed his own wounds were fatal and he did not stop the shooter at this immediate time he would escape or possibly take refuge in a nearby house where he would have access to hostages. The officer made the deliberate decision to neutralize the shooter but realizing he only had one round left decided to get closer. When the officer attempted to get up, he discovered he had no control over the lower portion of his body. Galassi, assuming the subject was going to shoot him again regardless of his actions, dragged himself across the lawn to a distance of approximately four (4) feet and fired his last round into the shooter's head. The officer saw the subject keel over and hit the ground. At this point, Galassi went semi-conscious and was not aware of the arrival of backup units.

It is felt any examination of the criteria described in the definition of awards discloses Officer Galassi is worthy of any or all honors the police profession could bestow on him. The presence of mind he displayed during the above incident coupled with the courage, self-control, and willingness to possibly pay the supreme price of his own life to save a fellow officer and other potential victims is deserving of the Medal of Valor.

The Chief of Police of the Gardena Police Department did not sign the above citation for the Medal of Valor, thereby Pete Galassi never received the award from his department.

* * * * *

Craig Knapp provided Pete Galassi with a framed bona fide military Purple Heart Medal.

Craig's experience on the Gardena Police Department was varied. In addition to patrol, he was on the S.W.A.T. team. He worked for major multiple-agency task force surveillance teams. He participated on pre-hire oral boards. After he retired from the Gardena Police Department, he worked eight years as a Deputy Coroner for Los Angeles County. He responded to numerous officer-involved shootings along with gang shootings, numbering in the hundreds. Craig knows of what he speaks, and he told me, "Those who decide whether someone is worthy of a citation for heroism, the administrators in the police departments, look at these incidents from a liability standpoint. They search for what the person did wrong, instead of looking at the heroism involved. They are worried about lawsuits instead of the outstanding, beyond the call of duty heroism displayed. The departments start looking at what you did right and what you did wrong in these life and death struggles. Then the politics enter the situation and become mixed up with the life and death gun battle, where people get maimed and die, and the heroism gets lost."

Craig petitioned a group of law enforcement officials from the National Footprinters Association to recognize Pete Galassi for his actions on the night of July 7, 1984. Several distinguished individuals, specifically Dale Pierce put forth the petition to recognize Galassi. This group was closely associated with the Los Angeles County Sheriff's Department and the Los Angeles Police Department.

About a year and a half later the National Footprinters Association awarded Gardena Police Officer Pete Galassi the Medal of Valor for his actions on the night of July 7, 1984. It is the highest award that can be bestowed.

Mr. Galassi said receiving the award was a great honor.

* * * * *

Mr. Galassi has successful children who he is very proud of. It took him a year to learn to walk and to heal up enough to return back to patrol. He credits his recovery to his wife, who suffered every bit as much as he did, and gave him her unwavering support and love. She is a role model for a cop's wife. She stood with him through thick and thin, through all the lonely nights and worries and injuries without complaint.

After returning to the Gardena Police Department, he eventually retired due to the nature and extent of the injuries he received the night he was shot.

Chapter 15

Making a Sandwich

Account of Michael F. Bobola
Los Angeles County Sheriff's Department

At the time it happened I had been a deputy for the Los Angeles County Sheriff's Department for four years. I was assigned to the old Lancaster Station. This station is the northernmost station in the Department. This was literally the wild west. For most of the six hundred square miles of this patrol area, it is a desolate desert, with jackrabbits, coyotes, antelopes, and rattlesnakes. Most of it is exactly as it was 150 years ago when deputies handled problems on horseback.

I had been at the station for three weeks. I was assigned to the three p.m. to eleven p.m. shift, and I was learning the ropes so to speak. Prior to going out to patrol, every shift throughout all the stations had a briefing. The briefing was meant to tell the patrol units of the crime trends and any new department information needed to be passed on. Briefing usually lasted fifteen minutes.

It was March 1986 when while in briefing, the call came out over the intercom system. When this happened, it meant there was a major incident that needed to be handled right now. When this call came out, the briefing came to an immediate halt. There was a woman who had been shot in the head.

I along with my partner sprinted to our radio car grabbing our war bags, containing ammo, extra handcuffs and other emergency equipment we might need for the shift. Driving with red lights and sirens through the desert at over a hundred miles per hour, it was still about a fifteen-minute drive.

The station had its own helicopter, which flew to the scene ahead of us. When we arrived, the helicopter had already landed in a field next to the house where the woman was. The two deputies from the helicopter were inside the house in the kitchen. One of the deputies was fixing a sandwich for a little boy who looked like he was five years old.

One of the deputies pointed to a closed door. He said, "In there."

I pushed the door open, and a woman was lying there on her stomach. She looked to be about thirty years old. She had brown hair, and she was wearing a light blue bathrobe, and it was closed and tied around her waist. Her ankles were tied together, and her hands were tied behind her back. Her ankles had then been tied to her hands; she was hogtied. There was a fire poker lying beside her. Blood was everywhere. As shocking as this whole scene was, the most horrifying part, the part I cannot forget is her head was pulled back. It was looking up toward the ceiling. Since she was on her stomach, her head should have naturally fallen forward. I could not help but think how uncomfortable she looked. I mean she was dead, but her position was so unnatural, and I kept thinking what kind of animals would do this to another human being.

I fixed the crime scene in my mind, burning it in my memory.

I stepped out of the bedroom and met with the deputy who had fixed the little boy a sandwich. It turned out the little boy was the woman's son.

The deputy told me, "He's been here all day. He's been going in and out of the bedroom. He told me he's hungry so I fixed him a sandwich."

If I was horrified before, now I was filled with shock and overwhelming grief. It took everything for me to hold it together.

The little boy had seen the suspect. He had seen the suspect enter the house through the garage. The deputy got a description of the suspect, and now we all knew what he looked like.

We were in the desert, everything was sand and dirt. My partner and I went outside to look for footprints. While we were outside, the deputies inside were able to get a hold of the woman's husband. He told the deputies their other children were due to get home from the school bus.

While we were outside, we saw some footprints. We called for a tracking dog, which arrived and got us pointed to the next house two and a half acres away. My partner and I got in our patrol car and drove to the house where the dog had alerted. The dog handler and my partner went to the front of the house, and I took the rear of the house alone, with a shotgun.

My partner made an announcement for everyone to come out. Two guys came out, and they were arrested. The homicide detectives were able to prove one of the two guys committed the murder.

After the men were arrested, I went back to the murder scene. Everyone was gone except a sergeant. My partner and I were tasked with sitting with the body until the coroner arrived.

It was cold. The afternoon had turned to night, and I had my jacket on. The sergeant had left and come back with some coffee for us. It was now a little before midnight, and the coroner had arrived and was in the house. When he came out, she was on a gurney. There was a sheet over her body, but I could see her outline in the cold of the night and the light of the moon. She was still on her stomach. The thought hit me again, harder this time, how uncomfortable she had to be in that position, outside in the cold. Her head was still facing upwards toward the sky, as were her feet. I was thinking how cold she had to be. I know it's weird to think because she was dead.

Sadness and despair overcame me, thinking of a little boy who must've been the one to call that a woman had been shot in the head. His mother.

Chapter 16

The Train Wreck

Account of Billy Lynch
Los Angeles County Sheriff's Department

At 4:23 P.M. on September 14, 2008, I was working as a Los Angeles County Deputy Sheriff assigned to motorcycles. I got the screaming call on my radio there had been a Metrolink Train Crash. I was in downtown Los Angeles when the call went out.

I jumped on the freeway and was racing over one hundred miles per hour get to the scene. The train crashed behind a house in a residential horse property area in Chatsworth, in the north end of the San Fernando Valley.

I pulled up to the scene, and a woman met me outside of her house. She told me the crash was behind her house and to go through the side of her house and through her backyard.

Nothing could prepare me for what I saw. The best way I can describe it was it was like a movie set. Nothing appeared real. Everything must have been set up. That had to be what I was seeing. A Metrolink commuter train had crashed into a regular train. The last car was the engine and was pushing the Metrolink train from behind. In other words, the front car of the train was a passenger car. This being the case, the passenger car was the first car to hit the oncoming engine of the train.

Of course, the fire department had been called and was on their way. The hospitals were notified.

The Metrolink's cars were lying on their sides at a forty-degree angle. Several of the freight trains' cars were lying on their sides also including the freight train's engine.

The back of the front passenger train obviously had the most damage. The front part of the train was crushed and mangled. The rear portion of the train, where the door would have been was missing.

I stepped into the rear of the train and there it was the human trash compactor. Not to call the people trash, that's not what I mean. But this name best describes the overwhelming complete devastation I saw. I was walking into death and dismemberment.

This is really hard for me to talk about…

Since the train was leaning three-quarters of the way over, I was walking partially on the sides of the seats. The end of the train I had walked into was not crushed, but it was in total disarray. The people still alive were in shock. For the most part, they were too shocked and disoriented to speak. They were all injured, some of them severely. Deputy Barry Ryan had already been there for fifteen minutes and had been taking people out of the train. He was soaked in sweat and had blood on his uniform, and he was completely spent. He had unbuttoned his uniform shirt. We spent the next fifteen minutes in the last one-quarter of the train getting as many people out as we could.

We cleared out the back of the train enough so we could finally get to the front three-quarters of the train.

Laying at a forty-five-degree angle, the front of the car was crushed and mangled. When it hit, it buckled and bent the car, so the car rose as you went forward to about ten feet in the air. This is where the car really began to be mangled. At this part was the cavern. It was a pathway or a crawlspace that led to the front of the car, but it was blocked. This cavern led into the front three-quarters part of the train that was terribly crushed. But you could not get through the cavern, there was luggage, poles, seats, metal and body parts blocking the path. I got to the crawlspace and worked my way through by moving and shoving and pulling things out of the way. It took about ten or fifteen minutes just to create enough crawlspace large enough for one person to enter at a time.

I was covered in blood and sweat. People were groaning. I was over-whelmed. I had been trained for riots, traffic accidents, shootings, fighting, but never for anything of this magnitude. The amount of carnage was horrible. By now others had arrived. The fire department passed up some Sawzalls, (these are portable saws capable of cutting through metal). We started cutting people out. We formed a conga line and began moving people and bodies out. Some were alive, some not. We were hot. I was sweating and exhausted. The fire department passed back bottles of water. I poured them over my head and down my shirt. I was trying to cool myself off, but it didn't work for long. The batteries kept dying on the Sawzalls, and they kept passing more batteries back. The fire department had started a generator for power, and we got our fair share of gas fumes.

I had a City of Los Angeles Fire Department Urban Search and Rescue guy with me. We would have to stop. I was panting and sweating, and there were lulls where we had to catch our breath.

A leg and foot was sticking up through the debris at us. There was so much debris and body parts that it was just something we had to work through. Then I heard something. I asked Deputy Barry Ryan if he heard it. He had not.

I yelled up to tell the fire department to turn off the generator. When they did, we both heard the faint cry, "Help me."

We moved a little bit of debris, and there was this man's head. His nasal cavity was separated from his head, and he was gurgling, "Help me." The leg that was sticking up was right next to the man's head.

We started digging and cleared enough debris away from the man's head so the Search and Rescue Firefighter could see down his body. He reached down toward the guy's body to remove debris, and he looked up at me and said, "Hey bro, that is this guy's leg."

He was talking about the leg next to the guy's head. The human body does not bend that way. Horror hit me, and I thought, "That can't be possible. There's no fucking way this guy could survive this."

I told the guy, "Hang in there we're going to get you out. You're going to be okay."

The body boards they were sending us were straight wooden boards with no railing. As we would recover a person, or a body, or a body part, we would place it on the board. Remember we were ten feet down in the car. We would pass the board to the next guys, up, up, up, and then the guys would pass the board down on the other side of the cavern. With all the debris, it was difficult to keep the boards level. Sometimes the people or bodies or body parts would fall off the boards. Sometimes they would fall onto me. It was like jelly.

With the amount of trauma, they sustained, the body's bones had been crushed. The bodies were like jelly.

After I had been inside the car for about an hour, enough fire personnel had arrived to relieve us deputies. I crawled out of the car and rested against the side. The sight that greeted me was horrible. I've never been in a war, but it was what I imagine war would be like. There were bodies covered with sheets everywhere. Helicopters were coming and going, blowing the sheets away. It was hard to imagine this was Los Angeles, California.

I hit the wall. I was exhausted, I had a headache, I was nauseous, and I was spent. My body shut down. A commander and a captain came to debrief us. They told us how they needed to do some training in major incidents or something like that. I don't know. I shut them out. I was angry. They weren't inside the car. They hadn't crawled through the cavern.

I got on my motorcycle and drove home. It was about a twenty-minute ride. I wanted to get home and take a shower before my family saw me.

When I got home my daughter, who was eighteen or nineteen years old at the time ran out to greet me, "Hey how are you?" Then she looked me up and down. I was covered in blood, and she started crying. I had tears in my eyes and couldn't speak. She later told me, "At that instant, I knew what my dad did for a living!"

Smells are the worst for me. To this day I cannot stand the smell of gas fumes, it makes me think of the crash. I relive the smells. The smell of the inside of the human body is something I will always remember. I will also remember the jellied body parts falling on me.

I had nightmares for four or five years afterward. They were dreams of the dead and injured beseeching me and talking to me. They have faded now, but sometimes in the dead of night when I least expect it, they come and haunt me, and I'm awake in a cold sweat.

* * * * *

Sergeant Billy Lynch along with four other deputies from the Los Angeles County Deputy Sheriff's Department were awarded the Medal of Valor for their actions on the afternoon of September 4, 2008. It is the highest award the department can bestow upon its members.

Billy, as he is called, told me the real hero that day was Deputy Barry Ryan because he was alone with the screams and the bodies, carrying people out until help got there.

Chapter 17

Fighting a Zombie

Account of David Carrasquillo
Inglewood Police Department

He looks fine. Especially after what happened to him.

* * * * *

A gentleman is the best way to describe Dave. He is the son of a preacher man. He was in the Marine Corps and is a highly decorated ex-cop. Dave is a powerlifter who on his best day bench pressed 605 pounds. He just had a horrible accident where he might lose sight in one of his eyes. He speaks of God, his will and how he is unafraid because the good Lord looks after him. And I would go into a gun battle with him anytime. He is writing his own book about the effects of stress from military and law enforcement service.

He is a brave and smart guy who believes in the Constitution of the United States and his duty to uphold its laws and to protect it.

* * * * *

"A death in the family dictated my dad move in with his two older brothers, my uncles when he was about fifteen years old. They were living in New York. He finished high school, and they all opened a barbershop in Manhattan. My dad then became a truck driver and always spoke of, 'That bad winter.' It turned out that winter would change his life. He told me how he was sick with a terrible cold and the windshield wipers went out on the truck. He and his brother had to roll their windows down and tie a string to the windshield wipers and pull them back and forth, one from the driver's window and one from the passenger window, as they drove in the icy snowstorm.

"That was it, my father decided to move to Los Angeles.

"My dad was a minister. On my mom's first visit to the church where my dad served, they met. It was love at first sight. They got married, and you know what happened next, here I am. I was born in Torrance, California.

"We lived in South Central Los Angeles. On April 12, I'm not sure of the year, but I remember the date because it was my dad's birthday. My mom and my sister and I were walking south from 103th St in the alley east of Vermont Ave. I was about 5 years old, and my sister was three years older than me. My sister and I were holding my mom's hand. A guy who was about 20 years old was walking toward us. When he was right in front of us, he smiled and said, 'Hi.'

"No sooner did he get past us when I felt a presence, like a shadow approach us from behind. Less than a second had gone by since the man had passed us. He hit my mom on her right temple, and she got knocked unconscious. Since we were holding hands, all three of us fell to the asphalt. The man grabbed my mom's purse and trampled over her to run south in the alley. All of this was happening very fast.

"As he trampled over my mom, I stuck out my leg and tripped him. He fell face first in the alley, and I was on him. I started hitting him as hard as I could, but what could a five-year-old kid do to a twenty-year-old man? He elbowed me and knocked me off of him. When he elbowed me, he knocked me a little senseless. I shook the cobwebs out of my head, and when I looked up, I saw him about twenty feet away running south in the alley with my mom's purse.

"I took off after him. He was running, and I was chasing him. I wasn't going to let him get away. He had knocked out my mom and stolen her purse. I was angry. I must have run about half a football field away when I heard my sister yelling at me, 'DAVID!'

"At five years old, I did what my older sister told me to do. So, I stopped. I went back to my mom. She was dazed but awake. Shortly after that two big L.A.P.D. cops came and took us home. We couldn't get in the house because the keys were in my mom's purse. I remember the cops lifted me up to the kitchen window and I crawled through. I ended up in the sink then jumped to the floor with both feet hitting the floor at the same time. I thought, 'WOW,' I'm like a superhero, helping the cops do something they can't do. I opened the front door and let my mom and sister in.

"When my dad found out what happened he was furious. He got my sister and a machete to go find the guy. Remember he was a minister, but he was also a two-tour Vietnam Veteran. I later found out he had won the Bronze Star for his heroic actions in the war. Anyway, he took my sister with his machete to go look for the guy. Luckily, he didn't find him.

"L.A.P.D. did find the suspect. He was a seventeen-year-old neighborhood kid. Of course, since he was a juvenile nothing much happened to him because about a year later he passed by our house riding his bike. He smiled at us and said, 'Hi,' as he rode by. Who knows if he recognized us? Anyway, it was the last time I saw him.

"We ended up living in South Central Los Angeles until I was eight years old. After that, we moved to Long Beach because the gangs were so bad. My dad is now dead but my mom is still alive, and we are close.

"Both my mom and dad were ministers in a church in Inglewood, and I was always there. When I was seventeen, I had had enough of going to church four days a week and twice on Sunday. I decided I wanted to be a Marine. So right after I graduated high school my mom signed for me, and I was in the Corps. My mom was reluctant, but my dad was a Vietnam veteran. He had two tours in Vietnam. He told my mom, 'Let the boy do what he's got to do.'

"I loved the Marine Corps. I gained a lot of experience. I matured and had a wide range of experiences. I served four years and was deployed in various areas during the Persian Gulf War, Desert Storm.

"When I got stateside in 1992, I was stationed at Camp Pendleton but was living at my parents' home in Long Beach and was commuting back and forth to Pendleton. I was at the end of my enlistment, and I planned to attend Long Beach City College and get my degree. The Rodney King riots happened, and the Marine Corps told me to stay home. I remember looking out of the back of my parents' home onto Artesia Avenue, and it was a war zone. People were just vandalizing everything, burning down the city. I saw the most amazing thing. I saw multiple refrigerators on the top of a car being driven down the street. This environment sparked my interest in wanting to be a police officer.

"I was checking into applying with different departments, but none of the departments were hiring. There was this huge hiring freeze going on. I waited to see if the freeze loosened up but a year went by, and still, no one was hiring.

"My dad had been working at the Veteran's Administration Hospital as a Bio Medic Technician. He would fix the X-ray machines, the M.R.I. Scanners and such. He told me about a job at the V.A. When I learned about it I said, 'Dad, that's a janitor's job! I've cleaned enough commodes and mopped and polished enough floors in the Marine Corps for a lifetime.'

"He said, 'Great, then you'll be good for the job!'

"I said, 'DAD!'

"And he said, 'Just do it.'

"And I said, 'Yes, sir.'

"And that was it, I was a janitor." Dave had a look of disgust on his face. I took it to mean he felt like he was going backward in life. "I was twenty-two years old, and I had a job as a janitor."

"About a year into my janitor job, my ex-wife and I came into some money. She wanted to open a coffee house. So, we did. Remember this was in the early nineties. There were not too many coffee houses around. There was no Starbucks Coffee; they didn't exist. Our coffee house was near Cal State University Long Beach. We were making money like you cannot believe. If you wonder how Starbucks makes so much money, it cost us 28 cents to make a cup of coffee. That was everything, the coffee, the cup, the sugar, the stirrers, everything. Our business went well for the first year. It was now 1994. But of course, nothing lasts forever. They had a major construction in the parking lot and because of this, cars had stopped coming in. We lost everything in our second year in business.

"It was 1996, and now I was out of a job. I had stopped being a janitor. Now, I realized I needed and wanted something a little more secure. My buddy told me to apply with the California Department of Corrections. I did and was hired after going through the academy. I spent three years with the department and decided I wanted to do more. I was tired of looking at naked guys bending over coughing, lifting their feet, and wiggling their toes and opening their mouths and lifting their tongues.

"I put myself through the Fullerton extended police academy. I went four nights a week and weekends for a year and graduated in 1998. While in the academy I bumped into an old friend of mine who was recruiting for the Inglewood Police Department. He told me I should apply. I applied to the Inglewood Police Department toward the end of the academy, and I got picked up.

"I learned a lot while working with the California Department of Corrections. I learned my people skills. I learned how criminals thought and behaved. No different than working for the Los Angeles County

Sheriff's Department in the jails, it gave me an opportunity to shine when I went to the Inglewood Police Department in 1999.

"I went to patrol, and two years later I was a training officer. One year later I interviewed to go to the gang unit. I came out number one on the list. The gang unit was a unit with nothing but guys who had been around a lot of years. No one left the gang unit. One of the guys had been there over twenty years. I worked as a gang detective for three years. I wanted to diversify my training and asked for a transfer to regular detectives and got it. I worked burglaries, robberies, juveniles, missing persons, auto thefts, you name it, I worked it. And I stayed in detectives until I medically retired in November 2012.

"On February 21, 2009, I was working a patrol overtime spot. It was Sunday morning. We had just finished a call of a woman chasing a guy in a parking lot with a machete."

* * * * *

I know, I know, you are wondering what happened to the woman with the machete call. It was just another call and not the main part of this story. You're shaking your head. You still want to know. Okay. The cops got there, pointed their guns at her. She dropped the machete, and she went to jail. The end.

* * * * *

"We were just finishing up the machete call when we got another call. It was a structure fire. It was a seven-story retirement home on the 200 block of Market Street. A man called and said he was stuck in his apartment on the third floor. He had lit a cigarette, and he had caught the place on fire. Apparently, he was in a wheelchair; the carpet around him and under him was on fire, and the apartment was catching on fire. He could not get out.

"We were all one-man units. I rolled from the machete woman in the parking lot call. A supervisor said he would be rolling. When I was half a block away, two other units arrived. There were three of us. The man was still on the line with dispatch, and he was now screaming, burning to death.

"The two units that got there before me were already making their way inside the building. When I got to the third-floor hallway, it was clear of smoke. As I was walking toward the apartment, the other two officers were already at the man's door. I was about thirty feet away. I could hear the man screaming in agony. Obviously he was in horrible pain. The officers shouted, 'We're going to kick the door!'

"I saw them. One of their legs came up. The leg came down against the door. In the next instant, they disappeared because I was engulfed in a cloud of black smoke that shot out from the burning apartment and I could not see. I hit the ground face first. It was so fucking unbelievably hot! Oh, my God, I thought I was on fire! I started low crawling back toward the elevator. I thought of the poor fucking guys that kicked the door. They had to be dead. I could not believe the smoke had filled the hallway faster than I could run, in less than a second."

Dave looked at me then rubbed the back of his head as if he was reliving the incident.

"As this was going through my head, and as I was madly crawling and horrified my back might be on fire, I heard frantic voices, '*GO, GO, GO, GOGOGO!!!*'

"The thought of going back for them never entered my mind. It made me feel a little better to hear their voices. I said to myself, 'Fuck it, I'm ahead of them.' The thing is the apartment was the last unit in the hallway. There was an exit door leading to a stairwell right next to the apartment. All they had to do was go out of the door. But they couldn't see it.

"All three of us got to the elevator, but we couldn't see it. We knew we were there because we could feel the door. We were coughing, our eyes were watering, we were feeling the sides of the elevator, frantically trying to find the button, and our hands and fingers were running into each other, but we couldn't find it.

"Then the door opened."

"It was the supervisor who was at the machete call. When the door opened, he yelled, *'WHAT THE FUCK??!!'*"

"He went down."

"It was hot! But our panic had subsided a little. We looked at each other and knew, we had to go back down the hallway. Even if it meant our death. If we didn't go back, a bunch of people, old people who couldn't help themselves would burn to death. Did I mention it was hot? We were the only ones there to help, and it was our duty; we were honor bound as peace officers to go back. Everything was smoke. We started knocking on doors, 'POLICE, OPEN UP!' we choked and screamed. As the people opened the doors, we grabbed them and carried and dragged them out of the building. There were five units on each floor. We emptied out three of the four remaining units on the third floor. No one was home at the fifth unit.

"Outside we formed a plan. We had to empty out the rest of the building. More guys had arrived. Now there were six of us. I told the guys, 'Let's team up. No one separates or leaves their partner in the building.' We all agreed. I teamed up with Caesar. And back in we went.

"The stairwells were full of smoke. We saw little old people trying to get out. We literally grabbed them and carried them out. I don't know how many trips we made.

"When we cleared the building, I asked the sergeant to do a roll call. And sure enough, we were missing Aguilar. 'OH, SHIT!' I looked at his teammate, 'Where's Aguilar?'

"'He told me he was coming right behind me! He's up on the seventh floor, I don't know,' he said in confusion.

"I told the sergeant to get us on the radio if Aguilar came out and then Caesar and I went back in.

"Caesar and I went floor by floor. We were yelling, 'Aguilar!' We were going down the hallway of the fifth floor. It was too smoky, and we couldn't see. It was so hot, too hot. Unbearable. We were actually stuck. We were going to burn up or choke to death. I said, 'Fuck it!' And I kicked in an apartment door. It was that or we were going to die. I found the bathroom and grabbed two towels. I put them in the washbasin and soaked them. I told Caesar, 'Wrap this around your head!' And we breathed through the towels and tried to stay as cool as we could. We cleared the fifth and sixth floor, and when we got to the seventh floor, we saw Aguilar. He was passed out in the hallway. Caesar grabbed one arm, and I grabbed the other. We dragged him out into the stairwell. 'Wake up wake up!' We slapped him around a little, 'Breathe, breathe bro.' Aguilar came around hacking and coughing and wheezing. After he started breathing, we dragged him down seven flights of stairs.

"We cleared out the building. The fire department showed up, and we were all outside smoking and crying. Not smoking cigarettes, we… were…all…smoking and choking, and we were all bleary-eyed standing outside of the building. Eventually, nine of us cops were involved in the incident. And we were all ordered to go to the hospital because we all looked like chocolate men. This is after us macho cops told the paramedics, through straw sized windpipes, we were okay. I didn't know it, but my blood pressure had skyrocketed.

"That same day I checked myself out of the hospital, like every other self-respecting cop who was there. I went back to the building. I went to the third floor and a big old Los Angeles County Fire Department Arson Investigator was at the apartment where it all started."

"He looked at me, 'Hey you can't come up here. We're conducting an investigation.'"

"The Inglewood Police Department, Forensic Investigation Unit, was in the apartment with the fire department.

"The department had sent another cop with me to make sure I was okay. He spoke up, 'Hey this guy was here at the beginning when the door got kicked in.'

"The arson investigator and another firefighter took off their helmets and came at me. I thought, 'Oh shit, we are going to get into it.'

"The arson investigator put his helmet under his arm and held out his hand to shake mine. He said, 'I can't believe you guys came into this. Let me show you something.' And he walked into the apartment. And there was the man. He was charcoaled all over, his bones were showing. The investigator looked at me and said, 'No not him. That's not what I want to show you. This, this is what you need to see.' He then pointed to a sign over the door. It was the exit sign, but I couldn't tell it was the sign. It was a mass of melted metal and plastic.

"He said, 'Do you know how hot it has to be to melt that sign?'

"I said, 'No.'

"He said, '1,200 degrees. It has to get 1,200 degrees to melt that sign.'

"I said, 'HUH?'

"'Yeah, your guys' lungs are singed. I can't believe you guys came in, and then...kept... coming in! You guys saved all these lives.'

"I was like, 'Just doing my job, sir, just doing my job.'

"And I told him, just like this, 'I used to call you guys a bunch of quiche heads and nozzle heads. I used to call you nozzle heads.'

"And he looked at me.

"And I looked at him and said, 'Yeah, I said it. But now? I have a lot of respect for the job you guys do because you know what? Fuck this!'

"He looked at me and said, 'Yeah but you guys deal with bullets.'

"I said, 'Bullets? The guy shooting at me? He'll run out of bullets, but this shit? It was the scariest shit I've ever been through in my life.'

"When it came out on the news they said we saved 100 lives. Fire is the real shit dude!"

Dave was reliving the event and had a grim faraway look.

* * * * *

"I was still working detectives. On October 4, 2010, I again decided to work overtime in a patrol car. This time it was a Monday. And it was raining. Usually, in the rain, not much crime occurs. It's usually traffic accidents. There is a little Carniceria, (a meat market that sometimes serves food also), at the corner of Lennox and Inglewood. It was breakfast time, and we were eating there. I had a big ass bowl of menudo. Mmm, mmm good."

* * * * *

"We were working a detail named T.S.T. Transit Services. The buses were notorious for the crazies. People mumbling to themselves, picking fights with other passengers, or just plain troublemaking gang members.

"A tone came out over our radio denoting a hot call was coming out. 'Shots fired possible robbery in progress at Simpson's Mortuary Flower Shop. On Manchester and Prairie.' Units started responding. We were detectives working overtime. Plenty of units were responding. We waited for further information and slurped down our menudo as fast as we could, knowing we would soon be leaving to help.

"When the units arrived, they put out they were going to clear the location. You know, make sure the robber was gone. Then one of the units put out additional information. 'Units stand-by, suspect description, robbery just occurred, shots fired, possible shooting victim inside, suspect is described as a male black around six feet two inches, 250 pounds, wearing black over black, black hoodie, black pants. Last seen westbound on Manchester Blvd. in a rusted colored Saturn SUV.'

"I looked at one of the guys eating menudo with me. He was working the robbery table.

'Hey man that sounds like your serial robber you've been looking for.' This guy had committed something like 27 robberies in one week. Those were just the Inglewood robberies. He had also committed some robberies in the Sheriff and L.A.P.D. areas.

"A few minutes later another call came out. It was another robbery in progress at a Radio Shack about a mile away from the flower shop at Manchester Blvd. and Market St. The robberies were moving in our direction. We left our chow and started heading in the direction of the last robbery.

"My partner Louie and I headed northbound on La Brea. The others divided and one unit went to the original call, and one went to the Radio Shack. The units at the Radio Shack put out a description of the suspect, and it was the same guy who did the robbery at the flower shop. I told Louie to head down to the 7-11 at Inglewood and Manchester. It's raining like cats and dogs. We can't see anything. As we are rolling west on Manchester up to the 7-11, I look over to my right. The 7-11, which is on the northeast corner is empty. No way. No way is this place empty, it's never empty. It's 9:30 in the morning. Everybody is grabbing a cup of coffee at that time. There were no cars parked in front, nothing. Something was wrong, and it was bad. The feeling was surreal because it was real.

"On the northwest corner is a women's medical clinic and there is a parking lot behind it. What do you think I saw as we got to the intersection? A large male black wearing black clothes. He was about six feet tall, and he was getting into a rust-colored Saturn SUV.

"I yell out, 'Louie he's right there!' as I pointed to him. We were already in the intersection and couldn't turn right. We made a U-turn, but now we were almost in front of the clinic, and the parking lot behind it and the suspect was out of our sight.

"By the time we got turned around, he was gone. We had just seen him. He was in the area. We went north to Queen Street. The air was busy, and I couldn't get on the radio. I finally broke through on the radio and told everyone we had just seen the suspect in the two robberies and he was in the area.

"We got back onto Manchester Avenue and went westbound again. We traveled two blocks west and stopped at the red light at Ash Street. There he was stopped at the next light in front of us on the overpass. He was set up to make a left turn to go southbound onto La Cienega Blvd. La Cienega parallels the 405 freeway on the west side.

"Another police car was driving east on Manchester approaching La Cienega facing the suspect. The police unit stopped at the red light and was just on the opposite side of the intersection facing him. The suspect who was stopped at the red light suddenly goes through the red light and makes a left turn on La Cienega. The unit east on La Cienega was closest, and he made a right with his red lights and siren blaring. We burned through the red light at Ash and got behind the unit chasing the suspect. We were now in pursuit. I was on the radio calling it. He got on the southbound 405 freeway.

"It was pouring rain. He's going back and forth between 80 to 90 miles an hour. I was telling our dispatch to notify all the different police agencies including the California Highway Patrol we were in pursuit. He was weaving in and out of traffic passing cars like they were crawling.

"The suspect sped up to 120 miles an hour. It was way too fast in the rain conditions. We literally could not see. Visions of hydroplaning and crashing at over 100 miles an hour went through my head. It was so scary driving that fast in the rain. I had seen people in car crashes.

Crushed bones or being paralyzed for life is not pretty. I pushed the thought out of my mind because the fear was paralyzing me. I couldn't think of anything but what it would be like to be crushed in the car. Apparently, the other unit felt the same way because both of us backed off. We lost sight of him. When we got to the 110 freeway, we didn't know if he continued south on the 405 freeway or got on the 110 freeway. We had lost him. I told the first unit to continue on the 405 freeway, and we would go south on the 110 freeway.

"As we got to the 110 on-ramp, I saw the suspect ahead of us. I saw a little splash on the transition ramp. He had kicked up debris next to one of those yellow barrels at an off-ramp. I got on the radio and told the first unit he was south on the 110 freeway not south on the 405 freeway.

"Now we were in the lead. The other unit that went southbound on the 405-freeway had to make its way to the shoulder and back up on the shoulder of the 405 freeway to get to the 110 on-ramp.

"The weather was starting to clear up a bit. The suspect got off the freeway and went through a red light at 70 miles an hour without slowing down. He didn't care about himself or anyone else. Now we were close enough for me to see the license plate. I put out a good description including the license plate. I informed everyone this was the same suspect I had seen at the 7-11. It turned out he had robbed the store right before I spotted him getting into his car behind the woman's clinic. So, in the span of a few minutes, he had robbed three places and committed attempted murder at the flower shop.

"We could not let this guy go. He was really bad. It was evident by his crimes and his driving he cared nothing for human life. We, officers, were holding it together. No one was out of control. Our radio transmissions were cool, and I remember looking at Louie, and he said to me, 'You are doing a great job.'

"I looked at Louie, 'You're a fucking amazing driver. Just like Mario Andretti.'

"It was the little breather we both needed. We calmed each other down and sobered up a bit.

"Then in a somber tone I said to him, 'You know we're going to get into a shootout with this guy.'

"He was somber as well. He answered, 'Yeah.'

"I said, 'Alright brother.' We both knew it was coming. The suspect had a gun. He was on this streak of crime, he had already shot somebody. He had no regard for any human life, his own or anyone else's.

"We knew what was coming. Louie's eyes met mine, and we nodded. To keep going at those crazy speeds and knowing what was going to happen, what was coming up, was nothing short of valor. Plain and simple. We knew…We knew. We were going to get in a shooting. I could feel the ice-cold paralyzing fear creeping in again."

Dave got that look again, the serious look like he was going into battle and there were no guarantees as to who would win.

"I pushed the thought aside as hard as I could. I could not be paralyzed and operate; I needed to be able to function, to think. I pushed the fear aside; I pushed the thought I was going to be in a shooting aside. There were no guarantees as to who would win. The thought…to know there were no guarantees…I could lose.

* * * * *

Folks if you don't believe this last statement here is the definition of valor: "Great courage in the face of danger, especially battle."

* * * * *

"We had the resolve he was not going to get away from us. This guy was a plague on society, and he was hurting people. He *had* to be stopped. It was just a matter of time before he killed someone. For the good of society, we could not let him go. I considered it as part of my oath as a police officer to stop and hopefully arrest this guy, and I could not, and I would not forsake my oath. If he allowed me to arrest him it would be that way, and that was the way I preferred it, but in my heart, I was prepared for battle. It was his decision as to which way it was going to go.

"He was going through the intersections, and he didn't care if the light was red or green. I remember putting out transmissions he was going 80 miles an hour down the side streets. It was crazy and so scary. It was apparent his attitude was, 'I don't give one fuck about anyone's life!' The realization he didn't care about anyone's life, including his own, made me realize again we were probably going to get into a shooting. Again, the fear gripped me and tried to clench me up, to freeze me, and again I pushed it away.

"I later learned the detectives at the station were hovering over each other, like a group of vultures, listening to the radio, listening to the pursuit. We were too far away for them to catch up to us. Every patrol unit at the station was trying to catch up to us. The detectives had to stay in the city because if a hot call or major crime occurred, the detectives would have to go in the field and handle it.

"We chased the guy up Sixth Street to the Little Company of Mary Hospital. He pulled into a driveway at Butte and Sixth and stopped at the entrance to a parking garage. We bailed out of the car with our guns out and put out our location. We put out he was stopped at the entrance to the parking lot on the east driveway of the Little Company of Mary Hospital at Butte and Sixth Street. When we finished putting out the call, he sped into the parking structure.

"We had three cars, one car was a single man car, and two were two-man cars. We jumped back into our cars and blocked the only way in and the only way out to the parking structure with our cars. When we got to the entrance of the structure, we could see the suspect's parked car about 70 feet away. I quickly assembled a plan. Gabe and Shea and I would go into the parking garage on foot. The other two guys, Louie being one of them, were to stay at the entrance in case the suspect got past us and tried to get out that way.

"We had no idea where the suspect was. The first obvious place to start looking was in the suspect's car. As we started walking in that direction, I saw out of the corner of my left eye the suspect climbing over a fence topped with concertina wire. This fence leads out to a huge parking lot.

"As I yelled out, 'There he is!' the two guys at the entrance to the parking structure yelled they will clear the car. The rest of us took off after the suspect on foot. In my mind, I was thinking I was going to have to climb over the wire, but then I saw a push bar door leading out to the parking lot. I hit the door and bam I'm outside. All this dumbass I was chasing had to do was go through the door like me!

"When I got outside I was on a walkway leading to the parking lot. However, the walkway did not directly go where I wanted to go, so I jumped over a metal rail bordering this walkway. When I jumped the rail my foot slipped, and I slammed my shin on the metal rail. I still have the scar where I scraped the skin off my shin. Have you ever been hit in the shin so hard your skin came off? It hurts pretty bad. It hurts enough to drop most people to the ground in agony. I was so intent on catching the suspect I hardly felt it. After I cleared the rail, I saw the suspect between two rows of parked cars. The parking lot has sets of parking lanes with parking spaces facing each other. He was about 200 feet away from me at this time between the first and the second row.

"The suspect was talking to a woman who was standing next to her car. I didn't know it at the time because his back was to me, but he was pointing a gun at her and demanding she hand over the keys to her car. Her keys were in her purse. This woman turned out to be married to a Los Angeles Deputy District Attorney, and she was an amazing witness.

"I was sprinting through the parking lot. My gun was out, and I was yelling, *'POLICE, POLICE!!! EVERYBODY GET INSIDE!!!'*

"Out of the corner of my eye, I saw Shea start to wing out to my right, moving to a flanking position in relation to the suspect. I was so focused on the suspect I was not sure where Gabe was.

"The suspect looked at us and realized he was running out of time. Another woman who was a couple of rows down was getting into her car. She had a baby with her who was in a baby car seat. She quickly threw her baby in the car, seat and all, and got in and locked the doors. He ran up to the car. You could see he was frantic and he was demanding she give him the car.

"He knew we were coming because I was screaming, *'POLICE PO-LICE!!!'* He was running out of time.

"A little way down was a lady who had just backed her car out of a parking spot. She was ready to drive off. She was about 70 years old. She had her 40 something-year-old son in the car with her. He had cerebral palsy. The suspect beelined it over to her. He opened her car door. As I was sprinting, I could see this going on, and I was catching glimpses of this changing unfolding scenario as I was running through rows of cars. I had been in a flat-out sprint, but now I slowed down. I was getting near and was trying to keep some cover and some concealment.

"When I got to within about 40 feet of the car, I saw the car door was open. His head was inside of the car, his feet were outside, and he was trying to pull the woman out. She was struggling with him. I was thinking how am I going to handle this? I could run up and try to pull him off of her. I could yell, *'POLICE FREEZE!!!'*

"That's when Shea, off to my right yells out, *'POLICE PUT THE GUN DOWN!!!'* He was in the middle of the driveway between the two rows of cars. From his angle, he could see the gun. I could not.

"The suspect pulled his head out of the car and spun to his right. When he spun, I saw his right hand with a gun in it.

"Time instantly went into slow motion as he started bringing the gun up in Shea's direction. Time almost stopped. That's how slow it was.

"My mind flashed back to Louie, and I saw his face when I had said during the pursuit, 'You know we're going to get into a shootout with this guy.'

"I saw Louie's face when he answered, 'Yeah.'

"In the next millisecond, I zoomed back to the parking lot. Even though I flashed back to my conversation with Louie, the suspect was still slowly bringing up his gun toward Shea. That's how little time it took me to relive and replay the conversation with Louie.

"I was now completely focused, and with total tunnel vision, started shooting the suspect, as Shea also did. Each shot was taking forever. It seemed like every pull of the trigger took almost a minute to do.

"Shea and I simultaneously started shooting. I was careful to put each round into the suspect. I was aiming carefully because from my angle the old lady and her son were in the car just to the right of the suspect. The last thing I wanted to do was accidentally shoot them.

"All my training, all my training in the Marine Corps, all my training in the police academies all focused in this slowed down moment. And I picked up my front sight and held steady and squeezed. I was efficient, I was shooting smooth, I had never shot so smoothly in my life. I had to hit him in the upper torso, over the car, so as not to accidentally hurt the poor citizens inside. I was afraid for the people in the car. I thought he was going to kill them. I thought, 'I can't let him take off with those people in the car with him.'

"As I shot, I could see the displacement of his clothes as my first bullet hit him. I saw dust fly off of him, and I could see the fray of material the bullet hole made. It was a slow poof as the bullet hit. Now that I think about it, it was amazing. I saw the material move, then I saw the material open, and I saw the thread of the material fray. From 40 feet, away.

"Time was now in frames, a picture of something then a jerk to the next picture. It was like you had a video on pause then hit the next frame button, then pause again, repeated over and over again.

"And I shot the next two bullets just like that. I burned into my mind where the first bullet hit and I put the next two bullets into the same hole as the first as much as I could. I did it in jerks of frames, frame by frame pictures.

"Sound was muffled in slow motion. Ever so slowly, a minute for each bullet firing, booooom, the material was poofing and fraying. Then I did it again, all over again. Time was forever, and it was so real, more real than anything I had ever experienced and such a dream at the same time. It was impossible it was so slow, that time was in jerks, in frames, in picture frames, but the sound was continuous but slow and muffled. I did this three times. Time was almost standing still, an eternity, forever and ever it was going on and on.

"As I was shooting, I could pick up Shea out of the corner of my eye, and I could hear his gun shooting in slow motion, again with the muffled sound, booooom, booooom, booooom.

"The suspect ever so slowly dropped his gun hand and turned back toward the car. Instantly with no warning, normal time came back now. I stepped away from the cover of the car I was behind. I still had my gun pointed at him, and I was walking toward him. I had seen the bullets go into him. *WHAT THE HELL??? HE WAS STILL STANDING!!!*

"It was a terrible dream. He was supposed to be down. He was supposed to be buckled to the ground. It was a terrible nightmare I was living. I was fighting a zombie.

"He reached into the car, and I was thinking he was going to try to take the car and get away.

"I perceived the threat and again with no warning, time instantaneously went into super slow motion again. My brain was acting without my will. It was changing time and vision and sound. I knew I had to shoot. As his back was to me, I shot again, another minute of time. And this time as I saw my bullet strike him, time froze. No movement, no sound. Time completely stopped. I saw my bullet go into his back below his left ribcage.

"It was like a picture taken at the exact moment my bullet hit him. It was a freeze frame of the material fraying caused by my bullet striking. Nothing moved. Everything was still.

"The picture frame unfroze and time went slow again. The suspect slowly turned toward the car and started getting inside. He was slowly trying to shove the lady over into the passenger seat. She was struggling with him. He had one leg in and his right butt cheek on the seat. She had now been shoved over to the center console. I thought, 'Oh My God, he's going to shoot this lady to get away!'

"I heard her scream, 'STOP!'

"Time now sped up. I lost a little time because somehow, I covered the last twenty feet in what seemed like a millisecond and I was right behind him. I could see his right hand on the gear selector. He was trying to get the car into drive, but I didn't see the gun. I didn't know where it was.

"Time was normal.

"I had to get him out of the car. While I was behind him, I reached over his left deltoid, or upper arm area, and grabbed his right breast shirt pocket with my left hand. I meant to rip him out of the car. My gun was in my right hand. I pulled hard, and I started lifting him out of the car.

"I saw the son of the woman in the car. He was shoved against the passenger door reaching up with both hands, and he was covering his face and head. He obviously thought he was going to get shot. I was yelling, *'PUT THE GUN DOWN!!!'*

"As I was ripping the suspect out of the car, I could see the suspect's right arm and hand between his body and the driver's car doorframe. And the gun was in his hand.

"Time slowed down to a crawl. I told him, 'Puuuttt…iiitt…doowwwn.'

"The suspect said, 'Okaaaay…okaaaaay…okaaaay.' Three times he said it. He heard me, and it was as if he was telling me he was done. He had had enough.

"Between the doorframe and the back of the right side of his body, I saw his arm lift, and then it crossed over the front of his body.

"In super slow motion, I heard a voice in my head, and it was my voice. I don't know if I said it or thought it, but it said, *'NOOOOOOO I'M FUCKED. I'M GOING TO GET SHOT!'* as he brought the gun over his left shoulder and pointed it at my face.

"I moved like Keanu Reeves in *The Matrix*. In super slow motion, but as fast as I could, I violently, and desperately twisted my head neck and whole upper body to the left. I twisted my head up and left as fast as I could. I also dipped my body downward trying to get away from his gun.

"Even though I saw what he was going to do, and I knew I was going to shoot him again, he got his shot off before I could get my shot off. And as fast as I was going, I couldn't move my head fast enough, and as fast as I was going, I couldn't shoot fast enough. I couldn't go fast enough to beat him.

"Imagine someone taking the palm of their hand, and smashing it into your nose and eyes as hard as they could…that's what it felt like. It felt like someone smashed my face into the inside of my head. I thought

I'm dead. He killed me. I was in shock. It was too unreal to believe this was happening to me.

"My nose was numb. I knew part of my face was missing. My gun was bucking in my hand, pointed right at his back, booooom.......
booooom...... booooom was the muffled sound of it. So slow, smooth and methodical, just a machine, but it was my only chance to live.

"An eternity later, hours it seemed, while I knew I was going to die, and while forever shooting him in the back three more times, and while wondering when this nightmare I was living in was going to end, and while believing it never would, and after an eternity... an eternity of my life, I finally felt his body go limp as I finished heaving him out of the car. He didn't look at me, but he looked up, and his eyes rolled up in the back of his head, and he fell to the ground on his belly. His gun was at his feet.

"He was still a threat to me. He landed on his belly, on his hands. I didn't know if he had another gun under there. I had shot him three separate times now. The first time I shot him three times in his chest. Then I shot him once in the back. Then I shot him three more times in the back. Seven times with .45 caliber bullets and it just seemed like he kept coming back. It was like I was fighting a zombie. I was fighting a zombie. He just wouldn't stop. Even after I shot him four times, he still managed to shoot me. Any normal person would have been down long before my last three shots.

"As he laid there, I was scared he was playing possum so he could kill me. He had to have been wearing a bulletproof vest. I was thinking to myself, 'Don't let up. Keep your guard up. Fucking stay on this motherfucker. He's going to try to kill you again.' And I couldn't feel my face. It terrified and horrified me wondering what had happened to my face.

"I was covering him with my gun. I was so enraged. Enraged that he had robbed and shot people. Enraged that he put my life and Louie's life and civilians' lives in danger by the way he drove. Enraged that he tried to carjack innocent people. Enraged that he wouldn't give up. Enraged that he made me shoot him. Enraged that after shooting him he wouldn't stop. Enraged that he said he would drop the gun and didn't. That he lied to me. Enraged he tried to kill me. I was enraged that my oath to my office and to the constitution, in my mind, prohibited me from executing him when he still had the gun in his hand as I was pulling him out of the car. Enraged that others who might judge me, had I executed him, would not think since he was facing away from me, he was not a threat. Enraged he ruined my face. I was so enraged, and I couldn't stop the intense anger. And I didn't recognize who I had become. I had never been this angry before. Ever. I didn't know who this person was. I was thinking, *I'm going to fucking shoot you mother-fucker, I'm going to kill you!!'* I didn't think he was done. All the thoughts intermingled into, 'If he makes any move I think is a threat again I've *got* to empty my gun on his head. He might be a zombie, but I'll make him a headless zombie.'

"I had no idea what was going on in the car. Every fiber of my energy was focused on the suspect. I was so pissed at what he had just done, that he had fucked up my face.

"As I was covering him with my gun, the guys came up to handcuff him. I told Gabe, 'Be careful he has a vest on.'" (A bulletproof vest)

"As Gabe went to check him out and Shea came with me to cover him, I thought, 'If this guy comes up I'm going to coup de grace him.' I thought, 'Fuck it, fuck it, prosecute me, this guy's a zombie; he won't stop, prosecute me, I'd rather live.'

"Gabe handcuffed him. It was weird, but the guy's index fingers were pointing upward. Gabe searched him, and he said, 'He doesn't have a vest on.'"

"I was incredulous. I was thinking, WHAT? He has to have a vest on. No one could take that many shots and still fight like he did. It was later determined each of the shots I had hit him with were life-ending hits. Yet still, he fought."

"I was still angry. You don't go from shooting someone to zero emotion as in an I don't care emotional state. It doesn't work that way. And I remember thinking. 'I have more respect for a cockroach than this piece of shit. A cockroach doesn't know any better. This piece of shit does."

"Neither Gabe nor Shea had looked at me. They were intent on the suspect. I told Gabe, Hey, brother, I think I've been shot.

"He looked at me and gave me that look. You know that *'OH FUCK!!!'* look.

"I was thinking, OH, SHIT, I'M FUCKED UP BAD!

"More officers were there now. Guys had caught up to the pursuit. Guys were handling the lady and her son.

"Gabe came up to me, 'Fuck, bro, you got a lot of blood on you. Where's it coming from?'

"My face, I dunno.

"I had been shot through the tip of my nose. My Red Dot was on the tip of my nose. Blood ran down my mouth and onto my chin. I had blood on my shirt from the suspect. I had lived, and he had died. It wasn't my day to go.

"The suspect broke the lady's arm. An officer helped the man out of the car and had gotten his walker out. The man came over to me, 'Sir I'm so sorry, I have cerebral palsy, and I couldn't get out of the car.'

"I felt so bad, and I was so angry, I turned and looked at the cause of all the incredible damage, at all the trauma this piece of shit had done, and I wanted to kick him in the head. I had visions of giving this guy CPR to bring him back to life just so I could beat him back to death. It's terrible I felt this way, but that's how angry I was. And I believe, 'Thou shall not kill.' I believe. I love people. I want to help people. I would do anything to help people.

"The lady later tried suing me. She said a shot I fired had fragmented and is what broke her arm. She had already collected from the city and was trying to double dip. Once that was dismissed I never heard about the case again.

"There was an immense amount of blood on the driver's doorjamb that separated the front door from the rear door. It was clotted in chunks running down the doorjamb. That blood could only have come from blowing out a major artery or the heart. That wound alone should have put the suspect down. The suspect sustained that wound before he got into the car and tried to put the car in gear and drive off. He sustained that wound before he struggled with the lady. He sustained that wound before he broke her arm. He sustained that wound before he shoved her over the center console. He sustained that wound before he shot me.

"But he did all those things after he should have been dead.

"He was a zombie.

"After this whole thing was over I called my wife to tell her I was okay. My mother in law had told her, 'Aye, mija, there were a bunch of Inglewood cops passing by me on the freeway. It was raining, but they were going really fast. It was so dangerous!

"My wife told her, 'That was David.'

'Aye, mija!'

* * * * *

Officer David Carrasquillo of the Inglewood Police Department was awarded the Distinguished Service Medal for Valor for his heroic actions on December 15, 2003. This is the department's second highest award that can be bestowed upon its members. This account was not included in this book.

Detective David Carrasquillo of the Inglewood Police Department was awarded the Medal of Valor for his actions on February 21, 2009, for heroism in assisting in saving the lives of over 100 citizens in a structure fire. This is the highest award the department can bestow upon its members.

Detective David Carrasquillo of the Inglewood Police Department was awarded the Medal of Valor for his actions on October 4, 2010, for heroism in saving the lives of two kidnap victims.

Chapter 18

Helpless

Account of Gloria Gressman
Los Angeles County Sheriff's Department

It was March 1981 I was assigned to the Lennox Sheriff's Patrol Station. The station had five patrol areas; the North end bordering Culver City and the Marina Del Rey, the City of Lawndale, Central area, which covered about a mile east of the Los Angeles International Airport, Gardena Park. It bordered the City of Gardena and the Vermont area which covered the unincorporated area ending at Vermont Avenue bordering the Watts area. It was 4:00 a.m. and I was working a black and white radio car with my partner Steve Gibbs in the Vermont area.

Even though it was 4:00 a.m. our windows were down. You can't do police work with your windows up. You have to be able to hear the sounds and smell the smells of the neighborhood.

That is precisely what happened. You know the saying, "Where there's smoke there's fire?" We smelled smoke. We followed the smell and found the house it was coming from. After calling the station for the fire department to respond, we knew no one had called them yet.

Another patrol car arrived to back us up. Now there were three of us at the house. The fire department had not arrived. We had a quick group discussion. Remember we had followed the smell of smoke, so the house had smoke pouring out of it. If there was anyone in the house, they were in real trouble, probably passed out from lack of oxygen. We decided we could not wait for the fire department to arrive; we had to get in there and search for people.

My partner and our assisting unit hit the door three or four times, and it caved in. We entered the house on our hands and knees with Steve right in front of me. Flames were rolling and roaring on the ceiling. The smoke was so thick you could hardly see one foot in front of you.

All of a sudden, my partner handed me a body. Then he handed our assisting unit another body, that of a five-year-old boy. I had a little girl about two years old. "Oh, Fuck, OH, GOD!!!" I thought. I grabbed her and took her outside a safe distance from the house. Laying her on the grass, I was going to give her C.P.R. She was wearing a cute pink and white jumper. I was on my knees leaning over her. She had the most beautiful eyelashes you could ever want. I could see her eyes looking up at me. They were half closed, half open…and they were lifeless.

She was lifeless. This was a baby, and took extra care when performing C.P.R. I concentrated, "Give the chest compressions with two fingers, so you don't break any bones. Cover the mouth and nose with your whole mouth. Blow little puffs of air, don't overblow or you will pop the lungs. Count the compressions, now puff air inside her." Every time I blew in air, I could hear her little lungs take the life-giving oxygen. "Please let me save her," I pleaded, "Let me bring her back."

I looked over, and there was our back up unit giving the little boy C.P.R. There was a woman, a neighbor, who had come out of her house. I yelled at her, "Is there anyone else in the house?"

She just looked at me. Again, I yelled at her, "My partner is in the house in the fire, is there anyone else in the house?"

Again, she just looked at me. I kept giving C.P.R. to the baby. The fire department arrived, and I tried to hand the baby to them. They told me to keep doing what I was doing because they weren't ready for her yet.

I ended up giving the baby C.P.R. for fifteen minutes. They rushed her to the hospital, but she was dead. It turned out they were the only two in the house. The mother worked at night and would leave the children alone. She would lock the top lock with a key. There was no way for the kids to have gotten out. They had tried because they were both at the front door when we found them. They were helpless. We couldn't save the children, they were already dead, we were helpless, we were all was helpless.

The fire was started because the boy was playing with matches. The mother was charged with manslaughter.

* * * * *

Gloria Gressman received the Medal of Valor from the Los Angeles County Sheriff's Department for her actions on the morning of March 1981. It is the highest award the department can bestow upon its members.

Steve Gibbs also received the Medal of Valor for the total disregard of his life in trying to save others and in his service to mankind.

* * * * *

During a subsequent autopsy, it was determined the little girl was sexually molested. This was determined due to trauma her vagina had sustained.

Gloria had held, and tried to give life to a baby who had suffocated to death, but who had unknown to her, suffered so much in her short life. This is so much more than sad to Gloria, and she has compartmentalized it and put it away, but from time to time it comes out of its box, and the overwhelming sadness hits her.

This crime was never solved.

Chapter 19

Killer on the Loose

Account of James, "Jimboo" Campbell
Los Angeles County Sheriff's Department

Google December 1988 Universal Studios shooting.

Let my long-time beloved, and close friend and ex-patrol partner Jimmy tell you about how he arrested this murderer.

* * * * *

"I was the lone Los Angeles County Deputy Sheriff working at Universal Studios on December 1st, 1988. I was in my little office underneath the Universal Studios Security office. My radio car was parked outside.

"Around 5:40 in the evening I heard the Universal Studios Security radio explode with voices. The radio traffic was there was shooting at the main gate on Lankershim Blvd. This was probably 100 yards from where I was.

"'Oh shit!' I thought. I mean you could tell by the panic in the voices this was real. My first thought was I had to get to the gate.

"I ran outside and got into my radio car. As I was backing up, I saw guys at the gate waving at me. They were waving me over to another security guy outside of the gate across the street at Valleyheart Drive. I thought, 'I'm not a doctor, what the hell are you going to do? There are plenty of people already responding to the security gate to give first aid. Something is going on out on the street. They want me out on the street, there is a problem there.'

"I drove to the gate, and I could see the security guy, I think his name was Hernandez, on Valleyheart north of Bluffside Drive. He was frantically waving for me to come over to him. I drove over to him, and he got in my car. He was beyond frantic. *'I SEE HIM, I SEE HIM! HE'S STILL THERE!'*

"There was a mist in the air, a light fog. There was also electricity in the air. I can't explain it. It was an eerie feeling permeating everything. It was weird, spooky. It was like it was a programmed movie. The whole scenario had such a profound effect on me it triggered me and put me on my guard. 'This is not fake.'

"Hernandez was telling me, 'There he is Jim, by the telephone pole.' He was pointing to a telephone pole on Bluffside Dr.

"I couldn't see him. I was looking and trying to make him out, but I couldn't see him. I was thinking, 'Shit, what is he looking at? How come I can't see him? I was looking at the telephone pole, and I didn't see jack shit!'

"Hernandez kept telling me, 'There he is, the guy in the khaki pants.'

"All of a sudden he stepped into my view. He was walking south on the west side of Bluffside. I was north of him on Valleyheart Drive. So, he was walking away from me on the opposite side of the street. There were cars parked at the curb facing north.

"I drove across Bluffside southbound onto the northbound traffic lanes, closest to the lane with the parked cars. The street was empty with no oncoming traffic. He wasn't acting right. He was so nonchalant like nothing was wrong. I already knew from the radio traffic he had just moments ago, shot two Universal security guards. I was trying to meld that information with the action of a man who was nonchalantly walking down the street, who had just murdered or attempted to murder two men. It was all too surreal.

"I was thinking, 'I don't like this. What's with this guy? He should be running. What the hell is going on?'

"The headlights on my radio car were off. I unlocked the shotgun. I looked at Hernandez, 'If anything happens and things go bad, use the shotgun if you need to protect yourself, use it.'

"I slowly drove behind him and watched him as I kept the parked cars between him and myself. My mind flashed to when I was a kid, and I played cops and robbers. I was being sneaky because I had come behind the guy with my lights off, and now I had cover with a parked car between us.

"I pulled up with my driver's door next to the driver's door of a parked car. He was on the sidewalk. While he slowly walked and as I slowly kept pace slightly behind him, I called out, 'HEY, HOW YOU DO- ING?' He wouldn't acknowledge me, he just kept walking.

"I pulled out my gun, and I got out of my radio car, and I said, 'Hey I want to…' and that's as far as I got. Things went into super slow mo- tion because he reached for his gun.

"He was wearing an open jacket with a wool sweater underneath. I saw him slowly pull out a revolver from his waistband from under his wool sweater. In what seemed to be slow, jerky frames of movement, his gun hand took forever to come up as he was trying to point it at me. As slow as he was moving, I knew I did not have the time to get my gun up on target and shoot him before he shot me.

"I'll never forget thinking, this is not going to turn out well. I'm glad I got this car blocking me from him.

"Everything about the gun was magnified. I could see it so clear. I couldn't believe I could see his gun so clearly and in such slow motion.

I thought, 'I'm not going to die because I can see everything he is doing, everything that is going to happen!'

"Before he could get the gun fully pointed at me, I dove to the ground. As I was going down, I saw the muzzle flash through the rear window of the parked car.

Time returned to normal.

"The round hit the roof of the parked car, exactly where I had been standing, and skidded off into the night. I was on the ground by the rear driver's tire. The parked car was still between him and me, and he was on the other side of the car. But in an instant, he was in front of me. He had to be moving at the speed of light because it seemed right after he shot at me he was six feet in front of me. There he was in an instant, pointing his gun at my head.

"My gun was bucking in my hand, and I was firing in faster than normal speed. My gun was three feet away from him, and I was firing into his body. There was no blood, no reaction from him. *WHAT THE FUCK?* He wasn't going down. He wasn't grunting or crying or reacting at all to me shooting him. I was missing him. I couldn't believe it. How could I be missing? It was impossible. Impossible. My gun was almost touching him. But I was missing him. He had an evil look of hate on his face.

"As I was shooting him, he spun away from me and took a step to run. I fired at his back, but he was still moving and starting to run.

"I was in an unreal nightmare, wherein this terrible dream of horror, nothing was working as it should.

Jimmy sat across the table from me and took a breath. He stopped and covered his eyes with his hand, and through a choked voice said, "This is so hard for me to talk about."

After a little while, he continued, "I got up, and I tackled him in a few short steps. I got the gun away from him and got him handcuffed. I turned him over on his back and lifted his sweater. There it was, pieces of his flesh in the wool.

"I searched him, and he had no other weapons, but he had five live rounds of ammunition in his pocket.

* * * * *

"A witness who heard the shooting later told investigators, 'It sounded just like a war.'

* * * * *

Several days before this incident, this loon killed three people in New Mexico. He went into a bagel shop and shot the owner, then his daughter in the head. The son-in-law ran outside and hid under a car. The murderer then calmly walked outside and shot the son-in-law in the head.

A cab driver who had contact with him said the murderer told him, "He received a message from God to kill a Nazi."

After the killings in New Mexico, the murderer caught a bus to Los Angeles. He went through the Universal Tours on December 1st. After he went through the tours, he exited the park and went to the main gate on Lankershim Blvd. He briefly spoke with the security guards there and asked to see the actor, Michael Landon.

The security guards turned him away, but he pulled out a gun and shot the first security guard in the head. A second security guard took off running. The murderer shot him in the head. He then returned to the first security guard and shot him in the head again. He then went to the second security guard and shot him in the head again. He killed them both.

Another security guard saw this and radioed there had been a shooting at the guard shack.

Jimmy's shots did not kill him. The murderer lived. When Jimmy shot, he was hitting him. Jim hit him two times in the stomach. Jim's third round hit the murderer in the arm and spun him around. That is when Jim saw him turn to run. Jim shot him again in the back. Jim threw two more rounds, which missed the murderer and went off into some parked cars.

The murderer had a five-shot revolver. At the time he engaged Jim, he had fired four rounds into the security guards and had not reloaded. He fired his fifth and last shot at Jimmy's head.

At trial, he was found to be legally insane and was sent to a mental institution.

Jimmy told me how after the incident he would run every night in the dark, where no one could see him. For months afterward, he ran, crying as he ran and as he relived the incident. He told me the reason for the tears. He felt like he let the families down of those five people who this guy murdered. He felt, and continues to feel guilty to this day. He told me, "I was the guardian between the righteous and the evil, and I failed." He is sorry he did not kill the murderer and bring justice as he sees it, for the murdered and their families. Now if this sounds cold-hearted, Jim is one of the most compassionate men you would ever know. He will literally give a stranger the shirt off of his back. I've never seen a man who cared so much about others. It broke my heart to see how this incident affected him so profoundly then, and even now after all these years.

As Jimmy told me, this guy just wanted to go around and kill people. And he had.

James Campbell faithfully and honorably served another 10 years with the Los Angeles County Sheriff's Department and retired as a detective in 1998.

Chapter 20

The Banker's War

Account of Steve "The Gibber" Gibbs
Los Angeles County Sheriff's Department

Nearly 34 years later, ghosts of the past emerged. The Los Angeles County Sheriff's Department hired me for the position of deputy sheriff in April 1983. This was the same month a sergeant from our Special Enforcement Bureau, our department's version of the S.W.A.T. Team was killed.

Somewhere around the end of June or the beginning of July 1983, I went on my first patrol ride in full uniform. I was still in the academy. In those days after passing certain academy tests, and as part of your academy curriculum, you went out on patrol as a quasi-partner with a deputy sheriff. The public didn't know we were still in the academy as we were in full uniform. They moved us around to different stations over about a month and a half to give us patrol experience. My first academy ride was at the San Dimas Sheriff Patrol Station.

After briefing, my "real" deputy partner drove to a residential area and parked the radio car. He told me, "Stay in the car and listen to the radio. If we get any calls honk the horn." He then left.

He walked into a row of townhome type residences and disappeared.

I sat there scared. We had just had an officer survival class. They had shown some gruesome pictures of an officer who had his throat slit because he couldn't get his gun out of his holster. The lesson had been you needed to be familiar with your equipment. I sat there with my head on a swivel. I was expecting for someone to come and execute me at any second. The radio had some traffic I could not comprehend. I was wondering if that had been a radio call for us. If it was, and I hadn't honked the horn maybe they would fire me for being incompetent. I was completely on edge. It was my first fifteen minutes in a uniform in a radio car in the field.

Like some little puppy excited to see his master I was relieved and happy when I saw my partner emerge from the row of townhouses. There was a woman beside him.

They both walked up to the passenger side of the radio car. They were chatting. The woman looked at me and gave me a "Mona Lisa" smile as she said something to my partner. The mood was somber. She softly said, "Oh my God, look how young he is." As she said it, she took her fingers and brushed the hair on the back of my head upwards. I had no idea what was going on except I instinctively knew she wasn't hitting on me or flirting with me. It was not like that. It was something else. It was a motherly gesture, and she looked melancholic. She brushed my hair one more time and removed her hand. She again softly said, "He's so young, he's just a baby," as if to say, "He has no idea what he is in for."

She turned to my partner, and he said to her, "Let us know if you need anything."

She said, "Okay," then turned and walked away back toward the residences.

My partner got back in the radio car. I had no idea what had just happened, and I was too green, too new to dare ask.

As we drove off, he looked at me. "Do you know who that was?"

"No, sir," I answered.

He looked at me and said, "Remember this last April? The sergeant at S.E.B. who was killed?"

"Yes, I do."

"That was his widow."

* * * * *

34 years later, this occurrence came full circle as I sat face to face with retired Los Angeles County Sheriff Steve Gibbs. We were sitting outside in the shade at a restaurant in Hermosa Beach. We sipped ice teas and watched the beautiful young women walk by, I could see Steve had lost none of his spark.

He told me the story.

"In April 1983, I had been a Los Angeles Deputy Sheriff for twelve years. My prior life before September 1971 was that of an ex-military man. I was twenty-three years old with a wife and two young boys to support. I was working on the freeway picking up trash and making the ice plants pretty. I was hungry to make decent money and have steady work. I applied to the Los Angeles County Sheriff's Department, and after going through all the testing processes, I was hired as a deputy sheriff in September 1971.

"After graduating from the academy, I worked the jail where I learned how to control people. I also learned how the bad guys moved, walked and talked. I learned how gang members and other hardcore criminals thought and fought. I was among the worst in society. I was locked in with murderers, rapists, robbers, burglars, and pedophiles. In a short period of time, I knew how to recognize a criminal, and I think my time spent in the jail gave me a great advantage when I actually went to patrol.

"I went to patrol at Lennox Station. It was considered one of the fast stations, containing areas heavily infested with gang members who robbed and murdered everyone. Just a little time at Lennox and my cop instincts were finely tuned. I felt my partner, and I could handle anything because we had handled most every type of dangerous situation you could run into.

"I applied for and was accepted to the Los Angeles County Sheriff's Department Prestigious Special Enforcement Bureau, S.E.B. This is the department's S.W.A.T. team. We were the best of the best; hands down. We had various names, The Last Call Guys, Rulers of the Night, and The Helmets. We had been in existence since the late 1960's and were continually shooting and fine-tuning our tactics. A deputy sheriff wanting to go to 'The Bureau' as we called it, was heavily vetted. He had to be in superb physical condition and known for being an outstanding street cop. After applying he was handpicked by a voting process by the other deputies. I was accepted into the bureau in 1981.

"At the time of my acceptance, I had already received the Medal of Valor for going into a burning house and passing two young children out to other deputies."

* * * * *

"1983 was a hectic time for law enforcement in Los Angeles. We were dealing with a high influx of crime, and we were anticipating the upcoming Olympics to Los Angeles in 1984.

"There was a lot of cocaine coming into the country during this time, mostly from Colombia. Los Angeles based Colombian gangs controlled these drugs and their sales and movements. It seemed everyone was using cocaine. It was the in drug.

"S.E.B. was serving narcotic warrants on a daily basis during the eighties. The Olympics were coming to Los Angeles and on top of serving high-risk search warrants, we trained. We trained, and we trained some more. Tactics, tactics and more tactics. Keeping in top physical shape was of paramount importance. S.E.B. was training a lot of outside agencies. These included the Navy Seal Teams, the Federal Bureau of

Investigation Hostage Rescue Team, the Army Delta Force and the 2nd Marine Reconnaissance Force just to name a few. Our expertise was the surgical clearing of buildings and other vessels. After some time with us, these units would return to their branches and train their personnel in what they had learned. The Los Angeles County Sheriff's S.E.B. and the Los Angeles Police Department Special Weapons and Tactics (S.W.A.T.) were world renowned as the best throughout law enforcement in dealing with hostage and terrorist situations. The saying at S.E.B. was, 'A runner or a lifter you must be, no one here rides for free.' I was a marathon runner and a triathlete competitor. We were all young and fit and ready for anything.

"In 1983, we had Emergency Services Detail, E.S.D., which were our tactical paramedics operating under the S.E.B. flag. These guys were part of S.E.B. and were cross-trained both as fully operational tactical S.E.B. guys and as paramedics. They went to every operation in case someone got hurt, be they a deputy or a suspect or anyone else. They were beyond good. In contrast to having great technical skills, they were deputies and were trained and expected to make decisions. If you mix bravery, extreme calmness under the worst scenarios and pressure, knowledge, and technical skills together, we were in the best possible hands ever.

"We got the address of the place we were going to hit. Scouting is a big thing. Proper Prior Planning Prevents Piss Poor Performance. Our team went out and scouted the place. While scouting and with years of experience in making entries, we saw everything and addressed the possible pitfalls of the operation. You want to know where every room in the location is, so you don't move around blind once you are in the house. Everything had to be taken into consideration, from how to approach the place, knowing if there were dogs and what kind of dogs they were, to where cover was available for perimeter/containment personnel, or if there were bars on the windows. No detail was too small to take note of.

"The location we were to hit was a single-family home at the rear of another residence. It was a stucco building with heavy bars over the front door and all the windows. We could easily handle this. We were going to pull the bars off of the window to the left of the front door, then break the window and slick as you please we would be in. This was an arrest warrant the narcotics bureau wanted us to serve. The guy was supposed to be a banker for the Colombian drug cartel. A banker? We worked out three hours a day. We shot constantly. We trained in moving as a tactical team to take down any target needed to be taken down. A banker? Any operation carries a risk, but in the back of my mind at least, I considered this to be a lower risk entry compared to those we had been handling. A banker? I remember someone saying we had the 'Milk Run.' Three other operations were being served that day, and our service was considered to be the least dangerous.

"After scouting the location, we returned to our S.E.B. headquarters in good spirits. We would be serving the warrant the next morning."

* * * * *

"It was on. It was seven in the morning on April 16, 1983. Our Sergeant Larrell yelled, 'GO!!!'

"My blood pressure elevated, my heart thumped in my chest, and I could feel the veins in my neck throbbing. My senses became acute, my vision narrowed and all my concentration was on my target. There was one single thing happening now, and it was to get in the stucco house and arrest the banker. The pucker factor was in effect. This is also known as, 'Your asshole is so tight it would take a sledgehammer to pound a nail into it' phenomenon.

"Once the paramedic truck backed up to the house, the time had started ticking. Time, time was of the essence. Things had to be done quickly and accurately.

"I watched as two E.S.D. deputies, our paramedics, ran to the front of the house. One of them had a long cable with a hook on the end of it. The other end of the cable was attached to the front of their oversized paramedic truck. The other E.S.D. deputy was there to provide cover fire in case someone started shooting at them. The deputy with the cable hooked it to the bars on the window to the left of the front door.

"Once the hooks were set, the deputies quickly but still covering themselves ran to the side of the house. They ran to the side of the house because they next yelled, *'ALL CLEAR!!!'* When that happened, the paramedic truck drove forward and pulled the bars off the window. They ran to the side of the house because you did not want to be in front of the cable or the bars as they violently came sliding and skidding behind the truck. If you were hit with this, you would at the least be seriously injured or possibly even killed.

"Now it was the S.E.B. guys turn. Our turn. We had to approach. Of course, anyone in the house would have heard the sound of the bars coming off the window. Time was of the essence. We had to get in quickly and make no mistakes. Larrell yelled, 'GO!' and we were off. We were exposed now. In the open, known as the kill zone. Cover was behind us, and there was no cover in front of us. Our cover was each other, we were now placing our lives in each other's hands. We trusted each other with an unwavering certainty no matter what, we would protect each other. Larry led, then Rich, then Larrell, then me, followed by Bill.

"One behind the other we quickly approached the front of the house, with each of us covering each other in case shooting started happening. With keen senses, understanding how vulnerable we were, we quickly moved toward the house, looking for any movement coming from any window or the door at the front of the house. If we saw any movement, we had milliseconds to assess the movement and decide if it was life-threatening. All my senses are on ultra-high alert, sight, sound, and even smell, as I understood how exposed we were in the open.

"My heart was beating, THUMP, THUMP, THUMP, almost out of my chest. I heard the expected crash, the breaking of glass. It was expected, but now my adrenaline was really pumping. Rich had shattered the window with a large metal pole and was raking the frame to get rid of any loose glass that could have cut us. It's close now, really close, it's almost time to go in.

"We were so vulnerable I wanted to go in. My head was screaming, 'Come on, let's go, let's get inside, let's do this!' It felt like I had been outside and exposed for hours, but the reality is it had been about 10 seconds. It's too long. From the time the bars have been pulled out to the raking of the window had been about 20 seconds. It's too long. It was enough time for a suspect to get armed and wait for us. COME ON LET'S GO!

"BOOOOM! Damn, I knew it was a flashbang.

"A flash bang is also known as a stun grenade or a flash grenade. It produces a blinding flash of light and sound more than 170 decibels. It was made to stun a person's senses and disorient them without causing permanent injury.

"It had been thrown through the window into the living room. We were now moving.

"Immediately after the flash bang went off, Larry was inside the window, followed by Rich. I heard, 'CLEAR!' This was a relief because it meant no one was in the living room and there was no threat. As the clear call went out from Larry, Larrell was going through the window, and I was right behind him, touching him. Larry and Rich had crossed the living room in less than two seconds and were looking down a hallway to the back of the house. Larry yelled out, 'Movement in the rear.' He'd seen or heard something in the rear of the house.

"My senses were heightened. What was the movement or sound Larry heard? Was it going to be a threat?

"We were in the living room, and I swept the living room with my shotgun, double checking for any threat. To my right was a darkened room, possibly a kitchen. There was a counter about waist high that ran the length of the darkened room.

"Another second had now gone by.

"I was looking forward toward Larry and Rich, with my shotgun held about waist high pointed to the right of Larrell. Larry and Rich were looking down the hallway obviously intent on taking care of any problems that arose from the rear of the house. Suddenly from my right, there was a loud explosion and a flash. The explosion was like a cannon going off.

"Gunfire!

"Time went to super slow motion. In the millisecond, it was taking my brain to process what was going on I thought, 'What the fuck, there are only four of us in the room?' I wasn't shooting, and neither were any of the guys. I was confused and could not understand what was happening. I knew it was gunfire, no question about it, but where was it coming from?

"I looked to my right, and out of the corner of my left eye, I saw Larrell go down. I was thinking he saw the gunfire and was getting down to avoid being hit. It's a natural thing to do, to get down. You know, get into a foxhole.

"Time is so slowed down it is taking forever to swing my shotgun to the right and locate the threat and fire. I was trying to turn to the right, but it was like I was moving in molasses. I was not thinking of Larry, or Rich or even of Larrell at this time. I was thinking I had to stop this threat to my right, and I had to do it now. But it was taking so long to get turned right.

"After what seemed like hours, I saw a person, a shadow, standing behind the counter in the kitchen. I had no idea if it was a man or a woman, and I didn't care. This person was holding something in their hand pointing it at me. The gunshot and flame of the gunshot had come from them, and was the threat. The devil himself was standing in the kitchen, spitting fire at me from ten feet away, and he was trying to kill me.

"I was in auto mode. I had killed hundreds if not thousands of targets during practice. This was no longer a living thing in front of me; it was a deadly threat. I leveled my shotgun at the silhouette, the target and I opened up on it. Now I was spitting fire in return, BOOOOOOM ever so slowly, BOOOOOOM, BOOOOOOM! Over and over I fired. To my left, I heard, Ratta, tat, tat, tat.

"I knew Larry and Rich were both firing. I was not sure who they were firing at. I was not looking at them; I could just hear them firing. I had no idea if they were firing at the same suspect as me. Remember they had movement at the rear of the house. Even though they are there firing at the same time as me, I was alone. I was fighting alone, I was fighting for myself now. If I were to get shot, I would get shot alone.

"BOOOOM, BOOOOM, BOOOOM! I kept firing. I knew I was hitting the suspect, I knew I was on target because since I had started shooting him, he had been dancing. He was jerking and moving with his arms and body dancing this way and that. He was jerking but not going down. He looked like a puppet. He kept dancing up and down and sideways; Helter Skelter like a puppet on a string being pulled and jerked by a puppeteer.

"The seconds were hours, and after what seemed like hours and hours, he slowly fell out of sight.

"The house now was so eerily quiet. Not a sound. My shotgun was still pointed at the kitchen. I was waiting for the devil to appear again. Silence. Through the darkness and quiet, I saw the vapors and smoke of my gunfire. It was lightly floating like little wisps in the air. I could smell the gunpowder from my gun. This was so surreal, like a movie or a horribly bad dream.

"Time went normal again. I glanced behind me, and Larrell was lying on the floor. He was on his left side in a semi-fetal position. He could have been sleeping, but in horror, I knew he was not. His head was in a large pool of blood, and his eyes were opened in a fixed stare.

"Just when my nightmare should have ended, my nightmare had just begun!

"I fought going numb. I had to act. Suddenly there were noises behind me. Shouting. I looked at Larrell again, I didn't see him breathing. Someone was shouting, 'Larrell's been hit!' Was it me yelling this? I don't know if it was or not.

"I knew I had to get Larrell out of the house. I bent down, and someone was there beside me helping me lift him up. He was a ragdoll covered in blood. I was silently praying and hoping against all odds he was going to be okay. I kept fighting the thought he was already dead.

"We carried Larrell to the open window and passed him to our paramedics. Please God, let Larrell be okay, I prayed to the good Lord.

"I was in a fog. I was outside now. Outside of the residence. How that happened, I don't know. Someone else took over the operation, remember there was movement inside the house and we had not cleared it yet.

"Then time moved on, and I was at S.E.B. headquarters waiting to be interviewed by homicide. I don't remember how I got there. I was so down in my spirit. It was the lowest I had ever been. I fought tears, and I was angry. So angry. I could not understand what had happened. I was completely drained mentally and physically.

"We finally got word from the hospital Larrell was in grave condition. He had been shot in the head. The bullet went into the lower rear area of his brain. The bullet had hit his brain stem.

"The continuous tape recording was playing in my head. I relived the shooting over and over again, and it wouldn't stop. The suspect jerking and jerking and dancing the dance of death. But it was too late, much too late. He had already killed Larrell. It was too late. I was too late. It was my fault. It played over and over again. It was my fault. It took over my mind and would not let go. I was numb. I wanted to kill the suspect, I wanted to murder him for killing Larrell. But I had killed him. I had killed him, but it wasn't enough because I was too slow. I was too late. The feeling it was my fault numbed me and was strangling me. I had let Larrell down. If only I had seen the suspect sooner, if I had reacted sooner, faster, Larrell might be okay. I knew how bad Larrell was injured. I was hoping against all hope he would live. The thoughts kept running through my mind and would not stop. They were driving me insane.

"Larrell was kept alive with the aid of a ventilator for a day or two, but he had no brain activity, and the decision was made to let him pass.

"When I got the news, I was devastated. I cried for many years after.

"The banker declared battle, and even though he died, he not only won the battle, but also the war."

* * * * *

"Larrell's death was the first death of a tactical officer in the line of duty in the State of California and the second tactical officer killed in the line of duty in the United States."

* * * * *

"The murderer was a Colombian who was associated with the Colombian drug cartel. I can't, to this day understand why he shot at us and killed Larrell. After he was killed, the house was cleared. There were two teenagers in the house; that was the movement at the rear of the place. When they cleared the house, they searched it and found nothing illegal inside. Nothing.

"Others, who had been in the house, later told me the kitchen counter I had seen did not exist. To this day I can see it, but it was not there."

* * * * *

"Larrell was a soft-spoken man who garnered respect when he spoke. He was considered an outstanding deputy sheriff and sergeant. He had learned his trade at Firestone Station, one of the fastest stations in the County of Los Angeles. He was an outstanding leader of men. I would have followed him to hell if he had asked and so would've all of his team. He had farm boy looks, with reddish blond hair. He had freckles and spoke with a slight country slang. He was raised in the country and chewed tobacco. He had a great sense of humor and enjoyed having a beer with us. He just wanted to finish his career and go back to the country afterward.

"Larrell's blue team members were his casket bearers. I helped fold the flag that covered his casket with tears flowing, cascading down my face. I still sometimes cry.

"Larrell K. Smith, Sergeant, Los Angeles County Sheriff's Department, Tactical Sergeant at S.E.B., will forever be honored by our department. He is and always will be part of the S.W.A.T. Blue Team and will forever be honored in the hallowed halls of the Special Enforcement Bureau."

* * * * *

Steve Gibbs, 'The Gibber's,' account of this shooting is made even more horrifying to me when I think of the wife of a slain hero, just several months after her husband's death, brushing my hair. She knew the hardships I would face. She, in a motherly and loving way said I was so young, 'Just a baby.' Who was she saying it to? To me? To herself, or just out loud in the breeze? To me? A new deputy sheriff, not even out of the academy, sitting in a radio car who moments before was waiting to be ambushed…me, not knowing I too, in the not too distant future, would also become a member of the Red Dot Club.

Chapter 21

On Fire

Account of Paul Adams
California Highway Patrol

In 1965, I was working as a California Highway Patrol Officer, and I was assigned to motorcycles. On this particular day, my partner and I were riding side by side southbound on what is now the 5 Freeway. We were exiting at the Artesia off ramp, and we could see off to our right some cars pulled to the side of the road. This was a frontage road with a field behind it. The field had dried weeds in it about eight inches high or so.

A group of people was frantically waving their arms at us trying to get our attention. As we continued driving, we could see a car was in the field and there was a small fire next to the car.

We tore through the dried weeds on our motorcycles and parked about thirty-five feet from the car. We saw the car had hit a wooden tele-phone like pole. Apparently, the crash had snapped a power line, which we saw was in the field. We couldn't see the end of the line because a woman was lying on it.

The fire was small, only a foot or so high but the woman was engulfed in it from the waist down.

My partner was just a little bit ahead of me. He got off his motorcycle first and ran to the woman. My impression was he was going to smoth-er the fire with his body or try to pull her from the fire. He was just over her and started to bend over when he was snapped with a cracking of electricity and thrown upwards and back about six feet. He landed on his back and was having trouble getting up.

I could hear screams; it was the woman crying out in agony. "Please help me, help me!" Things were happening in seconds. When I saw my partner get thrown backward I knew there was a lot of voltage coming from where the woman was lying. I ran to my partner. The woman was screaming for help, and she was smoking. The smoke from her burning body was blowing right into me. She was slowly cooking alive, and I could smell her burning flesh. It was almost like being at a barbeque and smelling roasting pork.

After seeing what had happened to my partner, I knew I couldn't grab her. The fire was slowly catching the weeds on fire, and the fire was slowly spreading up her body. I was praying she would stop screaming. I was praying she would die. "Please God let her die!" I wanted her to die because she was so burned, and she was screaming so loudly, and so plaintively I almost couldn't stand it. I wanted her suffering to end. I couldn't imagine nor would I want anyone to suffer trying to recover from those injuries.

While I was running to my partner, I saw the flames had spread beneath the car. Whereas I had been worried about my partner maybe being killed, and how to save the woman, I was now terrified the gas tank would explode. I was thinking this while I ran to my partner. I was hoping the gas tank wouldn't explode and I wouldn't get electrocuted when I got to him.

I grabbed my partner from under his armpits. I lifted him and dragged him about twenty-five feet away from the car. He was out of it. His leather gloves had been burnt, and I had no idea what type of condition he was in. He was half conscious and half unconscious.

The woman was still screaming. I looked, and her clothes had burned off. Her buttocks had now split open from the fire. She was totally engulfed in flames.

After dragging my partner away, he kind of came back to life, but he was physically shaken.

There was a lot of refuse in the field. I looked around for a board so I could move the wire from under the woman, but I couldn't find anything.

It seemed like forever, but it was probably just a minute or a minute and a half after we arrived, but the woman's screams became less intense, and they finally stopped altogether.

The Buena Park Fire Department arrived and put the fire out. The woman was dead.

I felt so bad. I kept thinking as my partner did, what we could have done differently to save her? The only thing we could come up with was we might have gone to our first aid kit and taken a roll of gauze and thrown it to the other side of the wire. Then we could have both grabbed the ends of the gauze and pulled the wire out from under her.

The feeling you could have done more is always there. It's there even if you know there was nothing more you could have done.

Of course, there is no second chance. You only get one shot.

Apparently, what had happened was she hit the pole, which snapped the live wire. The wire landed by her left rear tire, which started a fire. She went to stamp it out but stepped on the wire. The electricity from the wire threw her to the ground, and she landed on the wire. She was getting shocked the whole time. The voltage from the wire was enough to incapacitate her, but not enough to kill her or knock her out or to keep her from feeling being burned alive.

It was just fucking horrible. I can still hear her screaming. I can still smell her burning. I can still see her blackened cracked skin. I guess I always will.

Chapter 22

More than a Red Dot...Much More

Account of Leonard Bacani
Santa Ana Police Department

Leonard was born in the Philippines and moved to Africa when he was a baby. But he has no accent, he is as American as anyone born in America. Looking at him you would not know his nationality.

By the time he was two years old, in the 60's, Leonard was living in the Rampart area of Los Angeles. This area has always been known as dangerous and violent. In some of the years in the 80's and 90's, it led the City of Los Angeles in murders. Here's his story through his eyes.

* * * * *

"When I went to elementary school, I had to walk several miles, or so it seemed, to school every day. It was dangerous. Even for a little kid. There were gangs everywhere. And there were stabbings.

"I think because I was so young, the gangs left me alone. I was lucky. But I saw it. I saw the gang fights, the guys getting jumped, guys getting robbed. This is just from walking to and from school. I was six years old, and kids my age were also getting robbed. By the time they were in third grade some of the kids were part of a gang. It was hard because they'd want to recruit you to be an associate or to just kick your ass. I remember walking by an alley and seeing all these guys running out. A guy was lying there. I found out later he had been stabbed. I have no idea if he died or not.

"When you are in Los Angeles and living in a rough neighborhood no one likes the cops. It's kind of strange because people from other areas understood the cops were there to help you. But where I grew up everyone had a goal. It was, 'Do something bad to the man. Take him out.' The attitude was, 'When I get old, I'm going to take him out.' There was an unexplainable hatred of cops, and it was passed down from their parents. It was generational. The majority of this attitude came from Hispanic gangs, and there was no shortage of them. They thought the cops were an oppressive organization whose sole purpose was to make you miserable and they needed to be stopped. This was in the late 60's early 70's. These criminals, these gang members hated cops. I think it's hard for someone who has been raised like that, someone who had generations of anti-cop influence, to come out of that environment.

"My mom was a maid working at the Beverly Hills Hotel. For a time when I was young, there were seven of us living in a one-bedroom apartment.

"There was a street, Benton Way, was part of my route to and from school. I walked it every day. This route crossed over the Hollywood Freeway. One day, I must have been about eight or nine years old, I stopped on the overpass and stuck my head through the bars looking down over the passing cars on the freeway below me. I started spitting and counting how long it took my spit to hit the cars below. Well someone must have called the cops because before you know it here comes a cop car. It stopped and out stepped this big old cop. I said to myself, 'Oh no here is the man.' Remember all my schoolmates hated the cops and told stories how they were mean and oppressive and should all be taken out. I hated them just because of who I thought they were and what my classmates said about them. The oppressors. I really believed they should all be taken out.

"This mountain of a man came up to me. He actually got down on his knees, and we talked eye to eye. He said, 'What are you doing? You're spitting at cars, huh.'

"I told him, yeah.

"And right there, eye to eye he said, 'How would you feel if you were in a car, with your dad driving, and someone spit on your car? You wouldn't like that, huh?'

"I said, 'No, I wouldn't.'

"And he asked me, 'So, do you think it's right you do it to other cars?'

"'Gosh I guess not.' I answered. He never scolded me. I had a lot of respect for him for coming down to my level and speaking to me like a human being. He showed me, kind of in a loving way, my mistake. That made a huge impact on me. That one contact changed my whole way of thinking about police. I no longer thought like my classmates. I wanted to have a job where I could do something to help people. That one incident, that one interaction was that powerful.

"So, in high school, they asked me, 'What do you want to do?'

"I said, 'I want to help people.'

"They started showing me the different jobs I could have where I could help people. I decided I wanted to be a social worker. When I graduated, I took college classes in social sciences. Well wouldn't you know it, a bunch of cops was in my class. They started telling me how exciting it was to be a cop. They were telling me their war stories, and then they said, 'We actually get paid more than social workers.'

"I looked at him and said, 'You're kidding!'

"But then I thought about it. 'I need a bachelor's degree to be a social worker. I don't need that to be a cop. Right then, I decided to be a cop. I changed my major to police science and then enrolled myself in the Fullerton College Reserve Police Academy. I was 18 years old. After I graduated, I applied with several police agencies. I then accepted a position with the Monterey Park Police Department as a Reserve Police Officer. I was only 19 years old and working patrol.

"I remember my partner and I did a bar check. I had never been in a bar before. I was underage. I remember looking at my partner and asking if I was allowed to be in there.

"He said, 'Yeah, you're on duty, man.'

"We walked in, and someone said, 'Sir, sir, excuse me, sir.' I looked around and realized the man was speaking to me. It was the first time I had ever been called sir. I was trying to act all mature and everything, and here I was a baby-faced 19-year-old.

"I did a couple of years with Monterey Park Police Department then got hired by the Santa Ana Police Department. After all those years I remembered the impact that officer made on the little boy spitting on the cars, and I wanted to be that person. I still wanted to make a positive difference in people's lives. That incident dictated how I treated people and how I did police work for the rest of my career. I felt if you treated everyone with respect, even if they weren't treating you with respect, you were doing the right thing.

"After getting off probation at the Santa Ana Police Department, I worked as a field investigator. This is a position where, while working in a radio car, you were assigned cases and did follow up on workable information. It was a precursor to detective work. I was also a field training officer. I worked a special enforcement detail called directed enforcement. Santa Ana had four areas, and each had their own directed enforcement team. I worked as a vice detective, involving crimes with hookers, lewd conduct in public, gambling, and bar checks. I was a drug recognition expert. Then I became a drug recognition expert instructor.

"Santa Ana had every drug category you could imagine. On top of the normal stuff like P.C.P., marijuana or cocaine, we also had the exotic drugs like L.S.D. and psilocybin.

"In the 60's, Santa Ana was largely a white community. Then it became largely a black community. It later became a sanctuary city. A large community of illegal Hispanics moved in mostly because they knew they would not be harassed for being in the country illegally. One of the police chiefs believed in the concept of the sanctuary city and did not want to help federal law enforcement, (Immigration), with their goals. So consequently, we did not notify immigration when we arrested illegal aliens. It was out of control with crime when I got there in the 80's. I would say the Hispanic gangs committed 90 percent of the crime.

"With a police force of around 300 sworn officers, it was not uncommon to have an officer involved in a shooting every week.

"A big reason for the rampant shootings was these illegals grew up in little ranches in the countryside. They were used to handling their own problems. There were no police in their areas, and the only way they knew to settle their problems or differences was to shoot the offender. Another issue was during New Year's Eve they would shoot in the air. We always had people shot from stray bullets coming down from people shooting in the air.

"On top of the shootings, and all mixed up in this was the fact Santa Ana was a major drug pipeline in California and for the rest of the United States. When the drugs came across the border, they would make their way to Santa Ana to get distributed throughout the country. It was a major hub. The major drugs coming into Santa Ana would be black tar heroin and cocaine. They also had local people manufacturing P.C.P. So, there would be drug deals, drug rip-offs, shootings and all the crime went along with the drug trade. I remember one night we had five murders. That's different than five shootings, that's five separate killings from people getting shot. And they were all unrelated to each other. I don't know how true it is, but I was told at one-point Santa Ana had 80 percent of all the gangs in Orange County.

"It was a dangerous area. Most nights we ran from one priority one call to another. We were handling constant in-progress crimes, such as drive-by shootings, robberies, officer needs help calls, pursuits, etc. One night in particular, after shift, after going to shootings and stabbings, and all sorts of just general mayhem calls all night, a bunch of us were standing by the gun locker where we checked in our shotguns. We were high fiving each other, congratulating ourselves, ecstatic and euphoric, that we didn't get killed, that we made it through the shift. If you worked there, you became a veteran in a short period of time.

"One evening I was driving westbound on 17th street west of Bristol in my radio car. My windows were down like all good street cops. And I heard off to my right, *'POW, POW, POW, POW, POW!!!'*

"In an instant, I heard bullets, the wind of the bullets, the concussion if you will of the bullets passing by my face. It sounded like bumble bees, bzzzz, bzzzz, bzzzz, passing my face. And I could feel the air being displaced by the passing bullets as they whizzed by. While I was feeling the buzzing air of the bullets, I could hear gunshots going off, *POW, POW, POW, POW, POW.* It was about seven shots. The bullets passed through the open passenger window to my open driver's window, and they all missed my head. One or more of the bullets hit my right front tire and flattened it.

"I put that one out," (transmitted the incident on the radio).

I looked at Leonard, and he was still speaking. He was going on to the next subject. But I was thinking about what he had just said, that he had, "Put that one out." Then it dawned on me. There were multiple shootings he was involved in.

"Wait," I said. "You had other shots fired at you that you didn't broadcast?"

"Yeah."

"Hang on, man, finish this story first." I wanted him to stop before he went into another horrific tale.

"Oh, okay. I advised I was getting shot at and I was driving out of the kill zone, out of the area. I set up a perimeter. We did a search, but we never found the guy. We couldn't find the bullet that flattened the tire. It wasn't in the tire. After the containment, and after we couldn't find the suspect, I called a tow truck and changed the tire. I then put myself back in service.

"I went to dispatch, and I remember a dispatcher asking me. 'How do you feel, aren't you stressed?' I said, 'Yeah but I got to go back to work.'

"And you didn't broadcast the other one?" I asked.

"Oh, that one, it was either fourth of July or New Year's Eve and everyone, all us cops were getting shots fired calls. It was just too many units, too many radio cars taking fire, getting shots fired calls in different parts of the city. The radio traffic was too busy with emergency traffic with simultaneous emergencies. Everyone was tied rolling code three and helping everyone else. I didn't want to add to the cluster and create another emergency, so I just drove out of the kill zone and never let anyone know."

"Yeah, but what happened?"

"Nothing I went back to work," he replied cold as ice.

"No, I mean how did the shooting go down?"

"I was just driving down the street, and I heard a shot. The bullet passed through the open front passenger and driver windows in front of my head. I just kept driving. No one could help me. Everyone was busy helping everyone else who was also getting shot at.

"It was a sanctuary city like I said. The Hispanic gangs were everywhere, drugs were everywhere. And like I said, one night we had five separate homicides. None of which were related to each other."

* * * * *

"November 22, 1997, on a Saturday. It was just before the sun was going down, about 4:30 or 5:00. It was a long time ago…a lifetime ago… but not that long ago.

"It was really busy. I got the call to assist Children's Services, but the call was out of my patrol area. It was in the north end, but it was so busy all the north end units were tied up on other calls. So, they had me respond to handle it even though it was out of my service area. My backup unit was a sergeant.

"The call came out as, 'Meet social services. They have a warrant to seize an infant child from their mother and to place the child in protective custody.'

"My sergeant and I met the social worker several blocks away from the house, and she told us what was going on. The background was the mother was paranoid/schizophrenic and had recently given birth to a premature baby. Since the baby was premature, he had special needs. There was a nurse and a social worker that went to the house every day to monitor the baby and make sure he was being cared for properly. The mother was not right in the mind. She believed the nurse and the social worker wanted to harm her baby. The day before, the mother decided she would not allow the social worker in the house, so they obtained a warrant to take the infant into protective custody.

"We went to the house and knocked on the door, but the mother wouldn't open up. We knew she was there and we kept knocking. Finally, after about five minutes, she opened the door. The door opened, and we were inside. A very short greeting to the mother and we were being led upstairs by the social worker to the baby's room. It was the social worker, me, the mother, and the sergeant.

"When we got to the room I saw the baby in the crib off to my left. The baby appeared to be okay, although we hadn't picked him up yet. I was then punched in the chest. I had been punched before, and this was certainly a hard punch, but nothing more than I had experienced before.

"I looked up and there off to my right was the mother facing me. In her hand was a blade, a butcher knife and it was coming down toward me. She was going to plunge the blade in my face. Instinctively I put my hands up and caught her wrist. I violently twisted her wrist and threw my leg out and tripped her to the ground. She was a three-hundred-pound woman, but with the instant violence of my action, I put her down quickly and easily. After she was on the ground, I wrestled the butcher knife from her grip and threw it. From the time, I felt the punch to the time I threw her to the ground, to the time I got the knife out of her hand was about three seconds.

"Because the woman was so big, it took both the sergeant and me to get her arms behind her back to get her handcuffed. She was completely silent.

"When I stood up I noticed my sergeant looking at me. He had a weird look on his face.

"He asked, 'Are you hit?'

"And I thought to myself why is he looking at me like that?' I looked down, and I saw a hole in my uniform shirt in my upper left chest. I saw a slow, ever-widening brown, red fluid spreading from the hole outward across my uniform, across my chest. I said, 'Yeah.'

"I had seen the blade when it was coming down and when I disarmed the woman. It was a ten-inch long butcher knife, and the blade was three inches wide. Apparently, it had gone in my chest most of the way. The blade just missed my bulletproof vest.

"The social worker got a towel. I was starting to bleed. She helped me get the towel on my chest, and they were laying me down. My sergeant was visibly upset, a little panicked. After I laid down my sergeant started talking on the radio, and he couldn't get out who he was, his unit identifier, where we were, what happened and what we needed. Robert, we put out stuff on the air all day long. Day after day, week after week, month after month, and year after year. Now he was having trouble transmitting basic information, stuff you shouldn't have to think about.

"I was lying on the floor, and I was putting pressure on my chest holding a white towel. I told the Sergeant 'They already know where we are, say 10-33 officer down, he's been stabbed in the chest, roll paramedics.' I was telling him what to say, but it was not coming out. The sergeant was mumbling and almost incoherent while transmitting.

"I remember units saying they were responding. The social worker had taken the baby out of the room. I was lying on the floor with the mother who was face down and handcuffed.

"I remember units arriving. The Santa Ana Fire Department Paramedics saw me, and they said, 'Forget about the gurney!' And they put their arms under my armpits and my feet and picked me up and carried me down the stairs.

"When we got downstairs they cut away my shirt and took off my vest. They loaded me onto a gurney.

"I looked down. There was no towel or shirt or vest to hide the wound. And I said to myself, 'Wow man, that's in the chest, close to the heart.' I was having shortness of breath. I knew at least one of my lungs had been punctured and was filling up with blood. I had seen the knife. It was ten inches long. I wondered how deep the butcher knife had gone in. I wondered what else had been punctured or cut. I wondered if I had been stabbed through the heart or a major artery. I knew I was bleeding, but I was wondering how badly I was bleeding inside my chest. I knew if a major artery had been cut or my heart stabbed, no one in the ambulance could save me.

"Every moment that went by was making it more and more difficult to breathe. I seriously thought I might die. I wasn't panicked, but I was worried I would die. I had young kids. I thought of them without a father. It didn't look good. The paramedics lowered the back of the gurney so instead of me sitting up, I was now laying down. When they did that, I couldn't breathe at all. I got it out, 'I can't breathe. It hurts.'

"Somehow lying down brought on a lot of pain in addition to not being able to breathe. 'Bring me back up,' I gasped. It was hard to speak.

"They brought me back up to basically a semi-sitting position and loaded me onto the ambulance.

"I am a Christian. I had accepted Jesus as my savior, and I knew where I was going. So, I was worried, but I had peace because I knew where I was going. So, I said to myself, 'Okay if I die, I know where I'm going.'

"So, besides the driver in the front, there was me on the gurney, a paramedic in front of me and a paramedic behind him. The only one I could see was the paramedic in front of me.

"I was still thinking, 'This doesn't look good. I'm going to die.'

"Things got fuzzy. My vision got fuzzy. I looked at the paramedic in front of me, and he had a worried look on his face. I knew this paramedic. I had been on numerous calls with him over the years, and I had never seen that worried look, that, Oh, shit! worried look on his face before. His look said he thought I was going to die.

"As I was looking at him, I instantly went to another place. Not physically but I should say I went to another place spiritually. I went to the presence of God. So, I was in two places at the same time. The one place was physically in the ambulance. The other place was spiritual, in the presence of God, my Creator. But it was still me. I was in two places at once. I was fully conscious. Fully aware. It was real. I had no fear. No apprehension. I was in two places living fully aware of both places at the same time. My time in the ambulance was normal human time. The other place had no time constraints.

"I was in a theater with the Lord. We sat in a theater together. I did not see the Lord's face, but I knew he was sitting next to me. We watched the screen in front of us. In a split second, I was in this physical state; I relived my life with God in the spiritual state. It was my life. My whole life. Everything I ever did. Everything I ever said was displayed. Everything I ever smelled. Everything I ever touched. Everything I ever tasted. All my behaviors. Fun times, sad times, all of it. All my conversations were replayed before me. I saw my whole life from beginning to end in the real-time I had lived it. Imagine seeing everything in your entire life. It's like an eternity. I was embarrassed by some of the things I said. I was embarrassed by some of the things I did. I had to face them. I had regrets because my maker was with me watching these things I had done. I relived my mother holding me as a baby and how good it felt for her to hold me. I relived this memory, but I couldn't even talk yet, and I was standing on a chair. While this was going on the Lord and I were talking to each other and discussing my life.

"I said, 'I'm okay with this Lord. If you want to take me, I'm okay with it.'

"While all this was going on, I saw the paramedic with a worried look on his face at the same time as I was with the Lord. Now, remember there was another paramedic behind the paramedic in front of me. As I was looking at the paramedic in front of me, I could see the paramedic behind him. This was physically impossible. I was on a gurney. The paramedic in front of me was blocking out the view of the second paramedic. But I could see him and everything he was doing. I could see him going through their paramedic equipment in the ambulance, and my view of him was from above the head of the first paramedic looking downward. The second paramedic was getting the paddles from the heart defibrillator, and he was working at a furious pace. So, while this was going on, I was reliving my life with the Lord.

"After telling the Lord I was okay with Him taking me, I thought of my three daughters. They were really young. I got really sad for them. I thought and said to Him, 'How sad they won't have a father help to raise and guide them. They won't have a father to see them graduate from high school. They won't have a father to walk them down the aisle when they get married.'

"As I was thinking and saying this to the Lord, I watched both paramedics feverishly working to save me. The look on the face of the paramedic who was in front of me changed. His worried look went away. A look of relief came over his face. At the same time, the second paramedic's furious pace relaxed, and he calmed to a normal working pace. Something changed.

"I have an explanation.

"God spared me. He spared me because my purpose on earth was not finished."

* * * * *

"My middle daughter got married a few months ago. She wrote something to me on a plaque. She wrote, 'Of all the walks we have had, this one was the best.' She was referring to me walking her down the aisle.

"I realized one of the reasons God spared me was to walk her down the aisle. And it was one of the things I said to God. It was right after I said this to God the paramedics relaxed.

"I rehashed this at the wedding during my toast to my daughter and said God has blessed and ordained this marriage."

* * * * *

"I got to the hospital. Thoracentesis is the name of the procedure to remove fluid from the space between the lungs and the chest wall. My lung had collapsed, and blood was filling the space between the lung and the chest wall. A needle or sometimes a plastic catheter is inserted through the ribs and drains the blood out. They said I should have been in the hospital for at least five days to two weeks. I was out in two days. A miracle? I believe it was divine intervention. I have no other explanation. I had 97 percent oxygen absorption. Impossible? That's about as good as it gets.

"About six years ago during a family gathering, I learned something that happened during my emergency operation. My family had been waiting in the emergency room when the doctor came out to brief them on my condition. During the gathering, my sister said, 'Do you guys remember when Leonard got stabbed? Remember the doctor came out and told us they had to resuscitate Leonard three times on the operating table?'

"'What!' I said. 'I died?'

"My sister said, 'Yeah they had to bring you back three times!'

"'You guys never told me that!' They never told me I had died. I never knew until the family gathering about six years ago. Leonard looked at me with wonder, as if he realized he was brought back from death.

* * * * *

"An investigation revealed the lady who stabbed me didn't answer the door right away for a reason. During the interview with police investigators, the lady said she saw the social worker and the police knocking at her door and went to the kitchen and got the biggest butcher knife she could find. She went upstairs and put the knife inside a shopping bag in the baby's room and placed the shopping bag next to the baby's crib. She then came and answered the door. She intended to kill the social worker and the police officers so they would not take her baby.

"She was found to be legally insane and was not responsible for her actions. She could not be held criminally liable. She was sent to a mental institution.

"I don't know if it is true, but I heard ten years after the incident she was declared to be cured or at least well enough and is now back, released into society.

* * * * *

"I will always remember my ride to the hospital. I had my radio on. I could hear the officers on the radio blocking all the intersections, so we didn't have to slow down. As we were driving, I had a front row seat looking out of the back window of the ambulance. As we passed all the intersections, I could see the officers stopping traffic in all directions so we could go through without having to slow down. After we got through the intersection, the officers would get into their cars and fall in behind us. The procession got bigger and bigger as we passed the intersections, and I could see all the beautiful red and blue lights following us. All the cops, all my brothers, and sisters were there taking care of me and showing me their support. And the sirens declared the unbreakable bond and love I was, and will always be a part of. The thin blue line!

* * * * *

Leonard Bacani is medically retired from the Santa Ana Police Department. He received the Purple Heart because of the injuries he sustained on the evening of November 22, 1997.

Chapter 23

A Senseless Death

Account of Robert Rangel
Los Angeles County Sheriff' Department

In 1987, my partner and I worked the West Hollywood Special Problems Unit. Our main purpose was to stem the illegal activities on the east side of the city. Santa Monica Blvd from about Fairfax Ave. to La Brea Ave. was rife with street walking male prostitutes and sometimes female prostitutes. This was no secret. Men came from all over, from other countries sometimes, to meet up with the streetwalkers. This was a seedy area.

We arrested many young men and women for a variety of reasons. The most common arrest we made was drug-related, mostly, "for under the influence of methamphetamine." This was the drug of choice for the streetwalkers. Everyone we arrested for under the influence, who gave us a urine sample, came back as positive for having "Meth" in his or her system.

A favorite hangout for the undesirables was a hamburger stand named, "Oki Dogs." Oki Dogs was located at Santa Monica Blvd and Vista St. This was the heart of the area where the drag queens and male prostitutes congregated, (Oki Dogs is no longer there). The food was cheap, and the prostitutes and drag queens hung out with each other and sold dope and ate cheap food.

We Los Angeles County Deputy Sheriffs who worked at West Hollywood knew this place to be a cherry patch, meaning you could make an easy, quick arrest there.

My partner and I frequently drove through the Oki Dog parking lot or walked through the joint to have a look see.

One day we saw a young girl there who we hadn't seen before. She was pretty and innocent looking with that fresh look about her. She turned out to be 14 years old. She was blond with braces.

We were always on the lookout for new faces, especially young innocent looking boys, and girls. The reason for this was many young people with problems at home would come to Los Angeles to become movie stars. They were mostly runaways. It didn't take them long to figure out they might be the best-looking person in their hometown, but in Hollywood, their looks were a dime a dozen. Once in Los Angeles, they had no other way to survive but by selling their bodies. If they were listed as runaways, in other words, underage and listed as missing, we tried to identify them as soon as possible and get them off the streets.

We contacted this young girl and learned her name was Michelle. After first contacting Michelle, another young teenage girl, Evelyn, came up and identified Michelle as her friend and schoolmate. We knew Evelyn from earlier contacts with her.

Knowing Evelyn was in junior high school and now knowing Michelle was also, my partner and I told them to stop going to Oki Dog. Of course, we had no power to enforce our demand. They were not doing anything illegal. The girls challenged us.

"We can come here. We're not doing anything wrong. These are our friends. You're not our parents. You can't tell us what to do."

Actually, we had a pretty good relationship with Evelyn. We sometimes stopped our unmarked radio car when she was walking just to say hello and see how she was doing.

Over the next several months we would sometimes see Michelle and Evelyn hanging out at Oki Dog. When we could, we would talk to them and sometimes almost plead with them to stop hanging out at the place.

One shift, it was about midnight, a fellow deputy stopped a stolen car. The deputy was holding multiple people inside at gunpoint. My partner and I drove red lights and siren to back him up. When we and other units got there, we started doing our thing. We got each occupant out of the car one by one. The last person out of the car was Michelle.

My partner and I were heartbroken. I chewed her out. Instead of coming around and admitting she was hanging out with the wrong crowd she again defended herself saying these were not bad people and they were her friends.

Fast forward three months or so. My partner and I were driving around in our plain car during the day. We saw Evelyn walking and pulled over to say hello. I think we both realized we had not seen either her or Michelle for a while.

Without getting out of our car I said, "Hi Evelyn, where's Michelle?"

She gave me a look of death, "STOP FUCKING WITH ME!"

Now she had never spoken to us like this since we had known her. I was perplexed. "Evelyn, what's wrong?

She snapped and barked at us, "You know!"

I looked at my partner then back at her, "Know what?"

"FUCK YOU, YOU KNOW!!!"

I was worried. I had this heavy sense of doom come over me. I asked her in a very soft voice, "Evelyn I don't know what you are talking about. I know what? What are you talking about?"

She looked at me, and it's as if she now believed me. "You really don't know do you?"

"No, what is it," my response was a near whisper.

"She's dead."

Instantly I was fighting not to cry. I swallowed hard and looked down and looked away from Evelyn.

"They raped and sodomized her for days. Then they suffocated her in a plastic bag and chopped her up and threw her down a hill in different plastic bags."

Things got fuzzy. I mean my vision kind of went away a bit, and my hearing was almost gone. The next thing I knew the car was moving. My partner was driving down the street. I was heartbroken and fighting not to bawl. I knew if I started I would not be able to stop. I tried to push what Evelyn had told me from my mind, and I concentrated on the wind hitting my face and pushing the vision of Michelle's face from my thoughts.

About fifteen minutes went by. My partner spoke first. "Bobby, I almost started crying."

I still couldn't speak. I could feel my partner's gaze upon me. I couldn't meet his eyes and instead looked out of the window. I nodded my head up and down in acknowledgment.

I remember her and second guess why I didn't get her address and go talk to her parents. I think maybe if I did just a little more I could have saved her.

It's a demon that never goes away, and I will live with it the rest of my life.

Chapter 24

The Piano Mover

Account of Chris Barrett
El Segundo Police Department

"Sick kids, dead kids, dying kids, all this other stuff, you're going down an alley, and you don't know if you are going to run into a pill head with a gun. He goes through the whole thing. In probably less than two minutes, Jack Webb, the famous actor from the television show *Dragnet* nails police work.

"Just like Stacy in your first book, that was me. I watched all the shows. The original *Dragnet. Adam 12. Police Story.*"

* * * * *

Chris and I were sitting in his living room. He was referring to Stacy Lim's account of what made her want to be a police officer in book one of The Red Dot Club *series.*

* * * * *

"Robert, I grew up on those shows. I didn't come from a law enforcement family. The closest I had to relatives who worked in law enforcement was my grandmother who had two brothers who were federal revenue officers in the 1920's. Both of them were killed in the line of duty, one in Tennessee and the other in Kentucky. One of them was run off the road, and the other was shot. They died before I was born.

"I was born in Van Nuys. My dad owned a furniture moving company, and I started out working at a young age moving furniture. Dad started me off easy. I had to move pillows from the sofas and chairs, but I very soon moved up the ranks, and in several short years, I graduated to moving pianos.

"We lived in a dinky little house in Brentwood, just about a block from where Nicole Simpson was killed. When I turned seven, we moved to the Pacific Palisades. I was living the southern California life in the 50's. I walked to the park to play baseball, and we went barefoot. Our feet looked like the bottoms of shoes when I was a kid."

Chris and I busted out laughing.

Chris then continued, "Laurel and Hardy did this one movie where they are moving a piano up these stairs. They move the piano up the stairs, and then they lose it, and it runs them over as it rolls down the stairs. Back and forth the piano goes.

"Well, this one day we had to move an electric grand piano. It is the biggest, heaviest piano I ever moved. It had to go up a steep driveway then up these wooden stairs to the wooden porch at the front of the house. We got it up the driveway and started moving it up the stairs. I was nine years old at the time, and I was at the top of the stairs with my brother, who was a year older than me, and we were holding a rope tied to a pulley, which was attached to the piano. My dad and some workers were below the piano pushing it up. When the piano was in the middle of the staircase, halfway up, we heard a loud creaking noise. The staircase was going to break. The guys helping my dad panicked and ran and left my dad alone below the piano. So, it was just the three of us. My brother and I were on top holding the rope, and my dad was below pushing against the piano. I knew the stairs were going to break, but my dad was under that piano. I wasn't letting go of that rope. I was going to be pulled through that pulley before I would let go. My brother and my dad and I were together, and if the stairs crashed we would die together, I had made up my mind.

"My mom was at this job and saw what was happening. My dad was beneath the piano holding it on his back. Her two sons were holding the rope at the top of the stairs, and if this thing went, we would be pulled up the rope and into the pulley. She started screaming at the guys that ran away. The men came back, and we finally got the piano up the stairs and set it up."

I looked at Chris and he had a Lee Marvin steel to his eyes, and his jaw was set. This guy was for real.

"I played football in high school. I was quick, and I was tough, and I hit hard. I played the middle guard, but I messed up my knee. In addition to working with my dad, I was cutting grass and working construction with my friend's dad I was growing up with. I also worked at Kentucky Fried Chicken when I was a senior in high school and during my first year in college.

"At some point my dad wanted me to take over the moving business. I had had enough of that, and I said, 'Thanks, but no thanks.' The war in Vietnam was going big time. I registered for selective service. Then I did something really stupid, I dropped some college classes. The next thing I knew Uncle Sam sent me a notice, 'Greetings, show up for your physical.'

"This thought entered my mind, 'They're not going to take me. I blew out my knee in high school football.'

"So, I reported to the Army induction center in downtown Los Angeles. We were doing our physicals, and there were about twenty of us guys. We were naked in a room waiting to get examined. Across the street was an office building with these windows and a bunch of office girls were there at the windows gawking at us.

"I got examined. I told them about my knee and showed them a stack of doctor's letters, and they said, 'You look good to me, you can walk, you can talk, you can carry a gun. Follow the yellow line.' I followed the yellow line, and I walked into this room, and there was this sign,

I read it, and I said, 'I do, I will. Amen.' There I was, I was in. I was twenty years old. It was May 5, 1970.

"That afternoon I was on a bus to Fort Ord. I got through basic training, and my knee was blown up to the size of a watermelon. They were like, 'Oh, that's too bad.' I was then sent to Texas to be trained as a field medic. One day my knee was really bad. I was limping all over the place. I went to see a doctor. He played around with it just a little and looked at me and said, 'Why are you in the army?' The next thing I knew I was out with an honorable discharge. It was October 26, 1970.

"I had been engaged to my wife at 19 years old in 1969. After I got out of the army, we got married in July 1971.

Chris said sarcastically, "I was back working for my dad, doing my favorite job."

"My wife was working as well, so we bought a little 800 square foot house. In 1974 the union representing the moving companies went on strike. My dad was non-union. One day he got a phone call, 'You need to take your son off the trucks, or something might happen to him.

"Now I was out of work, I had an infant son, and I thought, 'I've got to find a job that isn't going to leave me disabled with a bad back. I want to play with my son.' I thought of those Adam 12 and Dragnet shows and decided to get my knee operated on.

"After my knee healed, I applied with the Los Angeles Police Department. When I took the oral examination, there were three officers on the board. One officer, in particular, was this big huge guy. He was about six feet four inches tall and weighed about two hundred forty pounds. I was wearing my suit with a tie, and I was doing everything right, 'Yes sir, no sir.' During the interview, the big officer said something I disagreed with, and I told him so. He fired back at me. I fired back at him. This verbal exchange went on for a little while. The other two officers were watching this like they were at a tennis match. Then I caught myself. I realized what I was doing. OH, OH. I was arguing with one of the officers on my oral board. I knew then I was done. I did the best thing I could do, I said, 'Sir I guess we'll just have to agree to disagree.'

"We finished the oral and I got up to leave. I had blown this oral, big time.

"I was in a room with all these other guys who either had taken or were waiting to take their orals. A secretary was there. Someone would walk out to her and hand her a note. She would read the note then call one of the guys in the room up to her desk, 'Mr. Johnson.' Johnson walked to her desk, and she whispered, but we could all hear, 'I'm sorry, but you failed your oral.'

"This went on and on. It was like one guy out of ten got the thumbs up. Almost everyone was failing. I was sweating so much you could ring my coat out. I was watching all these guys failing, and I was thinking, 'You might as well just get up and leave, you know you blew it.'

"About the time I was ready to leave, here comes the big cop I had disagreed with. He slowly strode across the room to the secretary. Just as he hands her the note, he locked eyes with me and gave me a little smirk with mirth in his eyes.

"I was like, 'Shit, he's just rubbing it in.' Several seconds later he disappears.

"The secretary opened the note, 'Mr. Barrett.'

"I looked at her, her face was blank. I walked over to her; I was numb all over. When I got to the desk, she said, 'Mr. Barrett, congratulations, you passed your oral. Here's your score, out of 110 you got 105.'

"I was speechless, but I was on cloud nine. I was like, 'Yippee, I, Oh.'

"At the same time, I was testing with the L.A.P.D. I was also testing with the El Segundo Police Department. In 1976 El Segundo picked me up as a reserve officer. I went through the South Bay Reserve Police Academy and graduated in December of 1976.

"On August 1, 1977, I got hired as a regular full-time police officer for the El Segundo Police Department. El Segundo sent two of us to the Los Angeles County Sheriff's Academy in East Los Angeles. We were in class #186. One of my classmates had previously been a New Jersey cop. One day we were standing at attention in formation and being inspected. One of the drill instructors tapped on his ammunition pouch, and it tapped back. There was something in there. The drill instructor opened it up, and there was ammunition that had been there for God knows how long. It was green and deteriorating. He said, 'What is this shit?' Then he dropped the green moldy mess at the cadet's feet.

"The drill instructors ganged up and yelled at him asking him questions like, 'How are you going to shoot anyone with ammo like this? What are you going to do, kill them by throwing your gun at them? How can you shoot them with this, the bullets won't even go in the gun?'

"At the academy, there was a wall with plaques listing all the peace officers killed in the line of duty in Los Angeles County from the beginning of time. He spent the whole weekend at the wall copying down every letter from every plaque of everyone who had been killed. Lesson learned."

"They never let up on us. Look, man, if you went through an academy and you made it, you accomplished something. The Sheriff's academy was cut and dry, you either made it or you didn't. It either killed you, or you made it. They hit you with so many different things all at once. If you were not physically fit you would not be able to recover fast enough to keep up with all the things you had to learn.

"I understand. I would ultimately go through three academies plus boot camp. I hyperextended my back in week number five of the Los Angeles Sheriff's Academy, and because I got injured, I would have to leave and hopefully come back to another class. In those five weeks, we had already lost about a third of the class.

"After I healed up from my back injury some spots opened up at the Riverside County Sheriff's Academy. El Segundo decided to send three of us to this academy. There was myself and another guy who had broken his wrist in the Los Angeles County Sheriff's Academy learning weaponless defense drills, and a third guy who hadn't been through an academy yet. It was a totally different academy. The Riverside Academy grounds were like in a river bed with fire roads leading into the hills. The academy was on the Riverside County Maintenance facility. Both of the other guys I went through the Riverside Academy with became lifelong friends. Max Phipps retired as a captain with the El Segundo Police Department and Kim Ruppert retired as a sergeant with the Los Angeles County Sheriff's Department. He was a recipient of the Medal of Valor."

* * * * *

"I graduated the Riverside County Sheriff's Academy out of class number 69, on November 30, 1977, and started working as a police patrol officer with the El Segundo Police Department. Probation was a stressful time. My tactics were great. My ability to communicate with the public was great. I could drive. But I couldn't spell worth a shit. I knew it. They knew it. Everyone knew it. I was afraid I wouldn't pass probation because I couldn't spell. I got home one morning about three a.m. I was just crawling into bed when the phone rang. It was the watch sergeant. 'I'm not accepting this report. Come back to the station and fix it.'

"So, I got up and got dressed and went back to the station. I had to write a memo as to why my spelling was so bad and how I was going to correct it. This was about my hundredth billion memo while I was on training. I hated writing memos.

"I stayed there fixing my report for a couple of hours. But some of the guys were worse spellers than me. However, because of me, they implemented spelling tests in briefing. Tell me I wasn't hated. Aha-ha!!!"

Chris had a huge smile and a glint of joy remembering this.

"The biggest thing we had going on were drunks. We had some residential and vehicle burglaries. Homicides were rare. There was a lot of dope. The major part of the city is industrial and aerospace companies.

* * * * *

"In 1935, an El Segundo Officer was killed after being struck by a car while he was directing traffic. In 1950 an El Segundo Officer was shot. He died a year later as a result of this injury. In 1957 two El Segundo Officers were shot and killed in the line of duty in the same incident.

"Four officers had been killed in the line of duty in the history of the department. The attitude of the department was nothing bad happens in El Segundo. This is Mayberry. You'll put more people in jail with a pencil than you ever will with a gun.

"In El Segundo, the attitude was, 'Don't worry, nothing ever happens here.'

"If you asked the question, 'Hey! How about those four guys killed in the line of duty?' they would answer, 'But that was a long time ago.'

"If you said, 'But it did happen.'

"They would come back and say 'Yeah it did, but all that stuff you learned, you can throw half of it away. This is El Segundo.'

"I had this Rolodex file in my head. All the things I learned in my college courses, all the stuff I learned in the academy, all the officer survival stuff, all the criminal codes, all the vehicle codes were all in my head. Things like what is the difference between homicide and justifiable homicide. All the knowledge that cops have to have is phenomenal. I'm not just talking about the academic world. When you add the world of psychology, it becomes an unbelievable amount of information you need to know. Then add all the tactics and procedures. Society almost expects the cop to be schizophrenic. One second you have to be just like Superman and look like Superman with all your leather and buckles shining and the next minute you're dealing with the pedophiles, the dope dealers and the guys who would kill you just because. But don't dare say a cross word to anyone because now you are unprofessional. You are supposed to be a robot and not a robot. It is the job that takes the most varied sets of skills there is.

* * * * *

"On May 6, 1979, I worked the 9:00 p.m. to 7:30 a.m. shift. The swing shift units were off duty at 2:30 a.m. When those cars went off shift, there were two cars left covering the whole city. There was one two-man car and one single man car. I was working with a partner, Cliff, in the two-man car. Greg was working in the one-man car.

"It's now the Sunday morning after Cinco De Mayo.

"It was not lost on me the night before was Saturday, and with the holiday where everyone could be a Mexican celebrating.

"The weekend before, my wife and I had gone to the movies and had seen, *The Deer Hunter*. When I came out of the theater something said to me, 'You're going to be involved in something that's going to be hairy.' It was the first time I had this feeling.

"When the call came out we were at Sepulveda and El Segundo Blvd. It came out as a disturbance at a business involving a customer at the Target Bar, 221 Richmond St. We were a mile and a half away. It was now about 2:50 a.m. Another call came out almost at the same time on the other side of town about two and a half miles away. It was almost identical. This call came out as a disturbance, with two men arguing at a restaurant in the parking lot.

"It felt like someone got a hold of the front of my shirt and was telling me, 'This is it, this is it. This is the big thing that's coming. The hairy thing.'

"I sped to the Target Bar. The doors to the front of the bar are double doors and are recessed back about six feet from two side walls. The walls extend out toward the sidewalk at a forty-five-degree angle. As we pulled up, I saw the one-man unit, Greg, who was on the north side of the bar, getting out of his car. His car was angled toward the front door facing south. I pulled up on the south side of the bar facing north and angled my car toward the front door. I got out of the car and went to the side of the forty-five-degree angle wall and faced the front door. My partner got out of the car and stayed by the passenger side door of our car facing the bar's doors. We had the front of the bar contained. But there was no one else in the field. There was no one to cover the back door.

"The door opened, and a woman came out and yelled, 'He's got a gun!'

"Greg called her over and spoke with her. He had her sit in the back seat of the radio car. When the woman stepped out of the bar, the door didn't close all the way. It remained ajar. Greg went to the crack of the door and peeked into the bar.

"This scared the shit out of me. I mean there was a guy inside with a gun. I wanted to yell, 'Hey man don't do that!' but I was afraid the guy inside would hear me and shoot Greg. I gritted my teeth and held my breath and waited.

"Greg retreated to the wall on the north side of the bar, and we started yelling for Juan to come out."

I looked at Chris.

"Robert, that was his name, Juan.

"We learned from the woman this guy Juan was her boyfriend. She was the barmaid. Well throughout the night she was dancing with other people, and Juan didn't like it. I'm sure there was drinking involved. One thing led to another, and she told him to leave. He threatened her, and she got the gun they kept in the bar. The gun was a two-inch barrel five-shot .38 caliber revolver. Of course, he took it away from her, and she called the police.

"In the back of my mind, I knew we still had the other call to handle at the restaurant. I was thinking we had to handle this call so we could get to the other call.

"My partner got on the air, 'We need a supervisor, we need back up, we have a man with a gun.'

"It turned out one of the units, Mike, due to be off duty at 2:30 a.m. had a late arrest. He had a reserve with him. He left the reserve at the station to finish booking, and he rolled to back us up. I got on the radio and told him, 'We have the front secured, take the back.'

"We were a block and a half away from the police station. As I continued to communicate, I heard Mike arrive at the rear of the bar. He radioed everything was all right, code 4. It was going good. We now had the front, and the back of the bar contained. Right after Mike arrived, our sergeant arrived. He pulled behind Greg to the north side of the bar.

"He signaled to me to go to the back of the bar. I assume he did this because there were now three of us in the front and Mike was alone in the back.

"I sprinted south on Richmond. There is a parking lot several businesses down which cuts west into the alley behind the businesses. The alley has a drain in the middle of it thereby forming a shallow, "V," with the middle of the alley at the deep part. Apparently, this was designed to carry away rain. When I got to the alley, I started running north toward the rear of the bar. My flashlight was in my hand. My gun was in my holster. Remember it was 3:00 a.m. The alley was dark but had some low light from the streetlights at the ends of the alley. All in all, it was pretty dark.

"As I ran north there was a car parked in the middle of the alley facing north, away from me. It was behind the bar. Weird....it was 3:00 a.m., Why was it there? The bars had closed an hour before. It registered, but it didn't register.

"So here is what I had. Mike had arrived at the rear of the bar and had said it was code 4. There was another call of men arguing in the parking lot of another bar. But that was somewhere else. I did not see Mike or his radio car in the alley. But I knew he was there because he said he was. He also said everything was okay. I just hadn't seen him yet.

"A man was standing in the alley outside of the driver's side of the car. There was a woman sitting behind the wheel of the car. It was a two-door Oldsmobile.

"As I was running down the alley toward the man, he looked at me then turned away like he didn't see me. Weird. A cop was sprinting toward him in a dark alley at three in the morning, and he acted like nothing was wrong.

"Now, I was at the rear of the car. No Mike. I should have seen him by now. What the hell? It was getting weirder with each passing moment. I approached the rear of the car, and I pulled on the trunk to make sure no one was waiting in there, and it was locked. I was ten feet away from the man, and he was ignoring me. He knew I was coming and he had to have heard me. But he didn't look at me again. Where was Mike, where was his radio car?

"I thought he must be hiding in one of the recesses in the alley and I just hadn't spotted him yet. I thought he must just be hiding in the dark somewhere so if the guy came out of the back of the bar he wouldn't see him. I mean he said he was there and everything was okay. All this was going through my head while I was checking the car and moving up the passenger side.

"I said to myself, 'I'm going to get these people out of here. I don't want them involved in the shooting.'

"Yeah, I said I didn't want them involved in the shooting. I didn't know there was going to be a shooting. Why did I say that to myself?

"I was cautiously moving up the passenger side of the car. Remember this was a two-door car. When I got to the rear of the passenger side of the car I bent over to speak to the woman. I hadn't cleared the back seat of the car yet, I didn't know if someone was hiding there. I was concentrating on the man standing at her driver's door, he was acting very weird, too nonchalant, it was spooky, and I couldn't see Mike. Then out of the darkness from the front of the car I saw something move.

"Then I looked and saw movement at the front of the car. I saw him. Coming out from a crouching position, out of the darkness from the front of the car was a male Mexican. His right side was to me. He had a stocky build, and he was wearing a white collared shirt and a blue jean jacket over it. And there it was. He had a two-inch blue steel revolver was in his right hand.

"Juan.

"Time slowed to a stand-still. A second was like an hour. In my altered perception of time, he moved in what seemed like hours from the front of the car to the right front fender. He slowly stood from his crouching position and walked directly at me.

"It was like someone took a bucket full of thoughts and dumped them on me at the same time. 'Where's Mike? Even though I knew it had to be Juan, I questioned myself, who is this guy? Who is the guy standing by the car? How is he connected to this guy with the gun? He must be part of it. How is he part of it? Part of what? What is the woman doing? Why is she so still? She must see the guy with the gun, but she has no reaction. How is she connected to this? What about the other call? Why had Mike put out it was secure when there's a guy with a gun back here? In those two seconds, each of these questions were full on conversations I was having with myself.

"All this was going through my head like someone took all the information in a Rolodex and dumped it into my brain. I was trying to make sense of things. All these separate, distinct questions and thoughts I thought out separately and pondered as the man with the gun was slowly turning toward me.

"Milliseconds were minutes and seconds were hours now. I could see the man and the gun slowly turning to face me. He had cleared the fender and was now on the passenger side of the car.

"I had to do something. He had turned around the right front fender, and he was now facing me. He was ten feet away and coming straight toward me. The gun was at his waist pointed at me.

"Probably two seconds had now passed since I first saw Juan. I said to myself, 'Chris you've got to do something, this guy's going to shoot you.'

"There were a bunch of cars parked to my right, just off to the side of the alley. As fast as I could, in slow motion, I pivoted to my right to run then jumped behind the parked cars for cover. It was as if I was turning in knee-high mud. I was twisted and had raised my right foot to run when out of the corner of my left eye I saw the flash. Then there was a slow booooom.

"*OUCH*! and then I couldn't breathe. The impact was so great it just knocked and forced all the air out of my lungs. If you take a match and drag it across the striker on the side of the box, that's what the bullet felt like as it traveled around my body. It was a thousand mile an hour fast red-hot zip tearing through me. But as it zipped through my body it was also dragging, like it was dragging parts of my body through me, inside me. The bullet tore into my left side and hit a rib. It then deflected off the rib and spun inward and ripped through my spleen. It continued on and nicked my left lung. It kept going on its red-hot path and it jammed into a couple of vertebrae in my back and stopped. When my vertebrae stopped the bullet, it was as if I was getting shot again. It jarred me so hard I thought of a wall being hit by a sledgehammer, and the wall was my body.

"It felt like somebody hit me with a baseball bat. My legs weakened, but I was instantly pissed like I'd never been pissed before. Enraged is an understatement. I was beyond rage.

"You *MOTHERFUCKER!!!*" I was so enraged I wanted to kill him. I forced aside the pain as the words, 'I'm going to kill you,' burned in my mind.

"I pivoted to my left and faced him. He was still coming at me, and we were now face to face. Everything was still in slow motion. I threw myself at him, and we collided hard and down to the ground we went.

"He still had the gun in his right hand. We both fell together sideways. As I was going down terror threatened to grip me because I was sure the other guy was involved. I just knew he was going to come and kill me. But I couldn't see him. I didn't know where he was.

"When I landed, I landed on my holstered gun and broke my hip.

"I was confused and scared. How did I get to this point? I was still wondering things like where was Mike and who were these other people? If the girl wasn't involved why didn't she drive off? With the complete rage was also terror. How bad was I hurt? Was I dying? My mind was not accepting this was happening. I couldn't believe it was happening.

"We were face to face. I was partially lying on my right side, and he was lying on this left. I can see it now, he slowly brings his right hand with the gun to my face. I was looking at the barrel of the gun. Ever so slowly the cylinder of the gun rotated, he was squeezing the trigger. No matter what I did, I would be too late to stop this from happening. Despair and rage seized me. The cylinder rotated lining up a bullet with the barrel of the gun. I couldn't get my hands to the gun to stop this. They were too far away. And then it happened, I saw the hammer drop. The gun went click. The gun should have gone off, it should have fired…but it didn't. I should have been shot through the front of my head, but the bullet didn't fire. It didn't fire.

"All of the I can't believe this is happening stuff went out of the window. I finally admitted to myself, *'Chris this guy is really trying to kill you!'*

"With my left hand, I reached up and grabbed the cylinder together with the frame of the gun. Now the cylinder wouldn't turn, and he couldn't line up another bullet to fire the gun. When I grabbed the gun, he pulled back a little bit, I guess to free my grip, but we were face to face. He couldn't pull the gun away. I rolled a little to my right and bit him as hard as I could in his left upper chest. I bit him hard and deep. I was trying to take a chunk out of him.

"This made him pull away a little more. He twitched a bit. As we struggled we were both grunting, but no one was saying anything. We were struggling hard against each other.

"I reached down and unsnapped my holster, and I pulled out my gun. It was a .45 caliber Colt. I rolled it to the right, and from the hip, I pointed it directly at him. It was lined up with his pelvis and, BOOOM, the muzzle flash exploded, I fired. Everything was still going in slow motion, and things were taking forever.

"He felt that. I know because I saw him and felt his body jerk and shudder. The grip on his gun lessened. I rolled my gun a little bit more and pressed it against his chest. BOOOOM, another bright slow muzzle flash in the darkness. I had fired again.

"He still had the gun. I was still gripping it to keep him from shooting me in the head. He was not done yet. He was still fighting. We were still struggling and grunting as we fought. I was convinced he still wanted to kill me and if I didn't stop him, I would die.

"A little bit ago I was thinking I was going to die and it was more real now than ever. I had to kill him because if I didn't, he was going to kill me. I put my gun to the side of his head. I knew I had one chance, and it was to blow his brains out. I wanted to take his fucking head off. I had to, he wasn't stopping. Then I got my senses. I stopped. I thought, 'Chris if you do this it will look like you did it on purpose and you will have to write a memo.'

"I hated writing memos. HATED it. I had written a hundred billion of them. This is what actually went through my mind. I thought I was going to have to write a memo."

I looked at Chris. Whereas seconds ago, I was fighting not to cry, now I started laughing. Chris and I were both dying laughing. To think someone who is definitely trying to kill you, and then you stop from killing them because you will have to write a memo, was too much.

"We had landed and were fighting with our upper bodies partially under the rear of some parked cars. I had been thinking I would put my gun against his temple and shoot him, but I was afraid the bullet would go through him and puncture the car's gas tank. The memo thing was still on my mind, so to avoid having to write a memo, and to not hit a gas tank, I lowered the gun from the side of his head and fired through the left side of his cheek. The round went through his cheek and knocked out his teeth through the right side of his cheek. The round lodged in his shoulder. He grunted loud and hard. I heard the breath go out of him with that shot he started gurgling.

"That final shot stopped him. He stopped fighting.

"I ripped the gun out of his hands and tried to scoot away from him. The thought went through my mind he might have another weapon but then after looking at him I wasn't too worried about it, he looked like he was done.

"I slightly rolled to my left and looked for the guy who had been standing at the side of the car. I couldn't see him. The car was still there with the motor running. By now it seemed like hours and hours had gone by.

"I thought of the man and the woman still out there. I said to myself, 'You knew this guy was here in front of your car. You knew he had a gun. You didn't warn me. You have not driven away. You must be part of this, and you are coming to kill me. I thought of someone picking me up and taking me hostage like they did in the movie *The Onion Field*. I was almost defenseless. I was hurt really bad and was having trouble moving around. This woman and this man were real threats and in my mind wanted to kill me as much as the shooter had. I fired at the car. There was a loud boom, and a slow muzzle flash and my round went through the passenger door. The round went through the door and shattered the window. It passed into the woman who was still sitting behind the steering wheel. It went into her right triceps and under her right breast then lodged in her left breast.

"I heard her, she let out a high-pitched scream and drove off. As she drove away I fired three more times, boooom, muzzle flash, boooom, muzzle flash and then once again. Those rounds hit the car but missed her.

"I had now fired seven rounds. I don't know how I did it, but I accidentally ejected the eighth and last round out of my gun.

"I pinned the suspect's gun under my body and reloaded my empty gun. I was looking for the man who had been standing at the side of the car, but I could not see him.

"Time returned to normal.

"I later learned when the first shot went off the man took off running. The weird thing was he knew Juan. They were from the same village from Mexico.

"It turned out the man in the alley and the woman had just come back from a date. She was dropping him off at the rear of his hotel. As far as I know, she had nothing to do with the suspect.

"The guys at the front of the bar heard the shots. Cliff put it out, 'shots fired.'

"The dispatcher repeated, '10-4 shots fired, 3:01 and ten seconds.' She had announced the time of the incident when she said 3:01 and ten seconds. This was the time of the morning the incident happened. If you subtract the ten seconds for the shooting to have occurred, and for Cliff to put it out, the shooting happened at 3:01 in the morning. 301 is my serial number.

"I had put out on my radio I needed an ambulance. I had put out the make and model and the license number of the car I read as it drove away. Help was on the way. I felt like the wicked witch of the west in the movie, *The Wizard of Oz*, in the part when the house fell on her. I was done. All the physical, emotional, psychological things I had just gone through hit me. All the things had happened to me in the last ten seconds had just dropped in my lap, just like that house.

"I was lying there screaming, 'God, help me. Please, God help me. It hurts, it hurts.'

"Mike heard the shots. He was that close, and that far. He was at the rear of a bar, in the alley…one block away. He had gone to the wrong location.

"Mike sprinted the block to me. I don't know why he didn't drive, he ran. Other officers told me he was a basket case. I can only imagine he was wondering if he was the cause of me getting shot.

"I saw the sergeant weaving through parked cars in the alley working his way to me. When he got there, I looked at him and said, 'That's the guy who shot me, I shot at the car, here's the guy's gun, I'm going to take a break.

"All I could do at this point was hang in there. I closed my eyes, right there lying in the alley. I controlled my breathing and slowed down my heartbeat.

"Things were now black. My eyes were closed so there was no sight. There was no sound. Nothing. I mean zero. As soon as everything went black, it went white. Everything was white. The white started to envelop me and tried to take over my entire status. It felt like I was being dipped into a glass of warm milk. It was serene, calm, quiet, and peaceful with no worries. Nothing. Moments before I had been in excruciating pain. It was gone. It was Heaven.

"My mind split. My conscious mind went one way, and my subconscious mind went another way. My conscious mind was going to the left. About that time music started playing. It was not drums, nor a guitar nor a harp. It was indescribable. It was the most beautiful music I had ever heard. It was not blaring. It was not overwhelming. It was just there. I was like, 'WOW,' and I wanted to go there. I wanted to go to the subconscious side. It was whiter there and brighter there.

"All of a sudden my conscious mind shouted, 'HEY.'

"Then I calmly replied, 'Leave me alone.'

"I drifted a little more.

"My conscious mind yelled louder, *'HEY!'*

"I got pissed, *'WHAT?'*

"My conscious mind whispered, 'You're dying.'

"I realized, 'I'm dying.' I stopped, and I think I said it out loud, 'Am I going to die?'

"I have no doubt this all happened and is completely true. Right in front of me, a voice spoke. It sighed as it spoke and said with an exhale of breath, 'No.' This single word was spoken, the word, 'No,' and the finality of the tone, the unquestionable assuredness of how it was said, how it was expressed, told me, and I knew I wasn't going to die.

"I was back. The two sides of my mind came back together, and I was back. The paramedics were putting the pressure suit on me, and the excruciating pain was back. I was in the alley with lights and cops and paramedics and people telling me to hang in there. I laid in the alley for what seemed like hours before they would move me. It was because I was hurt so bad and bleeding so bad they were afraid to move me.

"The experience changed my whole perspective. I knew I wasn't going to die.

"After they got me in the ambulance we were flying down Imperial Highway to the hospital. The driver was screaming, *'Get the fuck out of the way, you, assholes!'*

"I got to the hospital, and I was having trouble breathing. I could hardly speak. I got the doctor. 'I…can't…breathe.'

"He replied, 'Of course not, you've got a hole in your lung.'

"They cleaned my skin at my ribs and took a scalpel and sliced me open. No anesthesia or nothing. They just cut me. Then they got a tube and slammed it into the side of my chest, not once, not twice, but three times. On the third slam, it went into my lung, and all this gore and blood came out and went on the floor. Immediately I could breathe and talk. My poor Chief was standing there in his bathrobe. He had rushed so fast to get to the hospital he hadn't even gotten dressed, and all this goop went all over the floor by his feet.

"As I was lying there, a nurse walked by pushing a gurney. I wasn't looking at the person on the gurney, I was looking at the nurse. She pushed the gurney against the wall and left. I looked at the gurney and it was the suspect, Juan!

"I woke up the whole hospital, screaming, '*YOU MOTHERFUCKER!!!*'

"I was trying to get up off of the emergency room table to get to him. I was going to kill him. I had completely lost it.

"Everyone came running in. 'What the hell is going on?'

"I pointed at the suspect, and the nurse went over and pulled the curtain closed. No one went back there. When no one went back to Juan to help him, I realized he was dead…and I felt bad.

"Then the words came to me, 'Thou shalt not kill.'

"The shot that killed him was the first one. The one in the pelvis. That round hit his femoral artery, and he bled to death. But not right away. That shot left him with enough energy to try to kill me. The other shots would not have killed him.

"Then I thought, you son of a bitch, you shot me, you shot my job, you shot my department, you shot law enforcement, you shot my family, you shot my kids, you shot my wife, you shot my mom and dad… FUCK YOU! I understood he had put me in the position where I had no choice but to do what I did. I then stopped feeling bad. It was all his fault. Happy trails, Juan.

"I awoke during my surgery. I remember hearing two doctors were arguing as to whether or not to take out my spleen. After seeing I was fidgeting, they realized I was conscious. They gave me more juice, and I went out. When I woke up, I learned the doctor who argued to take out my spleen had won.

* * * * *

Mrs. Barrett told her experience. "I was asleep when I got a call from the police department. I was told Chris had been in an altercation. To me, that means he had been in a fight. It didn't sound all that serious, but they wanted me to go to the hospital. We had two children. One was seven months old, and one was four years old.

"I told them I had two kids and I couldn't just leave.

"They were insistent. They asked me if I could get a neighbor to watch them and I said, 'You know it's four o'clock in the morning.' They told me they would send over an officer and his wife to watch them.

"It started dawning on me maybe this was serious. What did they mean by altercation?

"The officer and his wife arrived to watch the kids. When I went outside to the police car, I saw a priest who I knew from the neighborhood church sitting in the front seat of the car. I asked myself, 'How serious is this?' They wouldn't tell me anything on the way to the hospital, and I was scared to ask how serious it was.

"When I got to the hospital there were several officers there. I then found out Chris had been shot. They told me a team of doctors including a neurosurgeon were there to operate on him.

"I went from sleeping in my safe, warm bed to being called by the department, to having to go to the hospital and having officers come to watch the kids, to riding with a priest to the hospital, to we need to tell you Chris was shot, so he had to go in to emergency surgery in a short period of time. I was numb, and my head was spinning processing all this.

"The police chief arrived in his bathrobe, pajamas, and slippers. We all sat together, myself, the police chief and the other officers.

"After the surgery, and for the several following weeks, I was numb. I operated on autopilot. So many people brought us food and offered to babysit the kids. My parents helped so much with watching the kids. There was so much love from so many people.

"This was a major life-changing incident."

* * * * *

Chris Barrett received the Medal of Valor from the El Segundo Police Department for his actions in the early morning hours of May 6, 1979. It is the highest award bestowed upon its members.

He retired as a result of injuries he sustained from this shooting on July 11, 1980.

* * * * *

Chris Barrett has an unbelievably cheery disposition. He went on to have a full career with Raytheon. He has two children who he and his wife put through college. He has four grandchildren. He has been married for 46 years. He coaches and has coached softball since the early 1970's.

Imagine the horror of fighting face to face with your would-be killer. Lying in a dirty alley grasping for any advantage.

Imagine having to fight while experiencing the horrid pain of a red-hot zipper piece of lead has bounced around the inside of your body dragging pieces of flesh, bone, and organs as it goes, and wondering if you were going to die.

Imagine the terror of looking at a gun in your face, with the cylinder turning to line up a bullet to kill you and your arms are too far away to stop it.

Imagine while doing this, you are also worried about two other people you are convinced want to kill you.

Imagine…imagine…imagine all this, but then imagine the last act of your legs, forevermore, was to pivot and lunge at your would-be killer.

Imagine fighting for your life without them, without your legs, and wondering if you would ever use them again because they refused to work while you were fighting…

Imagine the strength and will of a little nine-year-old boy, a piano mover, who would not let go of a rope, even if it meant his death, now a man paralyzed and wheelchair-bound forever since 3:01 on the morning of May 6, 1979.

Imagine May 6, 1979, at 4:00 in the morning, an hour later, a young woman named Kathy Barrett, sitting in the hospital was told her husband might never walk again.

Imagine her steel will as when recalling that night in the hospital she told me, "You have to keep going," and her wedding vow she kept, "For better or for worse…"

Chris still holds the rope, and now Kathy holds it with him. I know they will never let go.

Those are heroes. They are my heroes.

Chapter 25

Hostage

Account of Paul Adams
California Highway Patrol

"I was out of the Air Force after serving in the Korean War. It was now 1957, and I had been a San Diego Police Officer for several years.

"On this particular day, I was working the three to eleven p.m. shift. Our normal shift ended with us coming to the station and typing out our reports before we went home. So just about fifteen minutes before eleven, there were nine of us at the station in the report writing/briefing room typing out reports. We were sitting at a long table, and our shift sergeant was sitting at the head of the table reading and approving reports.

"The briefing room was accessible to the public, meaning civilians could walk into the room from the front lobby. Technically this area was for police officers only, but anyone could open the door and would be inside. Whenever a civilian walked in, we asked them if we could direct them to where they wanted to go and shooed them out. Even though they could walk in the room, it was off limits to civilians.

"So, we were sitting writing our reports when this big, in shape, crew-cut, blond haired young man walked in. He walked to the wanted poster board and looked to be reading the posters. A couple of us cops looked at each other and mumbled to each other, 'Who is that guy?'

"Some of the guys answered, 'I don't know should we tell him to leave?'

"Then someone mentioned, and we remembered there was an academy class going on and he was probably one of the recruits. I mean he looked like a recruit; he was young and in shape, and he looked like he knew the station and belonged there. So, we ignored him.

"Well as quick as a blink he was beside the sergeant. He pulled the sergeant's revolver from his holster and slick as you please he had it cocked and pressed up against the sergeant's right temple.

"We all saw it happen, but the guy was so fast none of us had a chance in hell of reacting.

"The room was dead quiet. We were all caught with our pants down. Our sergeant was pale as a ghost and had a blank stare in his eyes.

"The man spoke, 'Don't any of you try and go for your guns or I'll shoot this guy.' His voice was steady, his hand was not shaking. He was definitely in control. He stared us all down. 'Now lower those gun belts to the floor. I'll be watching, and I'll shoot the guy if any of you try anything.' He was so calm and serious. I don't think any of us had a thought of going for our guns.

"The sergeant didn't say a word. I think in half a second he locked eyeballs with all of us. Through his now pale narrowed eyes, and with an almost imperceptible nod, he silently pleaded with us to do as we were told or he would be dead.

"We all lowered our gun belts to the floor. The man just stared us down and made sure we were doing what he told us to do. 'Now get your hands flat on the fucking table!' he ordered. *SHIT, MAN*, he was serious, and we did as we were told. No one doubted he would do as he said he would do.

"Now none of us had our guns. We were all sitting with our gun belts on the floor, and our sergeant had a cocked gun to his temple. We might as well have been sitting there with our pants and shorts around our ankles. What good was a cop without his gun? The sergeant was pale as a ghost. The man wasn't saying a lot. He wasn't making any demands.

"All of a sudden, there was a bang, an explosion, and almost instantaneously there was a second bang as the man violently jerked and shot into the ceiling. We had no fucking idea what had just happened except the man was now on the ground and had dropped the sergeant's gun. The sergeant was making a mad scramble to the floor to get his gun while we got to our guns. *WHAT THE FUCK JUST HAPPENED?* I expected to see blood and brains from my sergeant's head on the floor, but he wasn't hurt. We were stunned.

"It turned out Officer Rucker was coming to work for the eleven to seven a.m. shift. He walked by the window that faced into the report writing/briefing room. As he walked by he saw us sitting with our hands on the table and our gun belts on the floor. He saw a man with a cocked gun to our sergeant's head. He knew he had to take action.

"The glass window had wires running through it which formed little diamond shapes in it. Rucker took his gun and pressed it against the glass and made sure the barrel was inside of the diamond shape. He said he was afraid the wire might deflect the bullet and he would miss. He took aim and shot. This was the first explosion we heard. We later learned the bullet entered the suspect's left ribcage and went into his heart. He was dead soon after he hit the floor.

"The man was a Marine stationed at the Marine Corps Recruit Depot. He had received a *Dear John* letter from his girlfriend who no longer wanted to see him. We surmised he wanted to commit suicide by cop."

Chapter 26

At the Movies

Account of Ray Garcia and Scott O'Connor
El Segundo Police Department

Chris Barrett recommended I speak with Ray and Scott about their shooting. He said it was a one of a kind story. He was right, but then again each of these stories are one of a kind.

Ray is quite the storyteller. He is articulate and self-assured. He has a quick wit and a little edge to him I instantly liked.

* * * * *

"I was the middle brother. I was the one who was in always in trouble. I had that little extra something. The little extra push for excitement. That little extra something. Sometimes that is a great thing for a boy. Sometimes it is not. People who knew me as a kid always asked, 'How could you be a cop after the type of little boy you were?' I was always in trouble. Nothing too serious, but trouble nonetheless. It was that little extra something.

"My dad worked seven days a week for as long as I could remember. He had a newspaper rack route. Every morning, seven days a week he would wake up at 2:30 in the morning and would be stocking the Los Angeles Times newspapers in newspaper racks. After delivering the newspapers he worked all day as a machinist five-days a week, but the newspapers had to go in the newspaper racks seven days a week. He never missed a day. He never missed any of my, or my two brothers' baseball games or events. That was his life starting when I was a little kid and through high school. Once in a while, and not every year, he would take us camping. He busted his ass for us. My dad is a great man.

"After my dad got home from work, my mom would get in her little Toyota Corolla and deliver the late edition of the Los Angeles Times newspapers to her newspaper racks. She did that five days a week. My mom was also our baseball team mom. She never missed a game either.

"My dad was the peacemaker in the family. My mom was the disciplinarian. She didn't need a belt. Why concern herself with such trivial matters? Anything nearby would do. One day while my mom was doing laundry I did something wrong. The nearest thing she could get her hands on was a hanger. 'Wham,' she hit me. That one really hurt. So, I sulked away. This happened close to the time when my dad was due to come home from work.

"I was sitting on the back-porch sulking when he got home. He came and sat with me. 'Hey your mom is uptight, you did something wrong, and you got it. Are you okay?'

"I said, 'That…WOMAN…hit me with a hanger!'

"Oh, oh, that did it, I've never seen my dad so mad. He picked me up by my hair and whipped my ass. He said, 'If you ever refer to your mother again as, *That Woman*, I will end you!'

"I had a happy childhood. We lived in a cul-de-sac dead end street in Norwalk, California. We played baseball in the cul-de-sac almost every day because there was no traffic going by. Opposite the cul-de-sac, the street ran alongside a chain link fence bordering the 605 freeway. Since we were always playing in the street, we saw accidents on it all the time. This one day we were outside, and we heard a crash. There was this van flying off the freeway, and it landed upside down, the wheels were turning. We ran to the chain link fence at the end of the street, and a man was standing on the other side of the fence. I was wondering, 'How did this guy get out of a van that had just flown off the freeway and landed upside down?' Another time I saw this woman flying through the air toward the chain link fence. She flew off of the freeway about 200 feet. She hit the embankment and smashed into the chain link fence. She was alive and moaning.

"The paramedics arrived and cut the chain link fence and cut the woman's pants off and she was wearing dirty underwear. I remembered what my mom had always told us, 'No matter what you have to wear clean underwear!'

"Then I understood why my mom had told us this. You just never knew. I was ten years old."

* * * * *

In southern California where so many have accents from other countries, Scott is one of the few natural born Californians still around. He was born in Hawthorne, California.

"My mom raised me. Her three sisters were always around, and it was the family I knew. My grandparents lived in Westchester until the Los Angeles Airport took their house. However, when they moved, they didn't move far enough, and the airport took their home again.

"My grandparents finally moved to the Lennox area close to 104th St. and Burl Ave. In the late sixties when my grandparents moved there it was not a bad area. In the early eighties, my mom fell on some hard times, and we moved in with my grandparents. I was a normal, little white kid from a middle-class home who ended up in an all Mexican area. I was…the…only…white kid in the area. I got my ass kicked on a regular basis by the Mexicans. I had to fight to keep my bike, which was stolen, robbed from me on at least several occasions. When we first moved there, I was like, 'Who are these guys and why do they want to beat me up?'

Scott and I were laughing.

"I was a ten, eleven, and twelve-year-old kid. I would ride my bike to the Melo Burger stand at Inglewood and Century and have to watch who was following me there and on the way home so I wouldn't get robbed. I got jumped on more than one occasion and had to fight. They were the type of guys who hung out on the streets and probably became gang bangers. They would get me cornered, and the fight was on. I was the only white kid against a bunch of Mexicans, so it never went well."

I looked at Scott, "You mean they did not fight you one on one? They had no honor?"

Again, we were laughing.

"They took my money or took my bike or both. I remember after one of my bikes was stolen, I was riding down the street on another bike I had to buy, and some was kid riding my stolen bike. He was with a group of other guys. I wasn't about to go and try to get my bike back, hell no, I wasn't that dumb."

Still laughing I asked Scott, "Why did they hate you so much?"

"I don't know," he laughed, "Maybe I just had a better bike.

"I moved into the area as a very naïve white kid. It was a little scary when I went out in the neighborhood. But by the time I moved out of the neighborhood three years later, I knew how to check my six, and I was always acutely aware of my environment.

"As hard as it was, it was good for me. It was a good life lesson. It's a lesson my kids today do not have."

* * * * *

Ray was a natural born storyteller, and I was having a blast.

"I hung out with an edgy group of friends. Not really bad guys but not angels either. I had a friend growing up named Jimmie. He was about two or three years older than me. For whatever reason, my mom wasn't too fond of him. When he got his driver license, he started driving his mom's Cadillac, sometimes without her permission. I was about thirteen years old, and my mom said, 'Don't you ever get in that car with that kid, ever!'

"One day, Jimmie came to the house on his bike. 'Hey, Ray let's go bike riding.'

"'Oh, okay,' I said. I got on my bike, and away we went.

"Well, it turned out he had stuffed his bike in his mom's Cadillac and drove it to my house and parked it around the corner. He then got his bike out and rode it to my house. When we rode around the corner, there was the Cadillac. He said, 'Let's go for a ride.'

"We stuffed our bikes into the trunk, and away we went. We got onto Studebaker Road. We passed a deputy, and he looked at us. The deputy hung a U-turn and Jimmie made a left and hauled ass. Now we were in pursuit, but we are the ones being pursued.

"I was screaming at Jimmie, 'STOP,' and I was hitting him anywhere I could.

"He yelled back, 'I'm not stopping, I didn't do anything wrong,' and he stepped on it even more.

"Jimmie finally listened to me and stopped. I mean I was just a kid, and I was scared. It turned out a neighbor saw us putting the bikes in the trunk of the car and called 911 and said two guys were stealing bikes. The thing was they were our own bikes!

"Anyway, the deputy proned us out on the hot street and sidewalk. Of course, the deputy gave me a ride home in the backseat of his radio car.

He went and knocked on the door with me at his side. Mom answered. You don't want to know what mom swung at me when the deputy left."

* * * * *

Scott continued his life story.

"I'd been working since I was fourteen-years-old pumping gas at the Chevron Gas Station at Manchester Blvd and La Tijera Ave. I worked there until I was seventeen-years-old. I was the attendant guy who pumped your gas, cleaned your windshield, and checked your oil. We had these little cash drawers in the middle islands at the gas pumps, and the people just pulled up, and we took care of everything right there. So, after we would pump their gas, we took their money and gave them their change without needing to go into the building.

"I was robbed three different times at gunpoint, and I distinctly remember each time. The first time I got robbed I was fourteen-years-old. They didn't care I was this teenage kid working until ten at night after high school. I would go home, 'Mom I got robbed today!' and then I would tell her what happened.

"She would say, 'Holy SHIT, you're going to quit!'

"I would go back to the gas station and tell the boss, 'My mom says I have to quit.'

"And each time he offered me a 25 cent per hour raise, so each time I agreed to stay. Then I would have to go home and convince my mom it was okay and it would not happen again."

I looked at Scott; I had to ask. "Who robbed you?"

He laughed, "I don't know they were these black guys."

I was laughing, "So you had Mexicans who robbed you where you lived, and now you had blacks robbing you where you worked!"

Scott was laughing.

"Yeah, I rode the buses. It was called the Rapid Transit District bus, and there were always fights on the buses. So, from ten-years-old, I was getting robbed, beaten up and working, but I was going to Catholic Schools where none of these types of people, criminal types went."

* * * * *

Ray had me laughing.

"Now here's how I got my first car. A few years later I got into the car with Jimmie. He was driving, and we were stopped at a freeway off-ramp. I heard this loud semi-truck horn. I looked behind us, and a semi-truck rear-ended us. It had lost its brakes. I won some settlement money, and I used the money for a down payment for my first car.

"After I got my car, I lost my car. Here's how it happened. A friend of mine and I went to a liquor store. We gave this lady some money to buy us some beer. We got the beer and put it in the back seat of my Volkswagen Bug. The lady told me, 'Don't put the beer in the back, the cops will see it.'

"I thought, 'Get lost, we don't need your advice.' I mean we had the beer already so now she was just, 'buttin' in.

"Sure, as shit while I was driving down the street we got lit up by a cop to pull over. I told my friend, 'Cover the beer!'

"The only thing my friend had to cover the beer with was his t-shirt. My dumbass friend took off his t-shirt and covered the beer.

"Of course, the cops found the beer and bingo I was handcuffed, and lickety-split I was in the backseat of their radio car. Shit! I was still in high school. They kicked my friend and his t-shirt loose.

"As we were riding to the police station, another cop car pulled up next to the radio car we were in. The guys were talking how they would all soon be off duty, they would meet up, and have some cold beer to drink after work. Those fuckers were going to drink my beer!

"When we got to the station, they asked me where I lived, and I told them.

"They asked me if my parents were home and I told them, 'No.'

"They asked me where my parents were.

"I told them they were bowling.

"They asked me when they were going to be home. I knew what was going on. I was a juvenile; they had to release me to my parents. But I had heard them talking with the other officers they were going to meet up and drink my beer. They did not want to wait around until my parents got home.

"So, with this working in my devious mind, I told them they wouldn't be home for hours, maybe not until one or two in the morning.

"I saw the hateful and crestfallen look on their faces. I had them. They had to let me go or wait for my parents. They weren't going to wait three hours for my parents, they were off soon and had some cold beer to drink. I was so cool, I knew I was going to skate.

"I had them...or did I?

"It turned out they outfoxed me. They cited me. Those bastards. They gave me a ticket and decided to let me go.

"I lost, but as a final last dig, I asked them, 'Can you give me a ride to my car? You guys drove me all the way here to the station. It's night-time, and it's dark, and I'm just a kid, and my car is all the way across town at the Tasty Freeze.'

"They hated me, but they had to give me a ride back to my car.

"Of course, my parents found out, and that's how I lost my car. My parents took it away from me for a while, and I was back to riding my bike."

* * * * *

Scott was as good as Ray at storytelling, and it was easy to see why they were such good friends.

He continued, "My wife is from El Salvador. She visited here in Los Angeles, and we met. After she went back home, I would go visit her. I've now been there twenty times, but I used to go down there to see her. Well in the Hispanic culture it is taboo to stay in the house of the girl you are dating. So, I would stay in hotels. I would see her, but at night after our date, I would go out and walk around the city.

"She was afraid for me. She would tell me, 'You are crazy, you're going to get robbed.'"

I couldn't help but look at Scott, the professional robbery victim expert, and laugh.

"Nothing ever happened. I had learned. I think if you look and are aware if you are looking, you are not an easy mark. People, especially criminals size you up continually. They are looking for an easy mark. I was walking around one night in El Salvador, and I was being followed. I made a turn, he made a turn. I made another turn, he followed. Finally, I just stopped and turned around and stared at him. He left. He walked away. I had learned how not to look like that guy, as the easy mark.

"After I got out of college I got this great job with an overnight courier service. I did everything while I worked there, and I made pretty good money, and I got to travel a little bit.

"But it was not a career. I started thinking about what I wanted to do. I mean I was making good money, I had an apartment at the beach, everything was good, but I wanted more. So, I started thinking. I wanted to do something exciting. I didn't want to be stuck inside in an office in a suit. I wanted to work with a team. I wanted to be outside. I wanted variety. I wanted to do something fun, something I could do the rest of my life. There is only one job like that. It was being a police officer. I thought it would be interesting and rewarding. I was street smart. I believed I would see interesting things. I thought I could be outside and I would get to meet people.

"In 1995, I was hired by the Los Angeles Airport Police Department. This was at the height of affirmative action and to be a white guy and get hired, you had to walk on water. I had gone through the LAPD testing process and had scored a 98. I told my background investigator, 'I must be in!'

"He looked at me, 'You're not in; you're a white guy. You need a 105 to be a white guy to get in. You need military experience to put you over the top. We're hiring other ethnicities; we're trying to balance the numbers.' Basically, if you scored lower, and lowered your standards, you could get hired if you were of a different race. That's what I was up against.'

"So, the Airport Police hired me. I got through the academy and started working. The department was good to me, but it was not really what I wanted. I wanted to work patrol. I wanted to serve a community. I wanted to go to the robberies and burglaries. The Los Angeles Airport butts up against the City of El Segundo. Naturally, I kept running into some of the El Segundo cops. I thought, 'These guys are squared away.'

"I applied and got hired in 1999. I've been here ever since.

"I moved around and worked different assignments with the El Segundo Police Department. On April 11, 2008, the night of the shooting, I had already been assigned for some time working with a federal task force with I.C.E. While my primary assignment was working with

I.C.E., occasionally I would sign up and work overtime at the El Segundo Police Department."

* * * * *

Ray continued.

"When I was getting ready to graduate from high school, I got my parents to sign for me to join the army reserve. After I got out of the Army's Basic Training and checked into my reserve unit in Los Angeles, I realized I had made a huge mistake. These guys in the reserves had very little to no military bearing. They were not a group I wanted to serve with.

"One day I met a Marine Corps recruiter at a party. I told him I was in the army reserves and I hated it. I told him the guys were not very impressive, and I wanted out, but I was stuck; they wouldn't let me out.

"The next morning the recruiter was at my house. My mom got me out of bed and said there was a guy in uniform at the door who wanted to talk to me. I got up, and we talked. He told me he could get me out of the army reserves.

"'How?' I asked.

"'Join the Marines Corps,' he answered.

"And just like that, I was in the Marine Corps. One week later I was in the Marine Corps boot camp. During my time in recruit training, I met the most impressive group of men, my Drill Instructors. Their uniforms were always immaculate, they did everything the recruits did, but they did it better and faster. Their command presence was unmatched, and they personified the image of a United States Marine.

"It was now January 1986.

"After I had been in for a little while I knew exactly what I wanted to become, a Marine Corps Drill Instructor. One of the prerequisites to becoming a Drill Instructor was you had to be a minimum rank of Sergeant. I worked hard and was meritoriously promoted to the rank of sergeant at 19 years old.

To even be considered for the position of drill instructor you had to be exceptional and approved by the Drill Instructor Selection Board out of Washington D.C. I appeared before the Selection Board when they visited Camp Pendleton, and I was accepted into drill instructor school in 1990. When I got there, I realized I was not the best as I thought I had been. I mean my classmates were career Marines. They were razor sharp. Squared away? Many of these guys were so sharp that I was just average in their presence. We were told on the first day of school, 'You guys are like cats hanging onto a drape. And we are going to shake the drape as hard as we can. Half of you will not be here when the school is over.' They expected you to do everything that any marine in boot camp could do but do it better. It was expected if we were competing against a recruit, we would beat him. I could run, at least I thought I could. They took us out on runs, and they were just that, runs. All the runs I had been on in the army reserve basic training, or in Marine Corps boot camp were more or less fast jogs. When I got into Drill Instructor school, I was in shape and could run three miles in less than eighteen minutes. That is three consecutive sub-six-minute miles. There were guys in the school who were running consecutive five-minute miles. These runs they took us on were for miles and miles on end. The physical training was insane. In my military life, I had never ever fallen out of a run. During one of the insane runs, they took us on at Balboa Park near downtown San Diego, I fell behind my forty-inch interval from the guy in front of me. I couldn't believe it. I was running as hard as I could to keep up, and I fell behind, and I could not keep up my interval.

"Another thing expected of us was to be able to do teach-backs. Teach-backs were where we had to be able to recite instructions such as the proper position of attention. There were about fifty different teach-backs, and we had to be able to recite the instructions verbatim without missing a word. We would scream these teach-backs across the parade deck to the instructor who was grading our volume and accuracy. Uniform inspections were insane. Every piece of accouterment was measured with a tape measure as to where it belonged on your uniform.

"Out of one hundred and thirty guys who started the school, sixty-three of us graduated. That's when it started getting hard. Out of us sixty-three who graduated, only fifteen made it through the two-year commitment as drill instructors. Think about it. When you are with a recruiting class, you are there seven days a week, day and night for three months. Every third day you are the night drill instructor. Everything out of your mouth, every instruction you gave, every demonstration you showed, always setting the example, they all had to be perfect. You could not show you were sweating. I learned a trick to not have my sweat show on my uniform. I turned my uniforms inside out, and scotch guarded the inside of them. All the sweat would run down the inside of my legs and into my shoes, but my uniforms were dry. Sometimes you only got a few days off between the time a class graduated, and the next one started. Before the two years were up, guys would burn out.

"I learned some things about myself and life. It was that perseverance, mental toughness, and perfection are things to continually strive for.

"As a police officer, people are always sizing you up. To this day, I don't think anyone has a better uniform appearance than I do. If there is a wrinkle in my uniform, I change it. If my boots are not perfectly spit-shined, they will be.

"On our physical training test, if anyone beats me on the run, they are lucky. Even now, even these young kids, I'm almost 50 years old, and they can't beat me. I'm slower than I used to be but I can still run a mile and a half in nine and a half minutes. It's not easy. I have to run every other day, but I have to set the example for my guys. I have to.

"I would not be alive without this attitude I developed from my life and the Marine Corps."

* * * * *

Scott continued.

"I was at the point in my career where I was thinking, 'I'm going to make it.' I'd been in enough situations where I could have shot people, and I didn't. I hadn't been shot at. I was seeing guys retire who had not been shot at or who had not shot anyone. I was thinking, 'I've been around. My skills are great. I know what I'm doing. I've seen and done a lot of stuff, and I'm going to be okay. I'm going to have a full career and retire. I'm going to make it.' By this time, I was married and had a couple of kids. Everything I did, and do, is for my wife and kids. I exist to work and provide for them. I want to make sure they can go to school and not have their bikes stolen. I want to make sure they can go to college and get a good job. I want to make sure I have a pension for my wife and me to live out the rest of our lives.

"I had signed up to work overtime at the Pacific Theaters, on the night of April 11, 2008, (the Pacific Theaters are no longer there). I had worked the theaters a lot of times. We were working the theaters because there had been an influx of dangerous criminals going there and hanging out. Gang members from Lennox, Hawthorne, Lawndale, and Inglewood and other south-central Los Angeles gangs were all going there on the weekends. There were guys dressed in baggy clothes, some were wearing blue, and some were wearing red. Most had tattooed arms, necks and heads. We had car thefts, burglaries, assaults and even some shootings. El Segundo is a great city. It is a safe bedroom community with little to no gang activity. The gang problems we had came in from outside of the city. I was going to work that night with Rudy who was a close friend of mine. We worked patrol together and got along great. For some reason, Rudy had to cancel, so I was going to work the detail alone."

* * * * *

"I was going to do six and a half years with the Marine Corps," Ray said. "When I had been in five and a half years, I started thinking about what I would do when I got out. A friend of mine told me he had applied to the Simi Valley Police Department.

I said, 'You applied to be a cop?'

"He replied, 'Yeah.' Soon afterwards he got hired.

"I thought, 'A cop. I can do that. The only department I knew was the Los Angeles County Sheriff's Department. They were the agency in the jurisdiction where I grew up. They were the guys who had constantly jammed me, detained me and handcuffed me when I was growing up. That was the agency for me."

We laughed.

"I applied. During the application process, they asked five hundred billion questions about my whole life. I told you I was not an angel. I fudged about one thing when I was a kid. It was a small thing, very small, and I lied because I was embarrassed about it. I disclosed all the big things except this one thing. During the polygraph examination, they caught the lie.

"They disqualified me right on the spot. Right now! We can't trust you, Ray!

"SHIT! I was out!

"I learned my lesson. These guys did not fuck around, not one bit. I decided right then I would be completely honest about everything.

"My friend told me the El Segundo Police Department was hiring.

'Who's that?' I asked."

"'I don't know,' he answered, 'but they're only taking 250 applicants so if you're interested you better go.'

"Literally, on the spot, I jumped in my car and drove one hundred thirty miles from San Diego to El Segundo. I filled out an application and drove back to San Diego. I had been applying to some other agencies, and the San Diego Sheriff's Department hired me first for the position of Correctional Officer. I was newly married; my wife was expecting, and I needed a job.

"I was going through the background process with the Long Beach Police Department and the El Segundo Police Department. The San Diego County Sheriff's Department had already told me I could have the next open deputy sheriff position when it came up. It just so happened that Long Beach and El Segundo both gave me a job offer at the same time. I wanted to be a cop, and El Segundo paid more so it was adios to San Diego and Long Beach and hello to the beachside El Segundo Police Department. I went through the Orange County Sheriff's Department Academy then graduated, and bang I was a cop. It was now January 1993.

"In my career, I worked patrol, was a training officer, a member of the SWAT team, a K-9 officer, promoted to sergeant and then to lieutenant. I came on the department with no college education, but the department encouraged us to get an education and paid for me to get my degree. I now have a master's degree.

"As a lieutenant, I was eventually assigned to be the Commander of the Special Operations Division.

"In the city of El Segundo, we have a multi-theater complex named the Pacific Theaters. Over a short period of time, we had a significant increase in crime occurring at this theater complex. We mostly had car burglaries, but we were getting killed with all kinds of crime. Despite having many nice family restaurants in the area, our main attraction for the undesirable element was the theater complex. This was a sixteen-theater complex, and we had gang members coming from Los Angeles County and the City of Los Angeles hanging out there. In addition to the theaters was an arcade area in the lobby. Because of the amount of crime occurring in the surrounding parking lots and businesses, mostly stemming from the theater attraction, I spearheaded organizing a two-officer detail to work Friday, Saturday and Sunday nights at the theaters. We needed a police presence there to try and reduce the crime. The position was a paid overtime position filled by officers who signed up to work it on a first come first serve basis. The location of the theaters is 831 S. Nash St. right next to the P. F. Chang's restaurant. Understand this is a nice area with fantastic restaurants around it. It's just the gang members would come and cause a lot of trouble.

"On April 11, 2008, the night of this shooting, I was the special operations lieutenant. At the rank of lieutenant, I usually do not work patrol overtime assignments and this night was no different. I was not supposed to be working. What happened though was one of the guys who had signed up to work overtime that night had to cancel, and we could not find a replacement. This meant my friend, Officer Scott O'Connor was going to work the position alone. That was not acceptable, so I volunteered to work with him.

"The night of Friday, April 11, 2008, was the fourth shooting we had at the theater complex. Three of the four shootings involved gang members, and one was an attempted robbery of an armored truck.

"The lobby of the theater is huge. The east side of the theater runs along Nash St. On this side is a glass wall with doors where you can enter and exit the theater lobby. On the southeast corner of the theater is the ticket office with glass windows where you can buy movie tickets from the outside. Inside the theater lobby was the back side of the ticket office where there is a counter where patrons can speak face to face with theater employees. The south side of the theater is another wall with other doors where you can also enter or exit the theater lobby. Inside the lobby and running from south to north along the west wall is the concession stand. At the north end of the concession stand is the area where the attendants take your ticket to enter the theaters. There is also an arcade area in the northeast area of the lobby bordering Nash St.

"You do not need a movie ticket to go hang out in the lobby.

"On this evening Scott had picked me up around six p.m. at the station, and we drove to the theater together. Several hours later, at just about 10 p.m., we decided to grab a cup of coffee. We were drinking our coffee and watching the crowd. The theater lobby was packed. We were standing at the concession near where the attendants took the theater tickets from the patrons. The ticket counter or kiosk was across the lobby from us.

"The theater manager approached us. She told us there was a man at the ticket counter demanding a refund for his ticket. She said she was not going to refund his money and he was refusing to leave."

* * * * *

Scott's mood was moving a bit from jovial and joking, to a serious one.

"Ray heard I was going to have to work alone. He knew how dangerous it could be and decided to fill the spot and work with me.

"We teamed up and went to work. Things were smooth, and just before 10 p.m., we decided to get some coffee. We went to Starbucks and came back and were hanging out in the lobby of the theater. We were in uniform so when people came in, they saw there were police officers there.

"We were standing at the end of the concession counter drinking our coffee. From across the lobby, I saw the manager walk toward us. When she got to us, she said, 'Hey there's a guy over there who is giving me a hard time, and I want him out of here. He wants a refund, I just want him to go away.'

"I looked across the lobby and pointed to the guy, 'Is it that guy, right there?'

"She told us, 'That's him.'

"The guy was leaning back against the counter with both elbows on the counter, and he was looking at us. To me, he looked like a guy waiting to tell his side of the story. He didn't look agitated or angry. I fully expected to walk up to the guy and have him tell us he wanted a refund.

"Okay, no problem,' I answered. I thought this is like any other manager customer dispute."

* * * * *

Ray was continuing on with the account.

"I thought, 'This would not look good if we were conducting official police business with coffee in our hands.' We both put our coffee down.

"Scott asked, 'Where is he?'

"She pointed him out. He was inside the lobby at the southeast corner ticket office windows. He was facing us and leaning backward nonchalantly with his elbows on the ticket counter. When I spotted him through all the people in the lobby, I saw he was watching the manager speaking with us. He was a black male wearing a black jacket, and he appeared to be in his early twenties. My eventual goal was to try and get the manager to give him a refund to end the situation.

"He had contacted her at the counter where he was standing, and he could clearly see she had walked over to us to talk to us. As she was talking to us, she was pointing at him, and he was looking at us. We were in uniform, he knew exactly who we were. Scott and I walked across the lobby directly at him, so he knew we were coming.

"Remember, before this evening we had already had three shootings. Other crimes were rampant. This guy was all bagged out. All his clothes were way oversized, and he had the look of a gangster. I decided before we did anything, we were going to pat him down for weapons.

"I made contact with him and was facing him off to the side a little. Scott stood to the man's left which was to my right. Scott was close enough to grab him if he took a step. I said, 'How's it going?'"

* * * * *

Scott relived the encounter.

"Ray and I walked over to the guy, and Ray started a conversation with him, 'Hey man, hey guy what's up?' I got on the radio and put out that we would be talking with someone in the lobby of the theater.

"Our dispatch came back with, 10-9? (please repeat, we did not copy the transmission).

"I got back on the radio to re-transmit, but as I'm broadcasting, I hear the conversation between Ray and the guy, and it is not going well. I noticed he had beads of sweat on his face. Ray was telling the guy to turn around and that he was going to pat him down. I then heard the guy say, 'Fuck you, you're not touching me!' Then I knew, oh, we're dealing with an asshole.

Ray said, 'No, we're going to pat you down, turn around.'"

* * * * *

Ray was talking with his hands as he described his and Scott's initial encounter with the suspect.

"He gave me that stupid look, a challenging look, where his chin was up, his eyes were low, he had the sneer on his face as he looked down his nose at me. It was the look that says, 'Who do you think you are talking to? I'm a badass!' I'd seen it before, it was the gangster hard ass look.

"I told him, 'Hey before I do anything, do me a favor. Turn around I'm going to pat you down really quick, and we'll try and get this thing resolved. You know why we're here.'

"He looked at me with a sneer said, 'Fuck you!'

"I said, 'No, no. That's not the way this is going to go. You've got to turn around; *Turn around! I am going to pat you down.'*

"He looked at me defiantly and said, 'You ain't going to fucking touch me!'"

* * * * *

Scott continued.

"The guy starts to make a move away from us, and as he does so, he glances over his left shoulder at me. There were people everywhere in the lobby. There had to be thirty people just around where we were. The guy's back was to me, and as he started to move away, I grabbed the back of his left wrist with my left hand. When I grabbed his wrist, I pulled back, and he pulled his arm forward. He did not break my grip, I still had him, and I yanked his arm back again and outstretched his left arm straight. While holding his wrist with my left hand, I started to push the upper part of his outstretched arm downward with my right arm to force him to the floor. We started going down."

* * * * *

Ray said, "He turned his head and glanced to his right as if he was thinking of making a move to his right. If he did, he would be heading toward the east side of the theater, toward the doors or the wall that leads outside to Nash St.

"I was thinking to myself if this guy is going to resist I'm going to tase him. The problem was he was wearing a loose jacket and t-shirt underneath. I wasn't sure I was going to get good contact with the taser.

"All of this is happening in seconds. From the time he said, 'Fuck you,' to me saying, 'That's not the way it's going to go.' To his saying, 'You ain't going to fucking touch me,' to the look to his right, to my thought of 'I'm going to tase you' and wondering if it was going to work, was probably no more than four seconds.

"Sure, as shit he took that step to his right, and Scott grabbed him. I remember he had him by the left arm and his collar."

* * * * *

Scott was showing me with his hands how he was trying to control the suspect.

"Suddenly the guy just exploded with power. He came back up from the waist and started turning toward me. I still had his arm. I thought, 'He is going to try to punch me.' I thought this because as he was trying to spin toward me, I could see he was bringing his right arm across his body. When he was partially turned, I saw a flash, a little glimpse of silver in his right hand."

* * * * *

Ray was animated as he explained, "He looked like he was going down, Scott had him, and I thought to myself, I got you now. I'm going to tase you. I could see his white shirt, which was closest to his skin, and that was my target. I had the taser in my hand, I aimed it and squeezed the trigger, and nothing happened. I cursed to myself, 'Son of a bitch it's on safe.' I depressed the safety with my thumb. He was bent over, Scott had his left arm, and the suspect was looking at me with his head to the left. His right arm was not controlled, and he was reaching into his waistband with his right hand at the same time I was depressing the safety of the taser. Then I saw it, he was pulling a gun from the front of his waistband. Time instantly went to super, super, super slow motion.

"Even though the barrel was not yet fully pointed at me, I could see the end of the barrel. I was so concentrated on the barrel of the gun, I could see the grooves inside the tip. It was a silver barrel, and he was slowly raising it toward my face. His arm and hand stayed close to his body, and he was raising the tip of the barrel to my face. My wife and kids instantly flashed in my mind. I believed I would no longer be part of their lives. It was as if someone was reaching into my chest and ripping my heart into pieces.

"You may not believe this, but I was calm inside because the gun was coming up so slowly and I had so much time to think. Slowly, ever so slowly it was raising toward my face. I said to myself, 'Your stupid ass, you brought a taser to a gunfight, you need to get rid of this thing.' Things were so slow in my head I thought, 'You have enough time, things are so slow, you can get rid of the taser and get to your gun.' I was no more than three feet away from him. My mind was working frantically. I said to myself, 'The good Lord has slowed time down for me and given me time to get to my gun.' What I didn't take into consideration was my movements were just as slow as the suspect's movements. The only thing not moving slowly was my brain.

"The cold realization I didn't have the time I thought I had was when I tried to pitch the taser. I saw my fingers slowly releasing the taser and was trying to move my arm to throw it, but it was taking forever and ever. I said to myself, 'This is not getting out of my hand, I should have thrown it by now. GET RID OF IT, GET RID OF IT, *GET RID OF IT!!!*' my mind was screaming, but I couldn't get fucking rid of it. I was arguing with myself that I needed to get rid of the taser because I was watching the gun coming up to my face.

"Now I was getting pissed at myself for not getting rid of the taser then realized, 'I'M NOT GOING TO GET TO MY GUN IN TIME!'

"I looked at the gun, the barrel was still coming up, and it hit me, 'The gun is too close, I'm not moving side to side, the barrel is coming at me, and I can't get to my gun. I'm going to get shot. How will my family handle this? My son's birthday is tomorrow.' I had an intense moment of grief because I wasn't going to be there.

"Finally, my arm released the taser, and I only focused on his gun. I said to myself, 'Where is he aiming, where is he aiming?' The gun was coming up coming up coming up and finally after forever it was aiming right at me.

"I accepted I was going to get shot. I said to myself, 'You're going to get hit, you're going to get hit. *WHERE* are you going to get it? *WHERE* are you going to get shot?'

"Since I had released the taser, I had been desperately trying to get to my gun, but my hand was moving so slowly I knew it was hopeless, but I still tried and hoped against hope that I could get to it."

* * * * *

Scott continued his story, "I anticipated a punch, so I juked right to avoid it, then *BOOOOOOM!!!* It was louder than shit! I knew what a gunshot sounded like. I knew what burnt gunpowder smelled like. In the instant that the boom went off I could smell the burnt gunpowder. In the very instant the *BOOOOOOM* started, time had gone to super slow motion.

"Then everything went black. 'Fuck I'm shot in the head! 'My brain is dying, I'm going to fire off a few more thoughts and then I'll be gone.' He had pointed the gun at my face point blank and when he fired it blew out and shattered my right eardrum. In addition to making me permanently deaf in my right ear to where they had to eventually graft part of a jaw cartilage and reconstruct my ear, it messed with my vision at the time, and I could not see.

"I thought of my wife and my kids. I hoped that they would be okay. I said to myself, 'Oh, God, I hope everything comes out okay for them.' Anguish and despair hit me, 'They're gone. They're gone from my life. I'll never see them again.' Hopelessly I thought, 'This guy just took my wife and kids from me, even though he didn't kill them, he took them from me.' He took my future with my kids and my wife. It was such a sinking feeling, a feeling of deep despair and fear that is indescribable…and I was scared.

"Part of me had a difficult time accepting it. I had this strange denial. Part of me was, 'No, no, no, this is not happening.' I believed I had been shot in the head and I was having my final thoughts. Everything was black. I was blind!!!"

* * * * *

The expression in Ray's eyes told me everything as he relived the event, "That's when it happened. I did not hear it, I saw it. I could not hear anything, it was if someone had turned off all the sound in the world. I saw it. If you think about the films we've all seen of the atomic bomb going off on Hiroshima, that's what it looked like, except in slow motion.

"As I was looking down the barrel of the gun, I saw a huge, slowly expanding orange and red fireball erupt from the end of the barrel. It started off as a little spit of flame at the end of the barrel then it got bigger and bigger as it slowly expanded to this huge ball of fire. Through the fire, I could see a shadow of something lazily and slowly spinning as it flew toward me. It continued to spin out of this brilliantly bright orange ball of fire toward me...

"In one fraction of a millisecond, I had seen the spinning object. In the next millisecond, it was gone, and I was hit full force in my face. It was as if someone took a full-sized concrete breaking sledgehammer and swung it as hard as they could in my face.

"The bullet hit me just below my right nostril. It traveled through my right upper lip tearing and pulverizing through my upper right row of teeth, gums and bones, and upper soft palate. It also tore off a chunk of my tongue. It ripped through my esophagus. The bullet traveled through the back of my mouth and mashed the bones almost to my right eye socket and to my right ear. Everything I just described was gone, well not gone, it was still in my mouth, but just not attached to anything anymore. My soft palate was torn and tattered to pieces. The bullet ricocheted off the vertebrae in my neck, chipping it, and continued on until finally stopping and rested by my carotid artery.

"It was the hardest hit I had ever felt. It was as if someone hit the inside of my head with this unbelievable pressure, and that my head expanded and blew up to three times its normal size, then came back to its normal size again."

* * * * *

Scott was telling me what happened after he was blind. "The next thing I realized was I was on the ground wrestling with the suspect. Everything was still black. Blinking my eyes did no good; I was still blind. However, I knew I was wrestling with him because I could feel and smell him. We were on the ground rolling around fighting. Time was so slow; seconds were like hours.

"I was yelling and screaming at myself in my head, *'GET UP, GET UP, GET UP!!!'* As I was screaming, I heard super loud shots being fired, *BOOOOOOM, BOOOOOOM.* I knew I was in trouble. I didn't feel the bullets entering my body, but somehow, I knew I was getting shot. I knew I was getting fucked up!"

* * * * *

Ray went on with his story. "When I woke up I was face down on the ground. No one was screaming, I couldn't hear gunfire; it was complete silence. My hands were beside me, palms down and my head was to the right. I saw Scott on the ground. I knew it was Scott because I read the back of his shirt that said Police on it. He was lying on his side two feet away from me. I noticed Scott's right leg was slightly bent and then I heard gunfire.

"The typical sound of gunfire at the range is a sharp, quick crack, but this gunfire did not sound like that. This was a super slow, long and loud drawn out sound of *BOOOOOOM, BOOOOOOM, BOOOOOOM!!!*

"I knew the first *BOOOOOOM* hit Scotty because I saw his leg jerk. I could not see where the shots were coming from. I could not see the suspect, but I knew Scotty was getting shot.

"When the second *BOOOOOOM* went off. I saw Scott roll a little to his right; I was horrified. Scott was being killed right in front of me.

"Rage welled up in me. I was so fucking mad…I was so fucking pissed!!! In my mind I was screaming, *'HE'S KILLING, SCOTT!!!'*

* * * * *

Scott took a drink of water. "When I came to the second time, my eyes were open. I was looking at the ceiling of the lobby. I could see. Toward the concession stand I could see all the cheesy popcorn and drink advertisement signs, and the purple and pink banners that made everything look like a carnival. I could hear sounds again. It was almost like parts of my senses were rebooting. Things were still in super slow motion. I turned my head to the left and saw the suspect lying on his back, shoulder to shoulder next to me. We were looking at each other. If this were a woman in bed, we would be having pillow talk.

"Everything then changed, I became filled with rage and anger. I'm normally a mellow dude. I grew up riding my bike to the beach, surfing, and stuff. Nothing makes me angry. I always talk my way out of any problem. I can talk anyone into handcuffs. I'm a mellow, easygoing guy who was now filled with the most intense rage and anger I've ever felt in my life. My mind screamed, *'HOW DARE YOU TRY AND TAKE ME AWAY FROM MY FAMILY!!! HOW DARE YOU TRY AND TAKE EVERYTHING AWAY FROM ME!!! YOU MOTHER-FUCKER!!! YOU'RE GOING TO DIE FOR THIS!!!'*

"Later I thought to myself, 'Holy shit, you became another person.' I had never wanted to kill someone before.

"Then it happened. He got up. He got to his feet and started turning toward the door. At this time in my life, I was running five miles a day. I was in excellent shape. I was on my feet in an instant, and as I was getting up, I made a smooth draw of my gun from my holster.

"He went out of the glass doors, and just as I was ready to shoot, I momentarily lost sight of him as he ran past the metal door frame. I was no more than ten feet away from him. I went right and there he was, still running. I started shooting and hit him four times. He went down just outside of the door.

"I had been moving forward as I was shooting and when he dropped, he did so quickly I almost stepped on his foot. He was on his stomach. *'I GOT HIM. It's over'* He then rolled over. I couldn't believe it, *'MOTHERFUCKER!'* Now I'm looking, I'm looking down this dark barrel. The barrel of his gun! My eye was lined up with the barrel, and it was as if time froze and I was having a staring contest with the barrel of the gun. *'MOTHERFUCKER!'* I screamed inside, *'FUCKING FUCK!!!'* I stared at the barrel of the gun in total disbelief...

"I was thinking I had just shot this guy multiple times with a .45 and he was down. I was positive he was finished, yet here he was pointing his gun at my face.

...and then it happened...*BOOOOOOM!!!*"

* * * * *

Ray was still speaking. "I was conscious again, and I realized I was just lying there. 'Hey stupid, you're not dead yet, so get your fucking ass up! Your family needs you to get off your ass, now!' I screamed at myself in an unbelievable rage, *'GET UP, GET UP, GET UP, GET UP, GET IN THIS FIGHT!!! GET UP, GET UP, GET UP, GET UP!!!'*

"I knew I got knocked on my ass. I knew I got shot in the head, but I didn't know where. I knew I was going to die, but I thought, 'You're not dead yet, you've got to get him before he gets away. Even though you're going to die, you've still got your arms, you still got your gun, you can still see, you can still breathe, get your fucking ass up and get this guy, he's killing Scott!'

"Time was black, and then I woke up again, and instead of being face-down by the ticket counter, I was just inside the lobby at the glass doorway. I was on one knee with my gun in my hand. I was looking out of the doorway, and the suspect was lying face down on his right hand on the walkway leading to the theaters. Scott was also outside sitting on the walkway with his back against the walkway rail. Scott was partially facing me but was pointing his gun at and looking at the suspect. We were both about five feet away from the suspect.

"'How in the fuck did I get here?' I was in total disbelief. Time was slow but jerky with starts and stops with parts of time missing. Things were not making sense.

"Scott had his gun pointed at the suspect. The suspect rolled 360 degrees to his left and faced Scott. He had the gun in his right hand. *HE'S GOING TO KILL SCOTT!!!*

"Scott started to fire. I started to fire. I couldn't hear our guns going off, but I could see Scott's gun bucking in his hand. Everything was still in slow motion, *BOOOOOOM, BOOOOOOM, BOOOOOOM.* We were hitting him. I could see his body and ass contort, and shudder and shake with each round we fired, and I could see his ass start to bleed. I remember the suspect then tossed his gun and it landed at his feet.

"Time now returned to normal. I could see the smoke in the air from my gun. My thoughts turned to my injuries. I started self-assessing. 'How bad am I hurt?' Blood was pouring from my mouth, and I couldn't stop it. I felt around the inside of my mouth with my tongue. All my right upper gums, teeth, and bones were gone. But the gore was still in my mouth, and mixed in with the blood that was pouring out was my pulverized teeth, gums, and bones.

"As I was breathing, I was inhaling chunks of bone, gum tissue, teeth, and blood. It was choking me, and I was sort of drowning in it. I started gagging and throwing up the gore. As I was spitting it out, I could clearly see my teeth, bone, and tissue coming out with the blood. It was not just coming out, it was gushing out. I began to wonder where the bullet went. It was so bad I thought, 'I bet the bullet went through my head.'

"I took my left hand and reached up to the back of my head and tried to find the hole where the bullet had come out. 'Okay, it didn't come out, where's the bullet?'

"Everything was quiet. It was the most quiet I had ever experienced in my life.

"I snapped back and realized, 'we need help, we need help.'

"I slapped my waist where my radio should have been, and it was gone. I looked, and it was on the floor about ten feet away. I yelled at Scott, but he wasn't acknowledging me. I don't know if I was making sense because I was spitting blood and bone as I spoke.

"Scott looked at me, and I sort of realized he could not understand me. I made the motion of my hand across my throat, trying to signal to him I could not put out a help call and for him to do it. He later told me he thought I was telling him, 'I'm dead.'"

* * * * *

Scott described the horrible nightmare he was living.

"It was as though I was in a second shooting. I juked left as his gun went off. Because of a bullet hole later found in the wall above me, we surmised the round probably went up and over my head. I ducked and moved right and fired four more times, striking him each time. He started rolling again to his face, and as he did so, he made a little flick of the gun, which landed by his side. The most stressful time of my life now started."

I'm sure when I looked at Scott I had a look of, "What the hell do you mean the most stressful time of your life was starting? What did you just describe to me?"

Scott was struggling to get this out.

Scott continued, "He was down on the ground, I knew these fuckers don't run alone. I thought, 'Okay, get ready.' I needed to reload.

"The situation was not over. I realized I might need the maximum amount of bullets. I dropped the magazine and reached for a full magazine to reload. When I went to grab the magazine, I realized my arm wasn't working right. My arm did not move fluidly, and it wouldn't go into certain positions easily. I felt bone crunching. Then it hit me, 'What's wrong? Why isn't my body working? What's wrong with my arm?' Finally, I was able to reload. I was still in hostile territory, but now I had more bullets loaded, and I was ready to fight. I looked down at my shirt, and there was this hole right over my heart. This scared the shit out of me. In a near panic, I wondered, 'Did that go through?' My shirt was frayed, and the material of my bulletproof vest was coming out of the hole. Although this round was stopped by my bulletproof vest and did not penetrate. It tore my chest muscle from my sternum, and it made mush out of my skin, it also caused my heart to swell. I looked at my left shoulder, and there was another frayed piece of uniform.

"While I had been fighting and moving, I knew I had been shot, but I hadn't time to think about it. Now, seeing the bullet holes, my arm not working, and the crunching bones in my arm and shoulder, it really hit me that I was shot. I started self-assessing. While I was coming to the realization of my injuries, I knew I had to get a broadcast out on the radio. In my mind, we still had other bad guys around. We could still get killed.

"I looked at the suspect, and he was moving and twitching. Even though he tossed the gun, that didn't mean he didn't have another gun on him. He was alive and still a threat. I couldn't hear a thing. My head was filled with the most insane ringing I'd ever heard in my life. I was deaf!!!

"I looked in the lobby. Ray was alone. He was about twenty feet away from me by the door, sitting on his hip almost on his side. His shit was everywhere. His face was sagging and bleeding. His face was drooped and distorted, sort of like someone who has had a stroke. He was pale. 'What happened to him?' I asked myself in bewilderment. 'Did he fall and break his nose?' He looked horrible.

"Ray made a motion with his hands across his throat, and I realized he was telling me he was dying. He was saying goodbye to me. I had a terrible decision to make. Do I take my eyes off this suspect and go to Ray? It took all my willpower to not go to Ray. I realized, 'No if you do that we're both going to get killed. This guy is not dead yet.'

"I remembered a video I saw of State Trooper Coates who died while asking for help on the radio. He was shot one time with a .22 bullet. I started wondering where the bullet or bullets that hit me were. Again, terror hit me. My whole upper left side of my shoulder, back, and chest was on fire. I wondered if I had only three minutes to live.

"By this time, I had squatted on one knee with my back against some hedges. I was sort of at a 45-degree angle to the lobby and the suspect. I was covering the suspect, but I had a visual on Ray in case someone came up to kill him.

"I had repeatedly practiced what I would say if I ever got shot. I practiced it because I knew if I ever got shot I might only have one chance to broadcast it. I took a deep breath, and I broadcast it perfectly. 'Officer involved shooting, I'm hit, looks like my partner is hit, suspect is down, send everybody.' Other guys who heard the broadcast could not believe it was real because I was so calm and there was no panic in my voice.

"There was this cloud of burnt gunpowder hanging in the air. I could smell it, and I was looking through it. I felt like I was at the end of a shooting in a bar in a western movie. The smell of gunfire, the smoke in the air, the bodies lying around me, it was carnage, and surreal. I kept wondering if I was going to die. The lobby seemed to have emptied out in seconds, and it had. Ray was bleeding alone in the lobby. The suspect was twitching and moving, and I was waiting for other people, the suspect's friends to come and kill us. My whole upper left chest was on fire, the gunpowder was slowly hanging in the air, the ringing in my head would not stop, and I could not hear anything; it was almost too much for my mind to process. And it was happening in such slow motion. What just happened? Is this real? Did this really just happen? This was just a manager and customer thing. I felt like I wasn't even there. My mind couldn't seem to catch up to the reality of the situation.

"I had decided I needed to keep the suspect covered until help arrived, then out of the second set of doors, a guy with two girls exited and walked right at me. What the hell? No one was around, and I mean no one. Where did these guys come from? The lobby was empty. We had just been in a gunfight. No one in their right mind would want to be anywhere near this stuff, and if you're approaching me while I have my gun out, you're either coming to kill me, or you're really stupid. At that moment, I was thinking anyone who comes near me plans to kill me, so I'm going to shoot them, period.

"I started screaming at them, *'GET BACK, GET BACK!!!'* I couldn't hear what I was saying but I must have said it right, and they must have believed me because they put their hands up and retreated back into the lobby.

"I got on the radio again, 'I need units now. I am being approached by other people.'

"I felt like I had to do everything. I thought the suspect was a threat. I thought my friend was dying. Again, I wondered, 'Am I dying?' Other people were approaching me. Then one of my patrol partners who was working in the city got on the radio, 'Scott I'm almost there.' How did I hear that through the terrible mind-numbing buzzing? It was like the weight of the world was just lifted off my shoulders.

"A Manhattan Beach Officer was the first unit on the scene. He came up the ramp with his shotgun, and I could see his mouth moving, but

I couldn't hear him. He was pointing his shotgun and walking around in little circles. I later learned he thought I was nuts. He was asking me if I was okay if there were other suspects, and I was ignoring him. He didn't know where to go or what to do because we could not communicate with each other. He was walking in circles looking and scanning for other suspects.

"As more units arrived, I took a step back and again took stock of what just happened. It was incredible to me. 'This is not what a shooting is supposed to be like. In the movies, guys shot at each other from twenty feet away and from behind overturned tables and from behind bars. In the academy, we shot at paper targets. We shot from behind barricades. No one told me I would be deaf and blind, lying on the ground, wrestling for my life. No one told me I would be right next to the man trying to kill me and that I would be shot from point-blank range. No one told me the man trying to kill me would be so close I would be able to smell him. No one told me there would be so much carnage and the shooting would seem to go on forever. No one told me I would lose consciousness, and then when I would come back, things would be different and that I would be in entirely different places. It was the most unreal experience of my life, but I was more alive, and my senses were more acute than at any other time in my life. I don't know if anyone could understand it unless they lived it."

* * * * *

Ray continued his account.

"Scott got on the radio and put out the call we were shot and needed back up and paramedics. All of a sudden, I hear Scott yelling at someone. I looked, and I saw a man in the lobby with a gun in his hand. There was a girl with him. 'OH, FUCK, this is not over, they're coming to kill us!!!' I turned and fired. The girl grabbed him, and they ran back into the theaters."

* * * * *

Ladies and gentlemen, this did not happen the way Ray remembers it. There is surveillance video of the incident, and Ray reviewed it. He told me the way it really happened.

Scott and the suspect were at the south set of glass doors. A black guy in a blue hoodie and two black girls walked out of the other set of glass doors, the northern glass doors, and started walking toward Scott and the suspect. During the subsequent investigation it was determined this group was friends with the suspect, and in fact, had gone to the theater with him.

An additional male black wearing a white pinstriped shirt was just inside the glass doors but did not exit outside. From his position, Scott could not see this second man. Scott yelled at the man in the hoodie and the two girls to get back. All four people, including the man standing just inside the glass doors, raised their hands and walked back into the lobby and out of the view of the video toward the theaters. Ray heard Scott ordering the people back but never saw anyone.

About a minute after the group raised their arms and left the lobby, you can see the man who did not exit the glass doors, return to the lobby with a gun. One of the girls who had been with the man wearing the hoodie was with this gunman. In the video, she appears to be tugging on his shirt and gun arm to get him to stop; as if she is trying to dissuade him from what he is about to do. It is supposed that Ray was right; this gunman must have come back to the lobby to try to kill Ray and possibly Scott. It is the only reason he would have gone back to the lobby with a gun.

In the video, you can see the man and the girl in the lobby, and you can also see red and blue lights outside, reflecting on the building. These were the red and blue lights of the Manhattan Police officer's car reflecting off the building. This was the first unit to arrive. The conjecture is the man realized other police had arrived and decided to retreat. This was when he left the lobby for the second time. If it wasn't for the Manhattan Beach Police officer arriving when he did, with his rotating lights on, it is probable the second gunman would have tried to kill Ray and Scott.

This second gunman was never identified, and Ray never shot at him as he remembered he had.

Time had slipped again, and Ray had been sitting upright on the theater floor unconscious for over a minute. Ray is not lying in the telling of his story. Just remember the horrific head injuries he had sustained and the emotional trauma of seeing your friend being shot. His mind was making things up. Given the circumstances, it is unbelievable that Ray was even conscious. A lesser man would have been dead from shock.

* * * * *

Ray told me what happened next.

"'Okay,' 'If I can stay conscious, I might survive this. Don't lay down. You can sit on your ass but...do...not...lay ...down!' I had to concentrate on my breathing. I had to breathe for my wife and kids. I sat on my ass and holstered my gun and put my hand on it. 'They might kill me, they might shoot me in the back of my head, but they are not going to kill Scott or me with my gun.'

"I heard Scott on the radio again, 'We're still in danger, we need help.'

"I could hear another unit responding on the radio, 'Scott, hang in there we're coming. We're almost there.'

"A Manhattan Beach Police Officer was the first to arrive. It was an instant relief. He came up the ramp with the shotgun. He was doing everything right, he was covering the downed suspect, but I was so worried about other suspects. 'Shoot into the lobby, shoot, get everyone back, shoot, shoot, shoot!'

"Shortly after, some of our El Segundo officers arrived. I knew by the gouts of blood coming out of me I didn't have long until I passed out. It was as if you turned on a faucet and it poured out with clumps and chunks of teeth, gums, and bone from my cheek. The most shocking thing was I could see my teeth on the theater carpet. Half of the gore had been blown down my throat, and I was throwing everything up. Every time I threw it up, I'd catch my breath and swallow more gore and chunks. Then I'd gag and throw up some more.

"Officer Corey McEnroe was the first officer who got to me. He saved my life. The last thing I wanted to hear was how fucked up I was. I also didn't want to hear I was going to be okay, like someone offering false hope, patting me on the back when I was going to die. He did something different. He came up to the front of me and leaned my head against his chest. I was gaging and pouring gore all over him.

"He said, 'Okay, okay, look at me, look at me.'

"I kind of looked at him and he got his flashlight and shined it in my eyes.

"He told me, 'I want you to take a deep breath through your nose.'

"So, I took a deep breath through my nose.

"He then said, 'Take a deep breath through your mouth.'

"So, I took a deep breath through my mouth. I was so dazed; half in and half out of it.

"He said, 'I want you to look at me. I want you to concentrate on me.'

"I started to gag again. He patted me on the back, 'It's okay, just get it out, just get it out.' I was throwing up all my shit on him.

"He looked at me, 'Concentrate, I want you to understand everything I'm going to tell you.'

291

"I responded, 'Okay.'

'Your eyes, your pupils are reactive to light. That's why I had the flashlight to your eyes. Your nose, your airway is clear. You can breathe. The bleeding has almost stopped. Do you understand all I've told you?'

"I mumbled, 'Yes.'

'You're going to live.'

"He did more than just come up to me and tell me I was going to be okay. He checked me out and told me each of the things he did. Then he told me the results and told me I was going to live. A light switch came on. I was no longer contemplating my death. I went from having no doubt I was going to die, to believing that I was going to live. I went from thinking I was going to die to thinking, 'Oh shit, I just need a few stitches. This just looks bad. I'll be home for my son's birthday tomorrow, and I'll be running next week.'

"The next thing I knew I was semi-seated on a gurney in the back an ambulance. The ambulance doors were opening and closing with officers checking in on me. Then the ambulance doors opened. My captain was at the crime scene in a Hawaiian shirt. I could see him on the street outside the ambulance. 'FUCK, they had called him off duty. How the fuck had he gotten here? He had the time to get dressed and come to the crime scene, and I'm still here? WHAT THE FUCK? Why am I still here? Get me to the fucking hospital!!!! As well as I could yell through the half of my face that was not gone, *'GET ME THE FUCK OUT OF HERE!'*

"I remember the doctor at the hospital telling me, 'We know where it is, we know where the bullet it is. We're going to get it. We're going to get it out, and you're going to be okay.' I remember waking up, it was two weeks later.

"There are hazes of time in the hospital. Purple colors flowing over all the hospital equipment, Visions of white when I opened my eyes. Then blessed bliss as I went under again, nurses coming and asking me if I was going to be good, as in not misbehave. It seems I had been trying to remove my tubes. I couldn't talk, but I didn't know exactly why I couldn't. I had tubes down my throat. Once I started healing there were all these things, tests, that had I had to clear, that my body had to perform. I got pneumonia that had to be fixed. I had a catheter they had to remove. When they came to remove it, I said, 'Okay.' I didn't realize how long that thing was, and the blood that came along with it. I almost passed out just from the blood.

"Several weeks later, I looked at myself in the mirror. I was emaciated, and I had a beard. I did not recognize the man looking back at me.

"I only had a hole in my face, a little red dot. However, if you followed the bullet's path to the back of my eye socket or ear, then you would understand it was so much more."

* * * * *

"Later in the hospital, my sergeant came to visit me. 'Scott, you did a great job, fourteen hits out of sixteen shots.'

"I panicked. I didn't say anything, but inside, I was dying. I shot sixteen times? That meant I reloaded and shot a bunch more times. What I didn't know, but found out later was Ray had also been shooting at the suspect while he was three feet away from me to my left.

"The suspect died at the scene."

* * * * *

The bullet that blew out Scott's eardrum and temporarily blinded him is the bullet that hit Ray in the face.

While he was lying on the ground, Scott got shot in the chest, which his bulletproof vest stopped. He took another round in the top of the shoulder. This round took out Scott's collarbone, it tore off his left bicep tendon, it blew out his rotator cuff, and it stopped right above his spine in his back between his shoulder blades. As a result of the damage, he had to go through a year of recovery to get back to work.

* * * * *

After Ray and Scott went back to full duty, they went back to work at the theaters again. The female manager was still there. She went up to them and gave them both a hug while apologizing and crying.

She explained what happened before she approached Ray and Scott on the night of the shooting. The suspect had been playing a shooting game in the arcade area. It was a dollar game, and on six different occasions he approached her and said the machine was broken and asked for a refund. She gave him the money six times. She finally became suspicious and checked the machine, and found it was working properly. Then he approached her and told her he wanted a refund for his ticket. He did not have a ticket stub or any receipt that proved he had bought a ticket. She refused to give him any more money. He threw a few "Motherfuckers" at her and demanded his money. She told him, "Sir if you don't leave, I'm going to go over there and get those two police officers." He told her, "Fine go get them." He then leaned on the counter and waited for Ray and Scott.

We later learned he was a gang member, in possession of a stolen gun and on parole. He was also high on P.C.P. He knew what he was going to do. Ray and Scott had walked into an ambush.

The suspect had gone to the theater with two other guys and three girls. One of the girls was his girlfriend. He had an argument with her in the theaters and left to play video games in the lobby. The two girls and the guy in the hoodie who approached Scott outside the glass doors, and who Ray never saw, were later connected to the suspect. They were part of the group who had gone to the theaters with the suspect. Scott believes they were coming to kill him. I do too. The man with the gun in the lobby was never found or identified.

The shooting, from the time the first bullet was fired to the last bullet fired, lasted seven seconds.

* * * * *

Lieutenant Ray Garcia was awarded the Medal of Valor for his actions on the evening of April 11, 2008. It is the highest award the El Segundo Police Department can bestow upon its members.

* * * * *

On the evening of October 28, 1999, Scott was at home when he heard an explosion. He ran outside and saw his elderly female neighbor standing outside. Her house was engulfed in smoke and flames. She yelled out, "My son is inside!" Her son was a mentally handicapped adult man who lived with her. Scott ran into the burning house, through burning walls and curtains and found the man in the rear bedroom. He guided him out. When Scott got outside, the woman, who should have been waiting for him, was now missing. Neighbors told him she had gone back into the house to look for her son. Scott ran back into the house, with the house more ablaze than before, and found her in the rear bedroom where he had found her son. He grabbed her and for the fourth time went through the burning house and guided her out to the front.

After the fire department got there, Scott went home. Sometime later, a letter arrived at the El Segundo Police Department addressed to his Chief. It was from the Los Angeles City Fire Department. The letter credited off-duty Scott O'Connor as having saved two lives from a burning building.

Scott's Chief knew nothing of the incident and told him he should have informed him and asked him why he never mentioned it.

Scott in his usual jovial manner said, "Chief, I just got here from the Airport Police Department. I just want to be an El Segundo Police Officer. I didn't think you needed to know. I'm not a braggart.

ROBERT RANGEL

* * * * *

Officer Scott O'Connor was awarded the Medal of Valor from the El Segundo Police Department for his actions on the evening of October 28, 1999, for saving the lives of two people from a burning house. Officer Scott O'Connor was again awarded the Medal of Valor for his actions on the evening of April 11, 2008. It is the highest award the El Segundo Police Department can bestow upon its members.

Chapter 27

It's a SET-UP!

Account of Joseph E. Holmes
Los Angeles County Sheriff's Department

"In 1978, I was working as a patrol deputy at Firestone Station. I can't remember why, but my partner and I made a traffic stop on 103rd Street near the Jordan Downs housing project.

"I was the driver, and so I approached the car on the driver's side. My partner Tom was a little behind on the passenger side, backing me up and watching the car.

"When I got to the driver's window, I could see both the occupants of the car were females. The passenger suddenly and with frantic speed opened her purse and reached inside. I went on high alert. The hairs on the back of my neck stood up. My eyes went wide open, and my eyes went into tunnel vision, focusing on the purse. Instantly, that icy cold lump hit the pit of my stomach.

I yelled at her, *"DON'T DO IT, DON'T DO IT!!"* My mind was screaming, *SHE'S GOING FOR A GUN!*

"I was sure I was going to have to shoot her. I drew my gun and pointed it inside the car at her. Well, what she pulled out was a vial of P.C.P. (Angel Dust a strong hallucinogenic.) I was so relieved it wasn't a gun. There was so much P.C.P. on the streets in those days, and we had made so many arrests with people in possession of it that as soon as I saw the vial, I knew what it was.

"She was trying to unscrew the lid so she could pour it out.

"With my gun still in my hand, I dove into the driver's open window, across the female driver and grabbed the vial with my left hand. I had to save the evidence. I was on the lap of the driver, and I looked into her eyes, our faces inches apart, 'Keep your mouth shut and sit right there. If you do anything, I'll kill you.' Remember my gun was in my right hand and she could have easily grabbed it and shot me.

"The female passenger was yelling and cursing at me as we fought over the vial. *'Motherfucker, let go, let go!'* As we fought, she suddenly lowered her head and bit me on the hand. She bit me as if she was trying to eat my hand like she was taking a chunk out of a piece of steak. It hurt like hell, and I instinctively jerked my hand back, but I did not let go of the vial. While she was doing this, I was trying to get my gun back in my holster so I could get both hands on the vial and rip it out of her hands. She was high on the P.C.P., which gave her superhuman strength and try as I might, I could not get the vial out of her hands. In what seemed like minutes, but in reality, was only a few seconds, I finally got my gun holstered and got both of my hands on the vial. I was lying on the driver's lap with my feet sticking out of the driver's window.

"By now, the passenger had succeeded in loosening the lid, and the outside of the vial was wet with the P.C.P. as it sloshed out of the bottle.

"We were struggling so hard that both of us somehow slid out of the open passenger door window. Tom was there with us now, and he was also trying to get the vial out of her hands. She was biting Tom's hands, and then she was biting me. Tom and I were jerking all around, trying not to get bit, but not willing to let go of the vial either. Each bite was excruciating, she was ripping and tearing open our skin, and we were both bleeding. After struggling for what seemed like an eternity, she managed to get on her knees. We were all still holding the vial. I got back on my feet. However, she then did the unthinkable. This crazed woman put her face in my crotch with her mouth open. *She was trying to bite my genitals!!!*

"I jerked to the left, as she latched onto my right inner thigh. Man, that really hurt. I pulled back in pain. Luckily my backward motion unlatched her choppers from my tender meat.

"I was semi-aware the driver had opened her door and ran off. By now the fight had moved back to the side of our radio car. Tom and I had blood dripping from numerous bites including the blood on the inside of my thigh. I finally got the vial out of her hand, and set it on one of the windshield wipers, out of her reach. There were several reasons why I put the vial on the windshield and not in my pocket. The main reason was that I needed to tighten the lid down because I didn't want P.C.P. leaking all over my uniform.

"But there was a second and more pressing reason…when I got the vial out of her hand and looked forward, there were about fifteen gang members from the Jordan Downs project coming at us. They probably wanted the P.C.P.

"My everyday holster had broken and was getting repaired. It was a low riding holster I had used for years and that I knew very well. Tom had loaned me a spare holster that rode higher than mine. I drew my gun from the unfamiliar holster, and I failed to clear the front of the gun from the holster. As my hand came forward, the front sight caught the front of the holster, and I lost my grip on my gun. My gun flew out of my hand and hit the front push bars attached to the radio car bumper. It slid into the street and landed right in front of the gang members.

"Time froze as they stopped and looked at the gun then at me. I reached into my uniform pants pocket and pulled out my backup gun. *'FREEZE!!!'* I yelled as I pointed my little five shot revolver at them.

"The gang members looked at me, then at the gun, then at me again. Not realizing I accidentally lost my gun, one of the gang members yelled, *'IT'S A SET UPP, IT'S A SET UPP, RUNNNNN!!!'*

"With one last look at me, they all turned and ran for their lives.

"I ran and grabbed my gun. Suddenly, I realized Tom was screaming, *'Joe help me, help me!'*

"I looked behind me, and Tom was still struggling with the woman who was fighting and cursing, and trying to bite him.

"I quickly grabbed the vial and tightened the lid and put it in my shirt pocket as I ran to Tom. After a little more struggling, we finally got her handcuffed.

So much P.C.P. had spilled into our cuts, and the smell was so over-powering that we got wacked (high on P.C.P.).

"Tom was walking around in circles asking me, 'Hey Joe, what's my name?' He would then start giggling.

"Our backup arrived along with the sergeant. He took all our guns away from us and got us to the hospital. Several days later Tom and I went to have some drinks. After we downed a few, we looked at all of our cuts and one of us said, 'Maybe we should use the incident as train-ing on how to make a good P.C.P. arrest and how to stop a gang attack!' We couldn't stop laughing."

* * * * *

On May 9, 2017, I was done writing this story, but then something happened, and I had to add this.

A world-renowned musical celebrity, a rock and roll superstar, came to our unit to be fingerprinted. Many sworn officers and clerical staff were so excited they left their workstations and went to the fingerprint station to get a glimpse of the musician. Many had their pictures taken with this person. It was like a bunch of kids were told that Santa Claus was there. Men and women officers and civilians alike were giggling like a bunch of kids.

Personally, I didn't understand the actions of the personnel, especially the sworn personnel. I did not like or dislike this musician. How could I, I didn't know him. To me, he was just another person who had come in to get fingerprinted. I pointed out to several officers, "Do you understand, you and the person next to you have made more of a difference in people's lives than that musician ever has? You're acting like this person is a hero. Is that what impresses you?'

This musician is a self-admitted user/former user of marijuana, acid, cocaine, hash, speed and heroin. He also admitted to talking a mother into letting him become the guardian of an underage girl so he could travel with her across state lines while on tour and not be arrested. He impregnated her and forced her into having an abortion. Really? This is what we idolize? This musician could have gone to prison for possession of drugs, providing drugs to a minor and for statutory rape. This musician could never pass a background check to be a peace officer. Again, I do not hate him, but when I was a deputy, I arrested many people under the influence or for having possession of the above drugs. I've seen people's lives and family's lives ruined by drug use. Perhaps if our parents told their children how abhorrent and shameful certain behaviors were, we could get our society turned around the right way. I would be ashamed to no end if my children saw me giggling and wanting to get next to someone of this character. According to his self-admitted history, he is a rapist and a drug user.

Is he talented? Millions say he is. Do I appreciate good music? Yes. Do I appreciate talent? Yes. Would you ever in your wildest dreams catch me idolizing or hero-worshipping a person of the above character? Never. I don't need my picture taken with them.

So, for everyone, I would like you to consider my point of view. We need to see the comparison between the musician and Joe Holmes. Joe, the average, not a world-renowned guy who used to sit down the row from me at work.

Here is Joe's history:

Joseph Holmes served with the Los Angeles Sheriff's Department for 30 plus years (1973-2004). During his tenure with LASD, he served 12 years as a street gang investigator, where he investigated over 2,000 street gang cases.

Joe served another 12 years as a homicide investigator. In that capacity, Joe was called upon to investigate over 50 officer-involved shooting cases. In total, Joe Holmes has been called to offer courtroom testimony in over 500 gang and homicide related cases.

He was considered an expert in street gang culture and in the behavioral patterns of street gangs and gang members, and the impact these gangs had on neighborhoods and communities.

Joe compiled and published an article regarding Black street gang culture for the Association of Los Angeles Deputy Sheriffs.

Joe trained and instructed deputies of the Los Angeles County Sheriff's Department regarding street gangs and homicide investigations.

Joe was a member of the California Homicide Investigators Association.

Joe was voted Homicide Investigator of the year for the State of California in 2001 by the California Homicide Investigators Association, his peers.

Joe did not tell me these things about himself, nor would he ever. I had to research it on the Internet.

When I read it to him, he was very embarrassed. He said, "Hoss, (Joe calls every man 'Hoss') how did you find this stuff about me? I never told you this stuff."

Joe never would, Joe does not brag about himself. I told Joe, "It's on the Internet."

He was shocked.

When I read to Joe what was written about him, he confirmed it was true. But Joe was adamant, he was no hero. He does not want that word associated with him. He did not want me to put this information about him in the book.

I told him, "Joe, it's on the Internet, and I want to tell the world what you, we, us cops do."

"It is? Hoss, how did they get that? Look you have my permission to use it, but please understand there are so many other guys who have done so much more than me. I am nothing compared to some of these other guys."

I told him, "Here's what I understand Joe, I understand that you went out there every day, rain and shine, day and night, weekdays and weekends, and holidays for over thirty years and faced it day in and day out. You faced all the broken families, all the dead people, all the blood and guts, all of it. You paid a heavy price."

"Yes, I did, yes, I did, but didn't you?" Joe was right. I did pay a price. I was only on for thirteen years, less than half of Joe's tenure, but I paid a price.

Joe added, "How am I different than anyone else?"

Then Joe started naming names of other people on the department. Some of the guys I knew. He called these guys his heroes. Guys who he said sacrificed more than he did.

To my eternal shame, he even named me because I got shot. In response I will say this; anyone can get shot. I just happened to be a guy who was forced to fight for his life.

You see Joe is my hero, to Joe others are his heroes. Joe gets ticked off when anyone calls him a hero. But consider this, strangers begged him for justice or looked to him to find their son's or daughter's, murderers. Other officers have looked to Joe to prove their shootings were justified. Joe held the weight of justice on his shoulders for decades. However, there is something he wants you all to know; he shared that weight with all other peace officers. We all paid a price. We all share it with him. It's the price we've paid and continue to pay. As Joe says, his prevailing emotion is regret. He wishes he could have done more. He feels he didn't do enough.

Do you see a common theme here? Gloria Gressman has regret. She couldn't save an already dead little infant. Thom Bradstock has regret. He couldn't save an already drowned man. Paul Adams has regret. He looked on helpless, unable to save a woman from burning to death. Robert McCrary has regret. He killed a man who had an empty gun. Steve Gibbs has regret. He could not save his friend and sergeant from being killed, and as he said, "it was my fault." I have regretted I didn't do more to save Michelle who was raped, sodomized, suffocated, and chopped up." We tried to serve our fellow man and wished we could have done more, but sometimes we were helpless. The guilt that we should have done more, even when we could not, threatens us.

Need I go on?

Joe Holmes was a street smart, book smart, court smart, people smart, procedure smart, peace officer. He spent many hard years sacrificing his own time and perfecting his craft. To say he was dedicated is an understatement. To what end? To make your, and my community a better and safer place, and to pass his knowledge on to others so they might carry the torch of justice.

The others are still out there. The other Joe Holmes, the heroes.

I'll say this; in comparing the Joe Holmes and the cops in this world to the rock stars, the Joe Holmes easily win. I'd rather spend a minute with a person of character, than any time with a drug using, child molester. Character is how I judge others, not fame. We should teach our children to admire and emulate those who work hard, and who possess the highest values and character. Our children should respect and revere integrity, honesty, and the sanctity of life. Caring and helping others are what matter.

When I see someone mentioned in a magazine article, a newspaper article, or a news segment honoring someone and even declaring them a hero for their acting abilities, their singing abilities or their sports abilities, I don't understand. I do not believe by virtue of a person's notoriety or talent alone that it makes them a hero.

Let's talk about the recent news reports of those shot by the police. When I see a person heralded as a victim when the police shoot them, I look at what led to those circumstances. Let the chips fall where they may. I will say this; cops do not just go around beating and shooting people because they feel like it. Something made them take action. So, look for the reason why the encounter turned violent. You need to understand what was going through the officer's mind. We see, in the overwhelming majority of these cases the officers were cleared in their alleged wrongdoings. Have you ever asked yourself why? If you missed the point, reread the pages in this book. In most cases, that person challenging the officer precipitated the violent encounter.

It makes one wonder where society's value system lies; where it's acceptable to violently challenge authority. It's just like I said, by not following orders the person has taken the encounter to the next level. Nothing good can result from that scenario.

Protesting is your right. Do it peacefully, folks. Peaceful protests mean you do not block streets or pedestrians. You don't burn or loot. It is not, "just," expressing yourself when people burn and loot. It is a crime, and those people, and or groups, that participate or propagate such actions should be held accountable to the highest possible degree. Additionally, those actions should be condemned in the press in the strongest possible terms.

Accepting burning, looting, drug use, rape, or any other criminal activity is not okay. This is not going forward. Quite the contrary. You have not reached a new state of understanding and evolution when you justify and accept criminal activity as okay. Everything is not okay. Throwing away integrity and lack of respect for others or the law is not freedom. It is chaos. Chaos is no way for a society to operate. It hamstrings society. How can these things be okay when they are detrimental to society? Drug possession and drug use is a crime. It is detrimental to society. Statutory rape is a crime. It scars that person and the families forever. It is not okay. When you see people accepting these things you do not see enlightenment, you are seeing the death of our family system and values. You are seeing the decay of our society.

We should honor those who have the scars. We should honor those who have sacrificed their bodies for their fellow man, for strangers. My friends walk with limps and move with care. Some of my friends have divots in their heads or scars on their knees or across their bellies. Sometimes the scars are not visible. Many times, they come in the middle of the night while they are sleeping…the nightmares. Sometimes only the spouses genuinely understand as they get hit while sleeping next to a person who is fighting for their life in their sleep, in their nightmare…these are the voices of the victims.

…A rock star? As they say in Spanish, "Que va?" or "Who cares?"

In my world, the rock star does not even rate to carry my war bag to my radio car.

Chapter 28

Final Thoughts: A Two-Way Street

It was the best of jobs, and it was the worst of jobs.

One night, I was forced to do something on the job as a deputy sheriff that was haunting to me. It was justified and necessary, but it was still bothering me. My ex-wife told me "You guys are not nurses or elementary school teachers."

Right and wrong.

She was right, and she was wrong. Chris Barret pretty much summed it up. Cops have to be everything at different times in their career. Personally, I have been a nurse, an elementary school teacher, a psychologist, a counselor, a peacemaker, a fighter, a racecar driver, an interrogator, a lawyer, a gunfighter, a preserver of evidence, an expert writer, and an expert testifier in court with complete, and accurate recall. I am positive I am leaving out some things, but you get the picture. While performing my duties, I have been brave, scared, sad, lonely and overjoyed.

It was the best of jobs, and it was the worst of jobs.

Dear readers, we want to help you. We are not here to harm you unless you force us to do so to protect ourselves or someone else. It seems like the word out on the streets would have you believe we are evil. So, let me put on my schoolteacher uniform and educate.

When an officer approaches you, he has no clue as to whether you are a good guy or a bad guy. So, he has a million things going through his mind. He might want to know if you saw something that he is investigating. He might want to know if you heard something he is investigating. He might want to warn you about your driving. He might want to issue you a citation for something. He might think you are a suspect in a crime. However, while doing all this, he still has no clue if you are a good guy or a bad guy.

While he is approaching you, he is watching your hands. Why? Because hands kill. Hands carry guns, knives, clubs, pokers, lead ashtrays, rocks, vials of acid, Molotov cocktails and attack Chihuahuas…you get my point.

The officer knows if you are going to kill him, it will probably be with your hands.

So… when an officer approaches you keep your hands plainly visible and away from your body. Why? Because you might have a gun, knife, poker, lead ashtray, rock, vials of acid or Molotov cocktails hidden on your body.

A sure way to get a gun pointed at you by an officer is to quickly reach into a pocket, waistband, under a jacket or sweater or any other item of clothing.

Let's talk about car stops. If you are in a car and an officer approaches you, turn off your car. We do not like getting run over. If it is nighttime and if you have time to do it, turn on your interior lights. Roll your window down. Place both of your hands on your steering wheel. Oh, and don't reach for anything in any compartment or under any clothing in your car either. If you have any questions, see above.

Oh, my God Robert, you make me feel like a criminal. Dear readers, I was a cop, and when I get pulled over, I do all of the things I just described. Get rid of that chip on your shoulder.

When the officer sees you do all these things he will either think you too are a cop or that you read my book.

Most importantly, get that chip off of your shoulder. If he asks you for your identification, tell him where it is. Wait for him to tell you what to do next. If he asks you to step out of the car, do it.

During an encounter with the police, it is possible he might be telling you to do something that under the circumstances he does not have the right to ask you to do, cops can be wrong. Words of advice, unless you are going to harm yourself by following their orders, do it. You can sort out the legalities later.

If you don't comply with their orders and the officer feels he has the legal right to give those orders, you have just taken the encounter to the next level. Just a word, you won't like the outcome.

To you officers like it or not, it is a two-way street. Here is how you can help. My son got pulled over, and the officer said he was on his cell phone. My son worked in construction at the time, and he was exhausted. He was driving while resting his face against his palm. Did the officer have the right to stop him?

Possibly.

Knowing my son as I do, he is not a sarcastic or nasty person. He doesn't have a tone to his voice or an attitude, especially after all the things I've told him about being a cop. He told the officer he was resting his head on his hand and that he was not on his cell phone, but he could understand how it might look like he was on one. He offered the officer his cell phone to check the call log. The officer did so and saw that no calls had been made. The officer went back to his car and reviewed his video. He came back and said, "It looks like you were on your cell phone. Put your cell phone away and don't drive while talking on the phone anymore."

Officers, it is okay to be wrong. If the officer had simply said that because of the way my son was driving it looked like he was on his cell phone and that's why he stopped him, good enough. A little follow up with an "I'm sorry for inconveniencing you; have a nice day" would be great. But to tell him to not talk on the phone anymore while driving left a bad taste in my son's mouth. As my son said, "His ego would not let him be wrong."

Just to let you all know my son holds no grudges.

To you cops, I love the way Leonard Bacani viewed police work and the public. He wanted to make a positive difference in people's life. His first encounter with a police officer, who treated him so kindly when he was a little boy as he was spitting on cars, dictated how he treated people and how he did police work for the rest of his career. He felt that if he treated everyone with respect, even if they weren't treating him with respect, he was doing the right thing.

Let's try to make this a two-way street.

A final thought. You officers and you Sheriffs and Chiefs across the nation took an oath. The oath varies depending on the state or agency you work for, but this following example pretty much sums up the oath of office. "I, _____, do solemnly swear (or affirm) that I will support and defend the Constitution of the United States and the Constitution of the State of California against all enemies, foreign and domestic. I will bear true faith and allegiance to the Constitution of the United States and the Constitution of the State of California. I take this obligation freely, without any mental reservation or purpose of evasion. I will well and faithfully discharge the duties upon which I am about to enter."

Other oaths speak of keeping peace in the community where they serve.

Peace officers, hold true to your oath. If your mayor, or city council members, or County Board of Supervisors pressure you to bend the constitution, hold true to your oath, for out of the words written in our constitution we the people are protected.

Chapter 29

To My Heroes

To all the men and women I have worked with and have met who have taken the oath, and have worn the uniform, you are my heroes.

We like everyone else have our prejudices. Despite this, every single time someone has needed help I have seen our officers do so. I have never ever seen an officer ask, are you gay, are you Mexican, are you lesbian, are you a transvestite, are you African American, are you Muslim, are you Chinese? I have never seen an officer not help someone because they belonged to any race or religion. We help because we are sympathetic to victims, whoever they might be. And we have and will jeopardize and sacrifice our safety and sometimes our lives for people we may not agree with. I have seen it time and time again. Life is precious.

On the flip side, we abhor criminals. Our job is to stop them. Why? Because we see firsthand the damage they do to good hard working every day great people. We see the damage done to your sons, daughters, and mothers and fathers.

Because of the violence we have seen we live in condition yellow. Condition yellow is a constant state of heightened alertness. We have done so for so long and for so many years, we can no longer live like an average person. I don't think we would want to anyway. We know too much. We live in condition yellow because we have driven around in a police car, most times for years always thinking someone might want to kill us. Now it is not as much a conscious thing as an automatic way of doing things. It is playing the "what if game" all the time. "What if" a man comes around the next corner with a gun pointed at me? "What if" the guy in the car that just pulled up beside me points a gun at me? "What if" the call I just got is not a burglary alarm call but is a burglary in progress? "What if, what if, and what if'n" all day long for years and years. I now know no other way to look at everyday life.

There are no guarantees.

It is touch and go.

There are no guarantees. None whatsoever. We have seen people go to the market and end up dead somehow. We realize that we, like you, can die. We know there are no guarantees.

Gunfights are touch and go. We study gunfights. We study gunfights, and we study them again. We practice our craft. We shoot, and we shoot some more. There are no guarantees. We can, and sometimes do lose. We understand that gunfighting is a sport for hard men and women. We understand criminals with no conscience shoot without regard for life.

Cops have rules to abide by, and we have a conscience. We look at what is behind our target. We will hold a shot if we think it is not safe for bystanders, even if it means we will be shot ourselves. We have a conscience and a reverence for life. Sometimes we hesitate, even when we shouldn't, just to be sure we are right. We understand to win in a life and death struggle we have to be more violent than those assaulting us, but we have to ramp up for this. We know that society will not understand how violent we must become and that they will castigate us for it. This is a hard price to pay. To know you are right and have the world falsely judge you for your actions without understanding why you were forced to do what you did hurts. But we pay the price every day. We are willing to ramp up to the violence we must use. This mostly takes just a millisecond, but in a gunfight, milliseconds are the difference between life and death. Milliseconds are precious. We understand that winning in a gunfight means that we are winning in the milliseconds of time within that gunfight. We understand that to win in a gunfight we are doing a whole bunch of little things correctly, millisecond by millisecond. And we win in fractions of seconds.

We are always playing catch up because we are always responding to the threat. Consider, first we have to realize the threat, then catch up to the threat, and then become more violent than the threat to beat it. At best, gun fighting is touch and go. And if anyone tells you differently, they have not been in a gunfight, but they might teach theories about gunfighting at a college with all the rules and regulations that go along with it. Or they might be a politician telling you don't need more than five bullets, or that your gun is too big.

Dear readers. Just because we cops have the ability to rise to extreme violence when we need to, we will not harm you. Unless you make us do so. Unless you give us no choice. If you force us, we are willing to go all the way. All the way. We are willing to do so to protect your husbands, wives, sons, and daughters. We are willing to do so because we don't believe there should be any victims in this world. We see victims all day long, and it hurts us. The victims call and plead with us for justice, day in and day out. We pay a hefty price to try and make things right. But we pay the price and try and make a positive difference. We are your neighbors. We sit next to you at church with our guns concealed. We are ready. We are the only thing that stands between civilized society and chaos. And stand we will!

To the heroes in this book, and I know you all hate that word, many tears were shed as you relived your accounts to put the words on these pages. As Richard Beardslee said in the book *The Red Dot Club*, "Oh, it's always there, right below the surface." A truer statement has never been said.

To you whose accounts are in this book, who were and are so brave to bare your soul, no different than if you were standing naked in front of the world, to tell it like it really is, I thank you. To you members of The Red Dot Club, to all the victims whose voices scream to the world from the pages of this book, you have my eternal and utmost profound respect and gratitude.

I, and the communities you serve are forever in your debt.

Robert Rangel

Acknowledgements

The words in this work are a compilation of experiences leading to a variety of feelings, horrors, and regrets that the storytellers live with. Many cops read this manuscript and relived their own horrors they saw and experienced that laid half buried. They ignored their resurfacing nightmares and tears and pressed on and finished the words. For their perseverance in finishing the manuscript, and for their brutally honest input I am eternally grateful.

I would like to thank my father Robert Rangel, who read every word and draft over and over again. Your continued support means the world to me.

Fred Bobola, once again you gave it your all. As you said, now you have an inkling what your father went through while he was on the job. Thank you for reading and re-reading all the words and for your fine editing.

Linda L. Barton founder and author of DeadlyReads.com, my friend whom I have not met in person, but who because of the long phone conversations we have shared I feel as though you are my sister, thank you for all you continued editing and feedback.

Once again I cannot thank the Los Angeles County Sheriff's Department of which I was a proud member enough. I truly understand why it is recognized as the finest law enforcement agency in the world. Thank you for all the years of fine training that made it possible for me to survive as a peace officer in the streets of Los Angeles.